FROM
MYTH
TO
FICTION

FROM
MYTH
TO
FICTION

THE SAGA OF HADINGUS

GEORGES DUMÉZIL

———

TRANSLATED BY DEREK COLTMAN

THE UNIVERSITY OF CHICAGO PRESS
CHICAGO AND LONDON

GEORGES DUMÉZIL, currently honorary professor at the Collège de France, has been professor of the history of religion at the University of Istanbul, of Indo-European religions at the Ecole des Hautes Etudes, and of Indo-European civilization at the Collège de France. A man of extraordinary erudition and literary productivity, his recent publications in English include the two-volume *Archaic Roman Religion* and *The Destiny of the Warrior*.

[1973]

Originally published as *Du mythe au roman*: *La Saga de Hadingus et autres essais*, © 1970, Presses Universitaires de France.

The University of Chicago Press, Chicago 60637
The University of Chicago Press, Ltd., London
© 1973 by The University of Chicago
All rights reserved. Published 1973
Printed in the United States of America
International Standard Book Number: 0–226–16972–3
Library of Congress Catalog Card Number: 72–89226

CONTENTS

PREFACE

The views put forward since 1938 on the structure of Indo-European theology as revealed by comparisons of the theologies and mythologies of the various peoples speaking the Indo-European languages have in most areas imposed and made possible a reassessment of the relative value attaching to the various documents involved. For example, much new light has been shed on the relationships between the Vedas and the Mahābhārata in India, and those between the Gāthā, the later Avesta, the Pahlavi treatises, and the "Books of the Kings" in Iran. And it is not always the oldest texts that have turned out to be the most conservative. As a consequence, all these research efforts have very soon run into the identical problem: that of the formation of the epics—or what amounts to the same thing in many societies, the formation of "the history of the origins," or again, when narration has become an end in itself, of the fictional narrative, with, naturally enough, a number of intermediate forms.

It was with regard to Rome that this problem was first formulated: as early as 1938 and in the most clear-cut terms. In a sense, Classical Rome no longer has any divine mythology, in that it no longer has anything to tell about its gods, even though their definitions and their functional relationships have remained perfectly clear; while in the "history" of its earliest kings, on the other hand, it presents us with figures, with stories, only a few samplings of which immediately made clear the double correspondence with both the theology and divine mythology of the Indians and with Roman theology itself. Romulus and Numa Pompilius, followed *chronologically* by Tullus Hostilius, in turn followed by Ancus Marcius, behave in the same way as Varuṇa and Mitra, then Indra, then the Nāsatya behave in their *hierarchic* order, and these various kinds of behavior are distributed among the provinces that are, also *hierarchically*, under the rule of the three gods associated to form the pre-Capitoline triad. How are we to interpret this double parallelism? Is the "history" of the pre-Etruscan kings a transposed divine mythology, transferred from heaven to earth, from the invisible world to the visible one? Or is it an extension, adapted to local Roman needs, of something that was already, long before Rome, a human mythology running parallel to a divine mythology, so that Rome was able to retain the human while discarding the divine? In the case of the first hypothesis, how are we to conceive the transposition? In the case of the second, the adaptation? And even before that, in either case, the conservation at once faithful yet flexible of the prehistoric content? Who was responsible for the preservation and methods of using such material? The colleges of priests? The *gentes*? Specialists of some kind? We are forced to admit that after more than thirty years all of these questions are still without answers: we are still at the stage of simply recording the results of operations whose mechanism we cannot describe and whose agents we cannot name.

Because of the richness and variety of the documents available, and thanks to our extensive factual knowledge of the social organization involved, in particular the priestly class, a credible solution became available for the corresponding problem in India as soon as it was posed. It was in 1947 that Stig Wikander observed that the central group of "good heroes" in the Mahābhārata, the five half—or almost —brothers known as the Pāṇḍava, were duplications as to their characters, their actions, and their relationships (beginning with the very order of their birth) of the hierarchized group constituted in the earliest Vedic mythology by the gods of the three functions, who are, moreover, explicitly described as the heroes' fathers: the just king Yudhiṣṭhira is modeled on Mitra (simply rejuvenated as Dharma), the two kinds of warrior, Bhīma and Arjuna, on Vāyu and Indra, and the two twins Nakula and Sahadeva, devoted squires to their elders and skilled veterinarians, on the Nāsatya twins. Step by step, over twenty years or so, the interpretative method thus disclosed proved capable of extension to most of the important characters of the poem, and even to its subject: it is an entire archaic mythology, more archaic on several counts than the Vedic mythology, that has been transposed to provide these epic characters and their exploits. The scope, the accuracy, and sometimes the ingeniousness of the transposition are in themselves sufficient evidence of conscious "authorship": in a world parallel with the religious life in which they continued to participate, offering sacrifices and reciting hymns, an entire academy of learned and talented priests, possibly several generations forming one "school," must have labored at the creation of this vast tapestry—I am speaking here solely of the first layer of material, not of later accretions—following a design laid out by one man or by a group of men possessed of what we can only term genius. Though all this must have occurred very early indeed, before writing, at the time of the four Vedas and the fifth; and we do not in fact know the true, humble, human, social status of the individual or team concealed by the fabled name Vyāsa.

Other Indo-European peoples have constituted the epic of their origins with the aid of an early divine mythology but retained the gods' own names. This is often the case with peoples of whose literary life we have a record just after their conversion to Christianity. In such cases the educated among them have been unwilling to let the valuable traditional material for which their religion could no longer find room just go to waste. So either from a simple wish to preserve it for its own sake, or because they wished to use it for the embellishment of their nation's or some dynasty's past, they have simply situated it in human times, just as it was, or at least with as few changes as were compatible with making it acceptable as a narrative of human events. The period of the Tuatha dé Danann in Ireland and the events covered by the fourth branch of the Mabinogi in Wales are of this type: Celtic mythology turned into history in one case and fiction in the other, still capable of reconstitution by a comparative interpretation of the two texts, Irish and Welsh, but as mythology beyond the pale. One can still glimpse what the authors of that admirable fiction or that strange history must have been like, anonymous and yet very individual: monks suckled on the lore of the filid, if not the druids, and perhaps themselves actually filid who had gone over to the new faith. But we cannot actually pin them down to a particular time, or place, or character.

The case of the Scandinavian nations is somewhat different: on the one hand the pre-Christian texts that we still read, the Scaldic or

Eddic poems, have preserved much of this area's mythology in its original form; on the other, a very talented and well-informed Christian Icelander has completed our pre-Christian documentation with two systematic treatises on the subject; and lastly, two authors— the same Icelander writing in Icelandic and a monk in Zealand writing in Latin—composed and put their names to human transpositions of this mythology purporting to be history. These latter are the first chapters of Snorri Sturluson's *Ynglingasaga* (to be precise, all that precedes the first quoted strophe from the *Ynglingatal*) and many passages in the first books of the *Gesta Danorum* of Saxo-Grammaticus. (In the present edition, quoted passages from the *Gesta Danorum* are taken from Oliver Elton's English translation first published in London in 1894.)

During the various phases of my past research, and often on more than one occasion, I have had to deal to some extent with these four diverse occurrences of the "myth and epic," "myth and history," "myth and fiction" problem—and some others too, which have proved most instructive, such as that presented by the legends of the Ossetes, the last descendants of the Scythians, about the Nart heroes. The truth is that the problem has been with me constantly: it has impregnated and often given their direction to all the theological, mythological, ritualistic, and sociological investigations I have been involved in. The epic or its derivatives are everywhere. For several years now I have been coordinating the results obtained in this fragmentary way. In the first volume of a series entitled "Myth and Epic," I have already made a summing-up of the present state of investigations into the great Indian, Roman, and Scythian epic expressions of the trifunctional ideology inherited from the Indo-Europeans. Nowhere has it proved possible to pinpoint exactly the "authors" whose existence we postulate from the quality of their work; but their intentions and methods have been examined as far as was possible. Two further volumes—one already published (1971), the other in preparation—dealing with the epics of lesser scope will be concerned with the same areas plus, in the case of some points, Ireland and Scandinavia.

But as I have already observed, Iceland and Denmark occupy a place apart, outside the great lines of Indo-European comparative studies, and permit us to make observations of a rare kind. Through

Snorri and Saxo it is possible to deal precisely and unambiguously with the "authors" problem that everywhere else remains no more than a watermark running perpetually below the surface in our examinations of such transpositions—the problem of their professional consciences and their imaginations, of their intelligence and the facts at their disposal, of their skill or lack of it, of their habits, even of their set formulas. In the case of Snorri I can only refer the reader back, after twenty-two years, to the first part of my own *Loki*, of which a radically revised edition is now in preparation. The present book contains—apart from the studies on Starcatherus, which has appeared in *Myth and Epic* 2 (1971)—all that a long familiarity, eventually becoming a sort of affectionate complicity, has taught me about Saxo's literary procedures.

I reproduce these essays—apart from a few corrections and a number of additions that in no way alter the theses put forward—in both the form and order in which they were first published or delivered. The reader will thus perhaps have the pleasure of discovering for himself or herself the progress, the hardening, of what was in the first place no more than a preference: in *The Saga of Hadingus* itself I had constantly made the reservation that possibly the alterations effected in the myth of Saxo's version were not his own but derived from his unknown Icelandic source. The later studies left less and less likelihood in this hypothesis and made it more and more evident that the Canon of Lund was responsible for them himself. Thus it came to be less and less as a source of evidence on Scandinavian mythology that he interested me (even though he is irreplaceable in that rôle in the many instances when he has worked on a since-vanished original), but rather as a source of evidence about himself and his method, through the examples he provides of the kind of "reinvestments" a distinguished and, moreover, religious mind could amuse itself with when the mythology of his forefathers had ceased to be anything more for him than literature: like Pope Honorius using the gilded tiles the Vandals left on the last Capitol for the roof of the first basilica built to Saint Peter.

The Saga of Hadingus, published in 1953 in the Bibliothèque de l'Ecole des Hautes Etudes, Section des Science Religieuses (vol. 66), contains the material of one of the two courses I taught in my first year at the Collège de France in 1949–50. I hope to have proved that in order to provide a content for the reign of Hadingus, grandson of Scioldus, in other words the third legendary king of the Danish Skjöldungar dynasty, Saxo simply reworked, though in great detail and encountering difficulties in the process that he resolved with a greater or lesser degree of skill, a Scandinavian account of the career of the god Njörðr, whom Snorri Sturluson, retaining his name, made into the second ancestor of the Swedish Ynglingar dynasty.

The appendixes that follow, also prepared for various courses of lectures, have already been published, apart from the second. The first elucidates a particular point in my investigation of the Hadingus saga. The next three apply the type of analysis developed for investigating the Hadingus legend to some of Saxo's other transpositions. The next two deal with the problem of the relationship between myth and folklore from two different angles.

I wish to thank the staff and my colleagues of the fifth Section de l'Ecole des Hautes Etudes who made it possible for me to publish this book once more, as well as the editors and staffs of the magazines and publications in which the appendixes first appeared.

University of Chicago Divinity School
March 1970

G. D.

THE
SAGA
OF
HADINGUS

To Malou Höjer and her children
in memory of Carl Henrik

INTRODUCTION

Of the author himself, that Saxo whose knowledge of literature later earned him the cognomen Grammaticus, we know very little. He was born in Denmark, in Zealand, toward the middle of the twelfth century. He was a *clericus*, chaplain and secretary to some highly placed personage whom he escorted on several short journeys; he may also have been canon of Lund, in Skåne. His death occurred later than 1216, though we cannot be more precise than that, and he died before he had completed the revision of his work the *Gesta Danorum*, a history of Denmark from its beginnings to his own time.

The saga of Hadingus forms the second part of the first book (chaps. v–viii) of these *Gesta Danorum*. It thus occurs early on among those "legendary books" that Saxo later added as a long introduction to the historic books proper: Hadingus was for him one of the very earliest Danish kings.

The interest of these first nine books is well known—as are their limitations. Though possessed of a classical culture sufficient to have earned him an enviable place in the world history of Latin literature, Saxo had not found in Denmark what Iceland and an eminent family had provided for his illustrious contemporary Snorri Sturluson: a sort of bilingual university providing a twofold source of learning and culture, a double tradition. In his youth, Saxo's masters must have made him compose a great many *contiones* and *carmina*, but he could certainly have been given no Skaldic verses to write, or any Icelandic essays, or even—to judge by the mistranslations that modern scholars are so proud of finding in his work—many translations from it. He certainly knew spoken Icelandic better than he knew German, but not all that well, and the precious and convoluted style of Icelandic poetry even less well.

3

As a consequence he never conceived any great design on the scale
of Snorri's—of which the *Heimskringla* (with its opening the *Ynglingasaga*) is only a fragment and what we term the prose *Edda*, "Snorri's
Edda," another—the intention of which was to give a new lease of life,
in a society now wholly Christian, to the literary tradition and vast
store of mythical material and images inherited from paganism, and
to do so without narrow and parochial patriotism, addressing himself
to all those cousins still in Norway or those scattered throughout the
northern islands as well as to his Icelandic brethren. Saxo the cleric,
Saxo the Zealander, less aware of being a Scandinavian, lacked any
such feeling of duty toward Scandinavian culture as a whole: he is
just as severe with the Norwegians as with the Germans, is constantly
scoring off the Swedes, and has praise only for Iceland, which he knew
about from the Icelanders he had met, all educated and fascinating
men. All he was really trying to do when he started out was to tell the
story of *his* Denmark and *his* rulers as nobly as he could, and then later
on to extend that narrative backward in time. And although the
second of these intentions led him to interest himself—rather late on
apparently—in the only Scandinavian literature then existing as
literature, that centered on Iceland, he nevertheless shaped, bent,
re-ordered everything he borrowed to the greater glory of Denmark.
Moreover, for lack of what we might term "philological preparation,"
he was obliged to content himself with garnering all his material at
second hand, or rather at second mouth, since it seems to have been
above all oral: from Icelandic poets traveling in Europe, some well
stocked and others more impoverished in their material, he perhaps
specifically asked for but certainly acquired an acquaintance with their
sagas, with their verses, and also with a mythology already "re-
thought" in terms of history. And it was with this material pri-
marily, refurbished with his rich Latin, cast at times in the meters of
Vergil or Ovid or Horace, that he composed his first nine books.

It must not be concluded from these considerations, however, that
Saxo is a bad source of evidence. Even if he were, he would nevertheless remain a necessary one, since his own sources have disappeared
to such a large extent and now remain accessible only through him.
But in fact it is not the case, and it is the object of the present work to
show, with regard to one important point, how on the contrary he is
able to reinforce our mythological documentation. For although he

may misunderstand words or things here and there, he does have one fundamental quality: he loves these old tales, these old religious errors, this paganism even, and is in no danger of committing the major error that so many philologists of our own day do not escape, scholars who may not so much as falter over a single word in a story, yet lack any feeling for its spirit and fail to perceive its structure and implicit philosophy. At whatever moment in his life he first began to pay heed to the Nordic fables, whether when he was about seventeen, as Axel Olrik believes, when he came into contact with an Icelander whose name (Arnoldus, or in other words Arnaldr þorvaldsson) is mentioned at one point in the *Gesta Danorum*, or whether much later, led to them by the requirements of his work, it is certain that as soon as he did begin to take an interest in them he did so with real sympathy and even—insofar as he could find a place for these fables to root on Danish soil—with pride.

I shall not delve very deeply into the question of his sources, into what was the great discovery and principal thesis, late last century, of the Danish scholar Axel Olrik: the distinction, where the legendary or fictional parts of the *Gesta Danorum* are concerned, between what is derived from Norwegian and Icelandic sources and what from Danish sources. Without eliminating it altogether, the criticism of the following years then much decreased the proportion allotted to the latter; and also, in the first group, decreased the proportion of the Norwegian sources as opposed to those from Iceland and the other western islands; and lastly, it restored some independence to Saxo himself in relation to his informants. I shall not, and do not need, to enter into any such discussion here, however, for the simple reason that the text we are about to examine is one of those that Axel Olrik himself assigned unhesitatingly to Iceland: it was not from the Danish tradition, regardless of the form we should envisage the bearers of it assuming in Saxo's time, but from the lore of the western *sagamenn*, either Icelanders or emulators of the Icelanders, that our author has drawn what he tells us about Hadingus. That is the most we can say, however: the original sources of that lore have not survived. As a result we shall frequently be forced—not for the sake of pedantic precision, but on the contrary in order to keep our irremediable uncertainty always before us—to resort to the phrase "Saxo or his source."

Our text is that of the edition of the *Saxonis Gesta Danorum* prepared by P. Herrmann and C. Knabe, professors at Torgau, deposited by them in manuscript form with the Royal Library in Copenhagen, and later published in a deluxe edition after further editorial work by Jørgen Olrik and Hans Ræder, in 1931, in a large quarto volume of 609 pages, at the expense of the Carlsberg Institute. This edition also contains a glossary of Saxo's work in four parts compiled by Franz Blatt. The preface to the edition as a whole, a sprightly piece of writing in straightforward Latin, sums up all that one needs to know about the history of the text—so let the reader resort to it in need. I shall here content myself with recalling the principal landmarks of that history: princeps edition in Paris in 1514; disappearance of any complete manuscript; the famous "Angers fragment" identified by Gaston Paris in 1877, published in 1879, and apparently deriving from a copy used during his revisions by Saxo himself; and lastly the successful efforts of three centuries of philology to improve the vulgate. The chapters with which we shall be concerned contain no important variants between editions; the emendations adopted by the 1931 editors are probable and, moreover, of no consequence to the content of the work. The "Angers fragment," containing a section of the first book, unfortunately stops before the saga of Hadingus.

As for interpretation, all the studies prior to 1920 were collated and utilized in a single, invaluable work by Paul Herrmann. As early as 1898, in the preface to his *Deutsche Mythologie*, Herrmann was saying that one indispensable "Vorarbeit" to any progress in our knowledge of Nordic mythology was a translation of and a commentary on the first books of Saxo. In 1901 he published such a translation; but it was not until 1922 that the essential part of his work appeared, the commentary, a book of almost seven hundred octavo pages, closely printed, a magnificent labor of erudition—against the conclusions and the method of which we shall be obliged almost constantly to protest. Let me therefore sum up here, as briefly as possible, the basis of my opposition to Herrmann's work.

Paul Herrmann was a distinguished mythographer and, though fascinated by Saxo, was nevertheless also rather suspicious of this Grammaticus who was so shaky on Icelandic grammar. In 1903, when he was right in the middle of his labors on our author, two years after the translation had appeared, he expressed himself in the presentation of sources that opens, not his *Deutsche Mytholgie* this time but his *Nordische Mythologie*, in these severe terms: (p. 20): "His mythology is the Icelandic mythology of about the year 1200, full of mistakes and corruptions. His nine books of legend are, as has been said before, a distorting mirror . . . The most extreme caution is therefore required when dealing with him." A strange love-hate relationship! Moreover, as his career developed, Paul Herrmann seems to have been increasingly influenced by the general tendency of his age: it is the very notion of "Scandinavian myth" itself that he apparently grows to mistrust.

The blooming of the *Märchenkunde*, the demonstration that a host of folktale motifs could be found in the stories about the gods Óðinn, Þórr, Freyr, Freyja, and so forth, and certain criticism of the narrative sagas, led at that time to a skepticism with regard to Scandinavian mythology that has left its mark on more or less all recent work on the subject. We must not forget that it was 1923, the year after Paul Herrmann's commentary was published, that saw the appearance of a manifesto by Eugen Mogk, the veteran Scandinavian mythographer who had edited the Germanische Mythologie in the *Grundriss*, and done so extremely well, but who had ended up by turning against it: fascicle 51 of the *Folklore Fellows Communications* of Helsinki devotes thirty-three pages to dismissing the value of Snorri's *Edda* as evidence under the significant title *Novellistische Darstellung mythologischer Stoffe Snorris und seiner Schule*. And it may be said that Herrmann's dense commentary ends up, in much the same spirit, by depriving mythology of the greater part of Saxo's evidence: twenty-four years of work had certainly fulfilled the program announced in 1898, but at the same time they had very nearly negated its interest.

In a number of studies opposing Eugen Mogk and his numerous followers I have attempted to rescue Snorri and rehabilitate his *Edda*: the present work is written on the assumption that their restoration is an accepted fact. I particularly refer readers to the final essay in my collection *Tarpeia* (1947), devoted to the war between the Ases and the Vanes, since it will be of considerable relevance to our present problem (cf. *La religion romaine archaïque* [1966], pp. 78–84; *Archaic Roman Religion* [1970], pp. 66–73), as well as to the extended discussion in the second chapter of my *Loki* (1948). Symmetrically, I hope here to show the great importance of the Hadingus saga as a document of "fictionalized mythology."

This does not mean, I must repeat, that Herrmann's 1922 commentary is not an irreplaceable monument. One may even say that whatever has been printed since then, in various articles listed in the invaluable bibliographies of the *Arkiv för Nordisk Filologi* and other germanistic publications, has merely gleaned the remnants of the old master's harvest. His book is called: *Die Heldensagen des Saxo Grammaticus, 2. Teil, Kommentar: Erlaüterungen zu den ersten 9 Büchern der dänischen Geschichte* (Leipzig). I shall refer to it hereafter under the abbreviated form, *Kommentar*.

1

HADINGUS IS NOT HASTING
THE VIKING

Between 1202 and 1216, having finished in his highly colored Latin almost chaotic in its richness the part of his *Gesta Danorum* that can be termed properly historical, or in other words what we know as Books 10 to 16, Saxo Grammaticus seems to have conceived a second project. Working backward through time, back to the very beginnings, he wrote the nine books, 1 to 9, that are of such value to us for the information they contain on the myths and epics of the ancient North. It is more or less agreed, on the basis of reasonably reliable criteria,[1] that the first book was one of the last written.

In Saxo's mind it is still—or already—history, and history without the perspective of hindsight. These first kings of Denmark certainly have more remarkable adventures than their successors, but the essence of the matter remains unchanged: they are all, without exception, leaders of the Viking era, engaging in battles, governing according to the accepted rules, even sailing all the sea-lanes familiar to the Vikings, from the "Byarmenses" of northern Russia to the great oceanic islands of Britain and Ireland. Their characters, the values they honor, the methods they employ are all the same. Saxo or his sources,[2] and very probably Saxo improving upon his sources, has assimilated their lives and times to those of Scandinavian warrior-kings in the Middle Ages, just as their contemporaries, the illuminators of the south and west, dressed the lords and ladies of both Testaments in medieval style.

It is in these terms that the last part of the first book, Chapters v

---

1. For example, the examination of doublet episodes, those that relate the same trick of war in several different places in the work. A study of the various treatments that Saxo has given us of a particular theme, emulating his former efforts and not always improving on them, sometimes enables us to decide which is the original and which the reworking.

2. See above, p. 5.

9

to viii,[3] relates the agitated story of King Hadingus, of which the following is a summary:

The Danish king Gram has been killed and Denmark annexed by the Norwegian king Suibdagerus.[4] His two young sons have been rescued by their tutor and entrusted by him to two giants, so that they may raise and protect them (v, 1). Of these two children one was later to make an act of submission and return to Denmark, where it appears that Suibdagerus—who in the meantime has also annexed Sweden—eliminates him, since we never hear of him again. The other, Hadingus, grows up in the home of his foster father, the giant Vagnophthus, determined to avenge his father (v, 7).

But between these two sets of facts Saxo has surprisingly inserted (v, 2–6) a systematic account of the mythological hierarchy. According to the northern fables, three different kinds of superhuman beings appeared in succession. First giants. Then wizards, physically less strong but superior in intelligence and magical know-how, who conquered the giants and passed themselves off as gods. Lastly a race born from a crossing of the previous two, inferior to the giants in strength and to the "gods" who had preceded them in magic, but good enough wizards all the same to achieve divine status themselves in the eyes of ignorant mankind.

After this parenthesis Saxo returns to Hadingus, who grows up with the giant Vagnophthus and is soon no longer a child. Entirely taken up with the thought of revenge he has no desire to experience sexual pleasure (vi, 1). But the giant's daughter, Harthgrepa, who has been his wet nurse, does all she can to awaken desire in him, expressing her intentions quite clearly in a little poem in which she gives what is in our eyes the least pertinent of reasons for her actions: "I have given you suck and am almost your mother: I am therefore the woman you ought to take as your wife" (vi, 2). Hadingus is persuaded in principle and sees no further objection other than his foster mother's size, whereupon she explains to him in a second poem that it is within her power to assume any size at will (vi, 3). And so, without further ado, they are able to couple.

---

3. The Latin text is given in Appendix 7. The passages important to this study appear in Elton's translation during the course of the book.

4. This name (borne by many characters, in particular by a king in one of the *Edda* poems) and those that follow are taken from various places in the Nordic tradition: Snorri, in his *Edda*, names a Svipdagr among the berserkir of the great Danish king Hrólfr Kraki, a Vagnhöfði and a Harðgreipr among the names of the giants, a Harðgreip among those of the witches. But Lokerus has nothing to do with Loki!

Since Hadingus wishes to go back to Denmark, Harthgrepa dresses in masculine attire and goes with him. On the way they enter a house where there is a corpse. Harthgrepa gives Hadingus a small stick carved with runes to lay on the dead man's tongue so that they may learn the future (vi, 4). Furious at being thus conjured, the dead man's spirit recites a poem, the third in the saga, announcing that Harthgrepa will soon be torn apart (vi, 5). This is in fact what happens, after a first danger has been narrowly avoided: the two lovers are in a wood in a hut made of branches when a gigantic hand, with long claws, comes down over them. Harthgrepa seizes hold of the hand and gives Hadingus time to cut it off. But the respite is brief: their anger increased, the invisible beings seize upon Harthgrepa shortly afterward and rip her to pieces (vi, 6).

Scarcely has Hadingus been widowed of his foster mother, if that's the right way of putting it, when a one-eyed old man (immediately recognizable on that account as the god "Othinus"), having taken pity on him, arranges for him to swear blood brotherhood with a Viking named Liserus, after which the two band together to launch an attack on Lokerus, king of Courland. But things go badly, and Hadingus has to run away. The one-eyed old man reappears, carries him off through the air on a magic horse, takes him home with him, gives him a strengthening cordial to drink, and tells him in verse what he must now do (vi, 7); he, the old man, is going to take him back to the place where he found him by the same means; Lokerus will make him a prisoner and put him in prison in order to throw him to a savage lion; but, with the aid of his protector, Hadingus will free himself, and before giving Lokerus the slip he will deliberately attack the lion, overcome it, drink its blood, and thus become even more vigorous (vi, 8). And that is how things turn out (vi, 9–10). Whereupon, fortified by the blood he has drunk, Hadingus besieges and takes—partly by trickery—the city of Handwanus, king of the Hellespont (vi, 10), then returns to confront his principal enemy, his father's murderer Suibdagerus, whom he kills in a battle near the island of Gotland (vi, 11).

Leaving his hero, and indeed leaving mankind, Saxo here inserts a purely mythological episode with no transition apart from the words *ea tempestate . . .*, "At that same time . . ." The episode concerns Othinus (now named and presented in his true status), the king of Byzantium, who prefers to live at Uppsala and has set himself up as king of the gods. As a tribute from the kings of the north, Othinus receives a golden statue of himself. His wife Frigga (the goddess Frigg was in fact the wife of Óðinn in classical Scandinavian mythology), out of cupidity inspired by this gold that Othinus has put under guard, commits unseemly actions, is false to her husband, and the latter, esteeming himself sullied by her behavior, exiles himself for a while (vii, 1). During this eclipse a wizard, Mithothyn, takes power, changes the usual sacrificial customs, and puts wizards from his own clan in power everywhere (vii, 2). When Othinus returns with his majesty refreshed and his brightness restored, Mithothyn flees, to perish wretchedly abroad, while the king restores the realm to what it was before (vii, 3). Then, by means of a simple *interea*, Saxo returns to Hadingus for good.

The hero wages a hard but victorious war against Asmundus, the son of the Swedish king he has killed. Asmundus, reciting two poems as he does so, fights back like a madman; but with the unexpected help of his former foster father, Hadingus overcomes him, though not before he has received a wound in the leg that leaves him with a limp. He honors his adversary with a fine funeral, before which the widow ritually kills herself (viii, 1–4). Hadingus is then obliged to return hurriedly to Denmark, where Uffo, the son of Asmundus, has created a diversion, and we are back where we started: Hadingus is once more reigning in Denmark but has been forced to evacuate Sweden, where Uffo, thirsting for revenge, takes refuge (viii, 5).

The narration of these wars is interrupted by a tale of a familiar type. His treasure, in Denmark, having been stolen, Hadingus resorts to trickery in order to discover those guilty of the deed: he has it announced that he will give the thieves great rewards if they declare themselves, and will even put them in charge of his treasure. They do declare themselves, first one, then the others. Hadingus keeps his word, rewards them as he promised, but then has them immediately executed (viii, 6).

The Swedish war begins again with Hadingus setting off in search of Uffo. But the Danish army suffers a terrible famine in Sweden that reduces it to eating horses, dogs, and even men (viii, 7). On the eve of battle two voices are heard in succession—in the form of poems, the seventh and eighth—two challenges emerging from invisible mouths (viii, 8–9). Then, during the night, while the battle is going on, two strangers, two horrible and bald old men, are seen fighting a duel by the light of the stars (viii, 10). Hadingus is defeated, but not disastrously, and goes bathing on a nearby beach to refresh himself. There he kills a weird sea-monster, which he bears in triumph back to his camp. A woman appears and tells him—ninth poem—that until he has expiated this murder (the monster was a divine being), wherever he may go, on land or sea, disastrous tempests will spring up and he will be driven from shipwreck to cyclone, from shattered house to further shipwreck (viii, 11). And these are the events we are shown, until he has offered up black victims to the god Frö, a sacrifice that the Swedes celebrated annually, Saxo says, under the name of *Fröblot* (viii, 12).

Then comes something quite different: the story of Hadingus's second marriage. He learns that somewhere beyond Trondheim, in Norway, a princess named Regnilda is being threatened with obligatory marriage to a giant. He hurries to her aid, kills the giant, but also falls badly wounded himself. The princess nurses him, and in order to be sure of recognizing him when the time comes to choose a husband, she conceals a ring in a wound in his leg. Shortly afterward, her father summons all her suitors, of whom there are a great number. Hadingus, now cured, is among them. Regnilda palpates their legs, identifies her rescuer, and marries him (viii, 13).

They have still not left Regnilda's country when a strange adventure befalls Hadingus. A woman rises up waist high from the flames of the hearth and beckons to him. He goes over, she throws her cloak over him, and lo and behold they are both down in the underworld. The hero returns safe and sound eventually, but only after having seen—among other sights—the happy fate that Óðinn has in store for dead warriors in the next world: they go on fighting forever, organized into opposing bands (viii, 15).

Hadingus and his wife set off for Denmark. During the voyage, thanks to the supernatural speed of their ship, they escape some Vikings who pursue them (viii, 15).

The Swedish war flares up again. King Uffo has promised his daughter to anyone who kills Hadingus, and a certain Thuningus, with an army of "Byarmenses," is marching against him. Passing the coasts of Norway with his fleet, Hadingus sees an old man (again it is Óðinn incognito) beckoning to him. He takes him on board, and the old man teaches him an infallible battle formation; then, in the battle, by means of a magical weapon and atmospheric counter-magic, he ensures his victory. As he leaves him the old man tells him that he will never die except of his own will and advises him to opt for glorious and distant expeditions rather than short and inglorious ones (viii, 16).

Having conquered Thuningus, Hadingus turns his attentions to Uffo. He counters a trick the Swedish king attempts to play on him, kills him, buries him with great pomp, and then places the dead king's brother, Hundingus, on the throne. And Hundingus at last provides him with a friend and loyal ally (viii, 17).

Hadingus returns to Denmark, where Saxo has him take part in a duet (ninth and tenth poems): Hadingus expresses his love of the sea, his nostalgia for ocean voyages, his horror of the views and sounds of land (viii, 18). Regnilda expresses the distress she feels when she hears the cries of gulls, the din of ocean storms, and sighs to be in the kind of landscape she grew up in (viii, 19). But this exchange of bitter laments does not lead to any event.

Hadingus is attacked by one Tosto, a Jutlander of low birth (viii, 20). There is a battle on land. Hadingus, beaten back at first, escapes out to sea in a ship, is pursued by Tosto, and by means of a very dangerous ruse (turning his ship upside down and hiding beneath it) persuades his pursuer that he is drowned. He soon reappears on land, falls unexpectedly upon his enemy, strips him of everything he has, and takes back his booty (viii, 21). Back in Denmark after a confused and shameful adventure with some Vikings, Tosto perishes in a duel at Hadingus's own hand (viii, 22).

Hadingus should now feel at peace, but does a saga hero ever feel that? So he has a dream in which his dead wife appears to him (we were not aware of her death till this event) and tells him in two couplets—the last poems—that his son will be a terror to his enemies and his daughter a danger to himself (viii, 23). He swiftly experiences the proof of the second of these pieces of information. Ambitious, impatient for the throne, the daughter incites her husband to plot against her father (viii, 24). In a long prose speech full of antitheses she praises the virtue of boldness to him, affirms the superiority in practice and even in law of the young over the old (viii, 25), and eventually convinces him: during the course of a banquet the son-in-law is to kill the father-in-law. But the father-in-law is aware of the plot, and when he gives the signal his men execute the traitor (viii, 26).

Last comes the death of Hadingus by his own will, as the one-eyed old man had foretold. Hundingus, his Swedish friend, having heard a false story of Hadingus's death, summons together all his nobles for a funeral feast. In the course of the drinking he accidentally falls into the huge vat of beer he has had filled and is drowned. Upon this sad news Hadingus, not wishing to be outstripped in magnanimity, summons his subjects and hangs himself in their presence (viii, 27).

Such is this strange biography, full of abrupt changes, burdened with two extraneous mythological passages (v, 2–5; vii) for which there seems little justification, and in which the "Odinic" warrior hero experiences several adventures that do not fit in with his type. What is its origin?

For the past half century or so, wisdom has seemed to consist in seeking to establish the history, the historical background, of everything. For more recent authors, therefore, Hadingus must be an authentic Viking whose career has simply been considerably embellished. Axel Olrik,[5] followed in particular by Gustav Neckel[6] and Paul Herrmann,[7] has gone further: Hadingus, he says, is the renowned leader whose life, in the second half of the ninth century, proved of such interest to the chroniclers of the West under the names of Hastingus, Asltingus, Alstignus, and so on. And this Hastingus was indeed a most turbulent and redoubtable character.[8]

In 866 he undertook a long expedition through Anjou, Poitou, and the Touraine, then, on his way back, met and slew in the course of a pitched battle two of the most valiant captains of western Francia, the counts Ramnulf and Rodbert. In 869, Salomon of Brittany was obliged to pay him tribute money in order to avoid being pillaged; and in the same year he once again extracted a ransom from Tours. In 872, besieged in Angers by King Charles, he achieved his freedom by promising to leave the country—a promise he did not keep, "unleashing his fury worse than before." And that same year he did in fact reappear outside Tours, so that the monks of Saint-Martin were forced to move out and set up a new monastery in Burgundy. In 874 he took part in a civil war in Brittany and was beaten. It was not until 882, after he had occupied the Loire basin for at least sixteen years, that King Louis forced him, or persuaded him with gifts of money, to leave France. He then disappears completely from history until 890, in which year he appears once more at the mouth of the Somme and begins making raids upon Amiens (891) and the Vermandois (891–92). He was then driven out of France by a great famine. During 893 and 894 he was making his presence felt in England. Then silence descends, without our having any idea where or how his death occurred. In England? Taking part in the great collective expedition against France in 896? In Denmark?

5. *Danmarks Heltedigtning* 2 (1910): 315.

6. In his article "Hamalt fylkja" in the *Arkiv för Nordisk Filologi* (1918), p. 323; also in the *Reallexikon der germanischen Altertumskunde* by Johannes Hoops (4 [1918–19]: p. 70).

7. *Kommentar*, p. 91.

8. I follow the account given by Gustav Storm, *Kritiske Bidrag til Vikingetidens Historie, 1, Ragnar Lodbrok og Gange-Rolv* (Christiania, 1878), pp. 63–65, since no one has improved on it.

His active career thus lasted from 866 to 894 at least, much longer than that of most of his ilk, though this does not mean that in 894 he was necessarily too old to continue.[9] His numerous victories on the Loire, on the Somme, and in the Islands, rendered his name particularly feared, and for the Franks he became the horrific archetype, of the Nordic predator. An energetic versifier has left us a portrait of him as such in verses that the learned Saxo would not have approved:[10]

> Hic sacer atque ferox nimim crudelis et atrox
> pestifer, infestus, torvus, trux, flagitiosus,
> pestifer inconstansque, procax, ventosus et exlex . . .
> ·
> Et tanto scelere ante alios immanior omnes
> quantus ad astrigerum tendit suspectus Olympum!

For most of the time he worked on his own, with his own army, and did not associate himself with the big cooperative expeditions. It was really only toward the end, during the attacks on England and Ireland, that he allied himself with other chiefs.

I have given Hastingus's history in detail so that it will become immediately apparent how different it is in every way from that of Hadingus. The latter, king of Denmark, solely concerned with winning back and keeping his throne, wages his wars solely in Sweden or Norway, against Courland, the "Byarmenses" or the king of the Hellespont,[11] which is to say in the north and the east, and is never in the slightest concerned with the western lands where Hasting passed the whole of his life.[12] And indeed the authors who have drawn parallels between the two careers have been rather hard pressed to find even a few points of similarity.

For instance, in the advice the old man gives Hadingus—to seek

9. Given the date of his first exploits, it may be supposed that he was between fifty-five and sixty when he disappears from view.

10. Dudo, De moribus et actis primorum Normanniae ducum, lib. 1, Hastingus, in Patrologie latine by Migne, 141, col. 621. There are eleven Alexandrines in the same tone.

11. A made-up name referring to some district in North Russia.

12. In fact, when there is a historical background behind one of his characters, Saxo is well aware of it. For example, the successor of Hadingus, Frotho I, apart from a few traits drawn from the mythical Fróði (the Danish Freyr), perpetuates in the geography of his campaigns, particularly in Scotland, and in certain episodes of his life, the memory of a real-life Viking named Fróði who lived in the first half of the ninth century: this fact was solidly and elegantly established in 1910 by Axel Olrik in the first appendix to Danmarks Heltedigtning 2: 314–16 ("Vikingesagen om Frode"); see below, Appendix 2, p. 159; cf. Paul Herrmann, Kommentar, pp. 130–31.

distant wars in preference to ones close to home (viii, 16)—Paul Herrmann has recognized an echo of Hasting's real-life history, since the words *bellis longinquis* are contrary to the story of the saga both before and after the advice. Since Hadingus never made any expeditions other than around Denmark, the words must have been suggested, Herrmann says, by some other, fairly powerful tradition; it means that the author knew that Hasting-Hadingus had in fact fought far from home, as we have seen that Hasting did.[13] But the weakness of such exegesis hardly needs emphasizing.

The same author also claims to have found a second concordancy in the two stories.[14] As we have seen, it was only later on in his career that Hasting seems to have practiced alliances and undertaken concerted expeditions. "This," Paul Herrmann writes, "is in accordance with the fact that Hadingus, in Saxo, concludes his pact of blood-brotherhood with the viking Liserus later in his career, not in his earliest youth." The interpretation is a rather bold one, as will be apparent if we reconsider the text (vi, 7). It is, on the contrary, when Hadingus is still young, at the *outset* of his career as a warrior and during the *first* episode of this new life that he and Liserus, at the instigation of the one-eyed old man, conclude this pact of brotherhood and become allies; until that point Hadingus had certainly displayed the taste and received a training for a warlike future (vi, 1), but he had not actually been in battle; on the contrary, he had spent his time in the embrace of his lovelorn wet nurse (vi, 3–4); and what parallel can we possibly find for this love affair between Hadingus and his giantess, or their return from Sweden into Denmark (vi, 4–6)—in other words, everything preceding the alliance with Liserus—in the solitary raids of the Viking Hasting along the Loire and the Somme?

Finally, it is no less bold to interpret the fact that Hadingus does not die during a campaign but at home in Denmark, by his own hand, as a recollection of the death of the real-life Hasting, since we know nothing about the latter's death whatever. In order to give color to his linking of the two deaths, Paul Herrmann observes[15] that from 894 onward Hasting "vanishes" (*verschwindet still*) from the history of western Europe. Yet he has told us himself, earlier on, that nothing at

13. *Kommentar*, p. 91.
14. Ibid., pp. 91–92.
15. Ibid., p. 92.

all is known of the how or the why of this disappearance. At that rate, one might also claim that the lifelong limp Hadingus had inflicted on him during his combat with Asmundus (viii, 3) is a reference to some wound, some infirmity, that might, despite our knowing nothing about it, have been inflicted on Hasting . . .

When one thinks of the sarcasm that such twentieth-century critics have heaped upon what they pityingly term Max Müller's "mythological school," it is sobering to consider with what flimsy evidence they are content to buttress the fantasies they claim to have been sired by this "historical spirit" of which they set themselves up as champions.

But does the similarity of the two names alone provide any authority for linking Hadingus and Hasting? Certainly not. Saxo never confused Nordic sounds to such an extent. If he had been writing about the Viking plunderer then his name—whether beginning with *Halst-* or with *Hast-*[16]—would have been found unchanged. And in fact later on (in 8. iii, 8) Saxo names a *Halsten* among the Norwegians who come to help Ringo against Haraldus Hyldetan; and (in 8. ii, 7) he names a *Hastinus* among the "proceres" who support Haraldus. So that *Hadingus* means quite simply *Hadingus*, and is not an approximation of something else.

It is not in the history of the Vikings that we should search for the events Saxo recounts. Despite the contempt of Paul Herrmann, we must address ourselves, along with several great nineteenth-century scholars, to mythology.

16. The best texts (*Annales de Saint-Bertin, de Saint-Waast*) write *Halstingus*. The chronicle of the counts of Anjou and the lords of Amboise says that in French he was named *Haustuin*, which confirms *Halst-* (Ferdinand Lot, *Romania* [1890], pp. 388–89). Dudo gives *Alstignus*. Later we find *Alstagnus*. Thus the forms *Hasting* (French) and *Haesten* (English) seem to have lost an *l*. I copy here almost letter for letter from the information given in the fascinating little book by Roger Dion, *Paris dans les récits légendaires du IXᵉ au XIIᵉ siècle* (1949), in particular p. 31, n. 2.

2

HADINGUS AND
THE GOD NJÖRÐR

(1843–1941)

To the best of my knowledge it was in 1843 that a list of the immediately evident analogies between the Hadingus saga and the myth of the god Njörðr was first drawn up—though in a humble capacity, as a subsidiary argument in an article with a different goal, as support for the confrontation of Saxo's two *Frothones*, the kings Frotho I and Frotho III, and the god Freyr. The article in question, which threw its net wide indeed, was entitled "Siegfried und Freyr" and was by Wilhelm Müller.[1]

The most outstanding of the analogies hardly required discovery; it is so evident that it would be a bold man who attempted to establish who first noticed it. "It has often been remarked," Müller writes, "that Saxo puts in the mouths of Hadingus, Frotho's father, and Hadingus's wife poems that are also recited, in Snorri's *Edda*, by the sea god Njörðr and his wife Skaði; and that the similarities are such that the verses in Saxo might well pass for a direct translation of the *Edda* texts."

This analogy has been frequently reiterated in later years, together with another that Müller was the first to point out: the way in which Hadingus and his wife Regnilda come to marry also recalls the way in which Njörðr and Skaði came to be married. Müller also thought he could discern other resemblances; but these justifiably have been allowed to lapse by subsequent scholars.[2]

---

1. *Zeitschift für deutsches Alterthum* 3 (1843): 43–53. Passage concerning Hadingus-Njörðr on pp. 48–49.

2. Hadingus as founder of *Fröblót*, the sacrifice to Freyr (Saxo, 1. viii, 12) linked to Njörðr and Freyr's creation by Óðinn as *blótgoðar* or sacrificial priests (*Ynglingasaga*, chap. 4). Daughters of Hadingus urging their husband to revolt against Hadingus (Saxo, 1. viii, 23–26), then against Frotho I, his brother (Saxo, 2. ii, 10–12) reminiscent of Freyja being accused by Loki of having incited the gods against her brother Freyr (*Lokasenna*, str. 32; but this is certainly a translation error: Loki says on the contrary that the gods caught

It was not until fifty years later, in 1894, that Ferdinand Detter, having recalled these first two similarities, pointed out a third relating to Hadingus's magical journeyings by sea and Njörðr's status as the tutelary god of the *sæfarars*;[3] this too has entered into the public domain, though no attention seems to have been paid to another important observation by means of which Detter was able to justify what at first sight appears to be one of the saga's most astonishing digressions: the conflict between Othinus and Mithothyn (vii, 1–3).[4]

Finally, in 1898, Rudolf Much pointed out[5] yet another correspondence, this time between the deaths of Hadingus and Njörðr, which are variously but equally "Odinic," marked with "Óðinn's sign" and oriented toward that god. Having been made the subject of mockery by Paul Herrmann,[6] this suggestion has since been generally ignored. Its force will nevertheless soon become evident.[7]

These are the three episodes in the case of which the analogy between myth and saga is generally recognized. To them we must add Müller's point of departure, to wit the fact that just as Njörðr in the *Ynglingasaga* has Freyr as his son and successor, so Hadingus has as his son and successor the first of the "Frothones" in whom Saxo in varying degrees has incorporated elements of "Fróði," the contemporary Danish doublet of Freyr.[8]

I. THE DUETS OF HADINGUS AND REGNILDA (SAXO, I. VIII, 18–19) AND OF NJÖRÐR AND SKAÐI (GYLFAGINNING, 12, PP. 30–31)[9]

Hadingus has married Regnilda, and after having defeated and killed his great enemy Uffo, king of Uppsala, he has returned to Denmark.

Freyja sleeping with her brother). Müller quite rightly hesitates to link the captivity of Hadingus (Saxo, 1. vi, 8–10) with the ill treatment meted out to Njörðr and alluded to by Loki (*Lokasenna*, str. 34): when Njörðr was sent to the gods as a hostage the daughters of Hymir used his mouth as a chamberpot (*hlandtrog*).

3. "Zur Ynglingasaga," *Beiträge zur Geschichte der deutschen Sprache und Literatur* 18 (1894): 1: "Njörðr und Skaði, die Nibelungen," pp. 72–82. In the same volume, pp. 198–201, Detter suggests a reconstruction—which smacks very much of the 1890s—of the "primitive form" of the Njörðr-Skaði myth.

4. See below, pp. 94–95.

5. "Der germanische Himmelsgott," in *Festgabe Richard Heinzel*, 1898, p. 276.

6. *Kommentar*, p. 107.

7. See below, pp. 141–45.

8 See below, Appendixes 2 and 5.

9. The *Gylfaginning* and the *Skáldskaparmál* are quoted (chapters, pages) from the critical edition, *Edda Snorra Sturlusonar* by Finnur Jónsson (Copenhagen, 1931): "*Gylfaginning*, 12, pp. 30–31" means "G., chap. 12 and pp. 30–31 of the F. J. edition."

18. Thus his enemy was now removed, and he passed several years without any stirring events and in utter disuse of arms; but at last he pleaded the long while he had been tilling the earth, and the immoderate time he had forborne from exploits on the seas; and seeming to think war a merrier thing than peace, he began to upbraid himself with slothfulness in a strain like this:

"Why loiter I thus in darksome hiding, in the folds of rugged hills, nor follow seafaring as of old? The continual howling of the band of wolves, and the plaintive cry of harmful beasts that rises to heaven, and the fierce impatient lions,[10] all rob my eyes of sleep. Dreary are the ridges and the desolation to hearts that trusted to do wilder work. The stark rocks and the rugged lie of the ground bar the way to spirits who are wont to love the sea. It were better service to sound the firths with the oars, to revel in plundered wares, to pursue the gold of others for my coffer, to gloat over sea-gotten gains, than to dwell in rough lands and winding woodlands and barren glades."

19. Then his wife, loving a life in the country, and weary of the matin harmony of the seabirds, declared how great joy she found in frequenting the woodlands, in the following strain:

"The shrill bird vexes me as I tarry by the shore, and with its chattering rouses me when I cannot sleep. Wherefore the noisy sweep of its boisterous rush takes gentle rest from my sleeping eye, nor doth the loud-chattering sea-mew suffer me to rest in the night, forcing its wearisome tale into my dainty ears; nor when I would lie down doth it suffer me to be refreshed, clamouring with doleful modulation of its ill-boding voice. Safer and sweeter do I deem the enjoyment of the woods. How are the fruits of rest plucked less by day or night than by tarrying tossed on the shifting sea?"

Njörðr, the sea-loving god, guardian of sailors, inhabitant of Nóatún, "The Enclosure of Ships," has married Skaði, daughter of the Scandinavian giants, who is in love with the rocks and forests of inland Norway. Their tastes are incompatible. Here is what Snorri writes:

Skaði wanted to make her home where her father had done before her, which is to say among the rocks, in the lands they call þrymheimr;[11] but Njörðr wanted to be near the sea. So they agreed that they would stay nine nights at þrymheimr and the nine following at Nóatún.[12] But

10. The lions in Denmark that appear here and earlier (vi, 8) must be an inappropriate reminiscence of some classical author.

11. The manuscripts have þrumheimr, þrymheimr and þrudheimr, "also entweder eine Stätte des Lärmes oder der Kraft" (Jan de Vries, Altgermanische Religionsgeschichte 2 (2d. ed.; 1957): 336).

12. Two manuscripts have nine and three nights (nœtr); a third has nine and nine nights; the fourth, followed by Jónsson, has nine and nine winters (vetr), i.e., years. But nœtr is guaranteed by the third verse of Njörðr's strophe, the alliteration demanding an n: nœtr einar níu; so Jónsson does not hesitate to reject vetr as an indisputable corruption.

when Njörðr came back down from the mountains to Nóatún, he spoke this poem:

> Harm the mountains do me.
> I have not been long there,
> Nine nights only.
> The howling of the wolves
> Filled me with horror,
> compared with the song of the swans.

Then Skaði spoke this poem:

> I could not sleep
> by the edge of the sea
> because of the sound of the birds.
> It wakens me,
> coming from the woods as I do,
> every morning, the sea-mew.

Then Skaði went back up into the mountains and lived at þrymheimr . . .

The analogy between the two situations and the similarity of certain details are self-evident.

2. THE MARRIAGES OF HADINGUS AND REGNILDA (SAXO, I. VIII, 13) AND OF NJÖRÐR AND SKAÐI (BRAGARÆDUR, 2, OR SKÁLSDSKAPARMÁL, 3, PP. 80–81)

A few paragraphs earlier Saxo has recounted how Hadingus came to marry Regnilda:

Hadingus chanced to hear that a certain giant had taken in troth Ragnhilda, daughter of Haguinus, King of the Nitheri;[13] and, loathing so ignominious a state of affairs, and utterly abominating the destined union, he forestalled the marriage by noble daring. For he went to Norway and overcame by arms him that was so foul a lover for a princess. For he thought so much more of valour than of ease that, though

13. Meaning, probably, a Haakon, king of Nidaróss, inland from Trondheim. Cf. Didrik A. Seip, "Når fikk kaupangen i Trondhjem namet Nidaros?" Maal og Minne (1929), pp. 35–44 (probably about 1200; Latin: Nidrosia).

he was free to enjoy all the pleasures of a king, he accounted it sweeter than any delight to repel the wrongs done, not only to himself, but to others. The maiden, not knowing him, ministered with healing tendance to the man that had done her kindness and was bruised with many wounds. And in order that lapse of time might not make her forget him, she shut up a ring in his wound, and thus left a mark on his leg. Afterwards her father granted her freedom to choose her own husband; so when the young men were assembled at banquet, she went along them and felt their bodies carefully, searching for the token she had stored up long ago. All the rest she rejected, but Hadingus she discovered by the sign of the secret ring; then she embraced him, and gave herself to be the wife of him who had not suffered a giant to win her in marriage.

And here, in Snorri's version, is how Njörðr had come to wed Skaði. She was the daughter of the terrible giant þjazi,[14] whom Óðinn and the other gods had just killed by guile:

Skaði, the daughter of the giant þjazi, took his helmet, his coat of mail, and all his battle armor, and marched against the Abode of the Ases in order to avenge her father. The Ases offered her truce and compensation. In the first place she was to choose a husband from among the Ases, but the choice was to be made without her seeing anything but the feet of those from among whom she was to choose. She beheld a pair of extremely beautiful feet and said: "This is the one I choose. None but Balder has no defects!" But it was Njörðr of Nóatún ... [there then follows a second clause that we shall have cause to return to but that has no echo in the Hadingus saga].

Here again the analogy is evident, despite important differences.

3. HADINGUS (SAXO, I. VIII, 15)
NJÖRÐR (GYLFAGINNING, II–END, P. 30) AND THEIR POWERS OF NAVIGATION

Saxo writes:

Then Hadingus turned back and began to make homewards with his wife; some rovers bore down on him, but by swift sailing he baffled their

14. Here, $z = ts$. See the translation of this entire story in my *Loki* (1948), pp. 24–26.

snares; for though it was almost the same wind that helped both, they were behind him as he clove the billows, and, as they had only just as much sail, could not overtake him.

Ferdinand Detter remarks of this passage: "It is hardly possible that Saxo meant that Hadding's vessel was more lightly built—the only other factor beside the number of sails and the favorability of the wind that would count. The words he has chosen show that what he had in mind was a *magical* speed, since it proves faster in identical *physical* conditions . . ." And one is reminded,[15] "since Hadingus is Njörðr" (*da Hadingus Njord ist*), of Snorri's definition of Njörðr's "*provincia*":

"The third Ase is the one named Njörðr. He inhabits that place in the sky known as Nóatún. He has power over the speed of the winds and can calm the sea and fire. His is the power to be invoked for sea journeys and fishing."

As we know, the Lapp mythology recorded in the eighteenth century by pietist missionaries there confirms this account of Njörðr's powers. Axel Olrik, in fact, identified[16] Njörðr with the Lapp god *Bieka-Galles* (or *Biega-*, *Biegga-Galles*, according to the dialect), the "Old Man of the Winds," about whom the Närö[17] manuscript, one of the principal sources of our information about Lapp religion, has this to say:

Their third great idol they call Bieka-Galles, "the Old man of the Wind." He is the same person as Aeolus. They represent him holding in his right hand a shovel with which he imprisons the wind in his caverns when it has raged enough, and in his left hand a mallet with which he drives the wind out to blow again. They pray to this idol both

---

15. Detter prefers to compare with the ship *Skiðblaðnir* belonging to Njörðr's son Freyr.

16. "Nordisk og Lappisk Gudadyrkelse," in *Danske Studier* (1905), p. 52; also dealt with by Kaarle Krohn, "Lappische Beiträge zur germanischen Mythologie," in *Finnisch-Ugrische Forschungen* 6 (1906): 172–75.

17. This report, written in 1723 by the missionary Johann Randulf, exists in many copies despite the loss of the original and was first published when Ivar Qvigstad determined to make such eighteenth-century observations universally accessible: *Kildeskrifter til den Lappiske Mytologi* 1, in the *Skrifter* of the Society of Sciences of Trondheim (1903). This intelligent missionary has been criticized for having failed to distinguish between his own personal observations and information derived from his master Thomas von Weston or his colleague Jens Kildal, and thus for having lumped together nomadic and sedentary Lapp communities, thereby exaggerating the Scandinavian character of Lapp mythology. His report, nevertheless, remains an extraordinarily important document, and was the sole basis of Axel Olrik's articles (*Danske Studier*, 1905, 1906) so convincingly using Lapp survivals to throw light on certain features of Scandinavian pagan beliefs.

when they are up in the mountains with their reindeer, asking him to calm the wind that is harmful to those animals, and also when they are fishing at sea and a tempest blows up, putting their lives in danger. They then promise to offer up a sacrifice on his altar.

The same manuscript says further on that the Lapps offer boats to Bieka-Galles. According to another source they also offer up wooden shovels to him. This shovel, which is almost certainly a misconstruction and should be an oar (reminding one, curiously enough, of the meeting foretold to Ulysses by Tiresias in the *Nekyia*: "When men shall take your oar for a winnowing shovel . . ."), and the error it constitutes seems to offer proof, according to Axel Olrik, of a borrowing by the landbound Lapps from the seafaring Scandinavians.

A similar interpretation is suggested by Scandinavian toponymy,[18] which moreover is also already in agreement with the description in Tacitus of the center of worship for Nerthus, the feminine Njörðr of northern Germania: *insula in oceano*. For whereas there are almost no place names in Norway having -*ey*, -*œy* as a second element for the other gods (none for Óðinn, one for Þórr at the entrance to Oslo fjord, none for either Freyr or Freyja), or with the second element -*vik* (bay) (none for Óðinn, none for Þórr, two for Freyr, two for Freyja), on the other hand from south of Bergen up to Œxnes in the Northland there are five places, especially islands in fjords or out to sea, with names deriving from **Njarð-ey* (När-ö among them!) and also, from south of Bergen down to Trondheim, four places with names deriving from **Njarð-vík* in which the *Njarð* seems to mean Njörðr. To which must be added two *Njarð-vík* in Iceland, one on the east and one on the west. And also in Norway, south of Bergen, there is an island named Tysnesœn that, thanks to Magnus Olsen,[19] has played a large part in the history of Scandinavian religions and that

18. I here give a précis of the account given by Magnus Olsen, "Hedenske kultminder i norske stedsnavne," in the *Skrifter* of the *Videnskabs selskabet i Christiania, h.-fil, klase* (1914, 4, pub. in 1915), pp. 50–62.

19. "Det gamle norske œnavn Njarðarlög," in *Forhandlinger of the Videnskabs selskabet i Christiania* (1905), 5, 29. All the first part, up to the interpretations (historic, mythological), is excellent, admirable in its precision and penetration; criticism by Anton Espeland, "Njarðarlaug—Onarheim—Tengstad," *Maal og Minne* (1919), pp. 62–65, of the second part of the article (para. 4, pp. 21–28), which Magnus Olsen considered wrongly as being the most conclusive, and of the reading *lög* in the toponym (in eighteenth-century documents the island is still called *Gierlou*: so we must take *laug* as the basis); cf. the same author's "Stedsnavnen på Njarðarlaug og i omegnen," ibid. (1920), pp. 103–10. Cf. below, **Appendix 6.**

formerly used to be called *Njarðar-lög* ("legal district of Njörðr"). All of which suffices to prove that in everyday life as in their theology the Norwegians looked upon Njörðr as the protector of seafarers and of the centers (islands, bays) of seafaring.

Such are the points of convergence that have so far become obvious between the myth of Njörðr and the saga of Hadingus.[20] According to the authors and schools concerned, the importance and the meaning attributed to them, however, have varied widely. But since I cannot give an account here of all the opinions that have been expressed I shall ignore all those of no more than anecdotal interest in order to concentrate on the principal ones, and those that have been or can still be maintained in more recent times.

Three-quarters of a century ago there was a tendency to rather sweeping assumptions in this matter: *Da Hadingus Njord ist . . .*, Detter blithely wrote. Hadingus thus "was" Njörðr," just as in chapter 16 of the *Ynglingasaga* Vanlandi "was" Njörðr" too, and again Agni in chapter 22 of the same work. It was the era when everything in the epic was endowed with a mythic origin, when against a background of uniformly naturalistic mythology (in which Njörðr was summarily defined as a "Meergott," just as other gods were simply "Himmels-" or "Sonnen-" gods), it was possible to set out without hesitation or qualm indefinite series of algebraic equivalences: Siegfried too, for example "was" Freyr . . . .

Then a reaction set in. Scholars became aware that the heroes of epic are not all transformed, humanized gods: Achilles, Agamemnon, Oedipus, Siegfried, all resist not only the "solar" or other explanations of naturalist mythology but also explanation "by the gods" in general. If we sometimes revert to using such interpretations today we try to be more cautious, and even when an epic hero presents affinities with a particular god we do not on that account immediately assimilate the one into the other: Romulus is not said to "be" the Jupiter who protects him; Numa, a devout exponent of *fides*, is not

---

20. On Njörðr see now Edgar Polomé, "Nerthus-Njord," *Handelingen der Zuidnederl Maatsch van Taal en Letterkunde* 5 (1951): 99–123, repeated in "A propos de Nerthus," *Latomus* 13 (1954): 167–200; Hans Ellekilde," Nærum, Guden Njords Hjem," *Søllerød-Bogen* (1952), pp. 57–95; Jan de Vries, "La toponymie et l'histoire des religions," *Revue de l'histoire des religions* 145 (1954): 207–30 (criticizing Magnus Olsen; see above, p. 25, n. 19), and Eric Elgqvist, *Studjer rörande Njordkulters spridning blard de nordiske folken* [1952]); see below, Appendix 6.

said to "be" Dius Fidius; even after Stig Wikander's[21] discoveries we do not say that the five Pāṇḍava, the heroes of the *Mahābhārata*, "are" the group of functional Indo-Iranian gods to whom they undoubtedly correspond. The reaction was therefore healthy in principle. Still, as almost always happens in such matters, it may well have gone too far.

And the risks of excesses in this direction were increased by the fact that at the same time, in the sphere of Germanic studies, it was beginning to seem possible that another kind of research might lead to the suppression, to the dissolution, of the majority of myths. For it was at this time in fact that interest was growing in "narrative motifs," in purely literary contents, in the incidents and formulas that can be traced from one saga or tale to the next and whose frequent recurrence in the adventures of the Scandinavian gods by then had been pointed out. A school of Germanists, whose most powerful spokesman was Eugen Mogk,[22] were led by their observations to believe that they had "laid" a great number of "myths" by this method, viewing them as no more than an artificial accumulation of narrative devices or motifs lacking any legitimate links and therefore devoid of any real subject matter. This concept was duly applied to the "mythical" story of Njörðr, with the result that its relationship to the Hadingus saga could be seen—and was seen—as being limited to one of three modes, one of which deprives that relationship of any importance whatever and two of which leave it much reduced:

a) The saga of Hadingus and the Njörðr myth have annexed the motives they share independently and fortuitously. Two of the motifs at least (the marriage by the bride's choice and dependent on a secret token for recognition; the magic power of swift sailing) are very widespread in other tales, and the third (the duo) may be a mere literary motif. This thesis is best represented by Friedrich von der Leyen, the initiator of this interpretation—or rather of this fragmentation of Scandinavian mythology with the help of the *Märchenkunde*.[23]

b) The Njörðr myth is a more or less direct lifting of motifs taken from an older form of the Hadingus saga, or at least from a narrative in which those motifs were already united and from which the saga

21. See above, p. viii.
22. See the discussion in my *Loki* (1948), pp. 81–108.
23. *Das Märchen in den Göttersagen der Edda* (1899), pp. 35–37, 81.

itself likewise derived them. This second thesis was for a time held by so notable a scholar as Jan de Vries.[24]

c) It was the Njörðr myth that first came into fortuitous being—like so many Scandinavian pseudomyths—by a combination of narrative motifs, and it was the author of the Hadingus saga—familiar with this literary aggregate—who borrowed this particular grouping of motifs from it. This last thesis seems to be that favored by Saxo's learned commentator Paul Herrmann.[25]

I hope to show that the first two of these theses are untenable; that the third alone is possible; but that this third thesis should be revised, first in the light of a less simplistic, less negative, more religion-oriented conception of the Germanic myths, and second in the light of a more attentive examination of the Hadingus saga itself, since the analogies already noted far from exhaust the parallelism that exists between the careers of Hadingus and the god Njörðr.

In his little program-book of 1899, *Das Märchen in den Göttersagen der Edda* (pp. 35 et seq.), von der Leyen attacked the analogy that involves the greatest number of differences, that of the marriages (No. 2, above, p. 22):

> The last story in the Indian collection *Vetalapañcaviṃçati* (*The Vampire's Twenty-five Tales*), runs as follows (cf. the author's *Indische Märchen*, pp. 107, 165): a king and his son see women's footsteps in a wood, some large and some small. The king decides to marry the woman with the larger feet, his son the woman with the smaller feet. They follow the trail. We then find that the women are a queen and her daughter, both beautiful, persecuted, and forlorn, but that it is the daughter who has the larger feet and the mother the smaller. This motif presents an undeniable kinship with that of the marriage of Njörðr and Skaði; as is only natural, it is in India that it has taken on the most delicate, the most elaborate form . . . .
>
> Saxo's story seems to me to be a reminiscence of the widespread story to which Reinhold Köhler has given the name "The Grindkopf story," a fairly exact masculine counterpart of the Cinderella story in

24. *Altgermanische Religionsgeschichte* 2 (1937): 255; in the second edition, 2 (1957): 175–77, Jan de Vries has gone over to my interpretation.

25. *Kommentar*, p. 107. Nevertheless, one sentence of Paul Herrmann's keeps all three of these in equal balance: "Die Möglichkeit, dass gleichzeitig dieselben Motive in verschiedenen Dichtungen zur Anwendung gelangen können, oder dass eine Sage sie der andern entlehnt, hat man früher kaum erwogen."

its crudest form (Grim, *Kinder- und Hausmärchen*, no. 65; Reinhold Köhler, *Kleine Schriften* 1 : 420), a form in which Cinderella is a servant in a king's palace, dances three times with him in magnificent clothes, and is identified thanks to a slipper left behind in his hands. In the same way, in "The Grindkopf story" a king's son is working as a gardener in another king's household and rescues him three times from great danger without being recognized; but the third time the king wounds his rescuer in the leg, so that having been recognized later by his wound the gardener is given one of the king's daughters in marriage.

Though the Saxo story derives from a "male Cinderella" story, one is tempted to look upon the *Edda* story as being a refined adaptation, and the Indian story an even more refined one, of a "female Cinderella" story, which is to say of the motif in which a king marries a girl he knows solely from her shoe, simply because he is so attracted by the shoe itself. This motif is extremely old. As early as Strabo we find it applied to an Egyptian king (rich bibliography in Paul Sartori, *Der Schuh im Volksglaube, Zeitschrift des Vereins für Volkskunde* 4: 160). But this is no more than a hypothesis to be handled with prudence. In any case, however, the motif could hardly have belonged to the original Njörðr and Skaði story; it seems rather to have been artificially and very clumsily inserted into it later; in the first place, in the other versions it is always, naturally enough, women's—not men's—feet and shoes that are recognized by their beauty; in the second place the *Edda* offers no justification whatever for the condition imposed on Skaði of seeing no more than the suitors' feet.

Moreover, it is von der Leyen's intention, in this section of his book, to show that the entire story (including the battles against and murder of the giant Þjazi) of which this scene is merely the epilogue is an artificial and unplanned agglomeration of other narrative motifs of the same kind.[26]

Twenty years later, in *Götter und Göttersagen der Germanen* ([1920], pp. 55, 199),[27] von der Leyen himself pointed out in all honesty, in the scene in which Skaði chooses Njörðr, a detail that may be linked, further back than the motifs of popular literature, with certain ritual practices, certain magico-religious representations that go deeper and are probably older than those motifs. It is at the sight of his beautiful feet that Skaði, making a great mistake, prefers her god to the others,

---

26. See my discussion in *Loki*, pp. 114–16.
27. Same author, *Die Götter der Germanen* (1938), pp. 43, 178.

just as in the Cinderella story it is the prettiest slipper (originally the prettiest foot) that decides the king's choice. "Now we look upon the diversely interpreted prints and pictures of feet occurring in several Scandinavian cave-drawings as fertility symbols, since we know that the foot radiates a sexual force and attraction (*eine geschlechtliche erregende Kraft*), and the foot of a god would naturally radiate a force even greater than the foot of a man." There is also a custom from the former French province of Berry, a popular ritual and never occurring as a narrative motif, that Felix Liebrecht related to the Njörðr-Skaði story as early as 1871:[28] on the night of the wedding, when it is time for bed, all the women present at the wedding feast lie down on the floor, their shoes and stockings are taken off, and they are covered with a sheet so that nothing but their feet and ankles are left showing. The groom must then indicate which feet belong to his wife. If he is correct then he is allowed to lead her up straight away to the nuptial chamber. If not, then he must wait till the following day. It is therefore possible, von der Leyen concludes, that the marriage of Skaði and Njörðr is evidence of a comparable custom with the rôles of the sexes reversed.

These reflections are interesting, but they still do not explain why this theme of possibly ritual origin was applied to Njörðr, to the marriage of Njörðr. In his *Skade und die Götter Skandinaviens* ([1941], p. 10 et seq.),[29] Franz-Rolf Schröder took up the question again at this point. Njörðr, he says, like his feminine and continental counterpart the Nerthus of Tacitus, was originally a chthonian divinity[30] and as such closely linked to everything to do with fertility, whether in plants, animals, or men. He is therefore connected to the "vegetable spirits" of many modern folk rituals, as for example the Russian *Jarilo*, who is celebrated on 24 June in White Russia: the young girls of a village choose one of their number to represent Jarilo; they dress her as a boy with a white cloak, a crown of flowers, and a bunch of wheat in her left hand; Jarilo has bare feet. They place him on a white

28. *Germania* 16 (1871): 217 (following Frédéric-Guillaume Bergmann, *Les Gètes* [1859], p. 247); and again in the collection *Zur Volkskunde* (1879), p. 408.

29. Second fascicle of the *Untersuchungen zur germanischen und vergleichenden Religionsgeschichte* (1941); and earlier by the same author, "Njörds nackte Füsse," in the *Beiträge zur Geschichte der deutschen Sprache und Literatur* 51 (1927): 31–33.

30. A word loaded with ambiguity and therefore to be wary of. Tacitus refers to Nerthus as "Terra Mater," but Njörðr, though a god of prosperity and wealth like the Vanes generally, does not have this precise specification; and he is even less an Orcus.

horse, and if it is good weather they lead him out into the fields, across the plowed land. Then, in the presence of the elders, his companions stand around him, also wearing flowery crowns, singing a song in his honor:[31]

> He goes everywhere, Jarilo,
> All over the world,
> Making the wheat to sprout in the fields,
> Multiplying the children of men.
> And wherever he places his feet,
> There is wheat by the stack,
> And wherever his eye rests,
> The shoots grow strong and green.

Schröder also recalls the Roman *Nudipedalia*, practiced in times of prolonged drought, an agrarian rite recorded by Pliny (*Naturalis Historia* 28; 78) in Cappadocia, in which the women are bare-footed, and also a modern practice in Lower Franconia. And he concludes: "Even if all the customs and traditions relating to bare feet cannot be exclusively explained by a single type of representation, it is certain that many of them fall into the domain of *fertility magic*, as in the case, we may assume, of Njörðr's bare feet."

31. This White Russian song was published by Drevlianskij in the supplements to the *Žurnal Minist. Narodn. Prosvêščenija* 1 (1846): 21. Through Alexander Nikolayevich Afanasiev, *Poetičeskie vozzrenija* . . . 1: 441–42, the ceremony and the song were included in the *Wald- und Feldkulte* 1 (1875), by Wilhelm Mannhardt (p. 415), who popularized them with the inclusion of what seems to me a curious error. Here is the text of the song:

> Valačyvsja Jarilo
> na usemu svêtu,
> polju šyto radziv,
> ljudzjam dzêcu pladziv.
> A gdzêž jon nagoju,
> tam žyto kapoju;
> a gdzêž jon ni zyrne,
> tam kolas zacjvice.

Mannhardt and his successors, including F. R. Schröder, all translate line 5 as "*wo er geht mit blossen Füssen*, where he goes with his bare feet." This means that they see *nagoju* as the adjective *nagoj*, "bare" (but then where do they get "feet"?), whereas it is simply the instrumental form of *noga* "foot" (notated *naga*, because unaccented *o* = *a*, as *plodiv* in line 4 and *kop(n)oju* in line 6 are notated *pladziv, kapoju*). The text says simply: "Where he [walks] with his foot, where he places his foot"; the bareness of the feet is there in the ceremony, but the song does not mention it.—Cf. also Bror Schnittger, *Fornvännen* (1922), pp. 101–3; the article "barfuss" (Eckstein) in Hanns Bächtold-Stäubli, *Handwörterbuch des deutschen Aberglaubens* 1 cols. 912–22; Hilding Celander, "Barfotaspringningar vid vårdag-jämningstiden," in *Folkminne och Folktankar* (1944).

Schröder reinforces his argument by an examination of the second clause in Skaði's agreement with the Ases. For not only does she demand marriage with a god before she will be reconciled to them, she also insists on something she believes to be impossible: that the Ases shall somehow make her laugh. Then, Snorri says:

> Loki tied one end of a cord to the beard of a goat and the other to his testicles, and then as each pulled and yielded in alternation they both cried out loudly indeed. Then Loki fell at Skaði's knees: she laughed, and so her peace was made with the Ases.

Von der Leyen, as early as 1899, had quoted parallels from other stories for this incident, though parallels so localized that, coming as they do from the Germanic and above all from the Scandinavian countries, one begins to wonder whether the connection ought not to be reversed and whether in these cases it was not the more modern stories that borrowed the motif from the myth.[32] Schröder, however, has recalled the numerous rites and myths linked to fertility cults and gods in which: (1) an angry or mourning divinity is made to laugh or to emerge from his or her retreat by the sound of laughter; (2) this result is obtained by a scene of ribald sexual exhibitionism: Baubô making Demeter laugh by disclosing her "female scallop";[33] or, in an Egyptian myth that some have seen as the prototype of the Baubô legend but that is probably merely a parallel formation, the goddess Hather uncovering her sex and provoking laughter in her father, the sun god Ra, who had been lying on his back for a whole day, offended, gloomy, and alone; in Japan, Uzume dancing an obscene dance and making the gods laugh so loudly that the sun goddess Amaterasu comes out of the cave to which she had retired in anger; and so on. And Schröder concludes that the second condition laid down by Skaði, and the manner in which Loki fulfills it, far from being just a narrative motif fortuitously attributed to a certain set of gods,

---

32. *Loki*, p. 115, n. 1.

33. See the delightful essay by Paul-Louis Couchoud, "Le mythe de la danseuse obscène" in *Mercure de France*, 15 July 1929, and also the classic bibliography of the subject quoted by Schröder: Kern, in the *Real-enzyklopädie* by Pauly-Wissowa, s. v. "Babou," vol. 3 (1899), cols. 150–52; Hermann K. Usener, *Kleine Schriften* 4: 127; Ludolf Malten, in *Archiv für Religionswissenschaft* 12 (1909): 438; Arthur B. Cook, *Zeus* 2 (1925): 131–33; more recently, Ernesto de Martino, "I Gephyrismi," in *Studi e Materiali di Storia delle Religioni* 10 (1934): 64–79 and especially 68–75); Isidore Lévy, "Autour d'un roman mythologique égyptien" (*Ann. de l'Inst. de Philol. et d'Hist. Orientales et slaves* 4 [1936], *Mélanges Cumont*), pp. 819–34: "Hathor, Baubô, Uzumé."

is a very suitable choice of motif indeed for a goddess who is about to marry, as Skaði is, a god of abundance and fertility like Njörðr. Despite almost universal approbation, he says, von der Leyen was wrong to see the whole myth of þjazi, Skaði, and Njörðr as nothing more than an aggregation of narrative motifs linked by a single loose thread, *eine Anzahl lose miteinander Märchenmotive (Das Märchen . . .*, p. 38); "Behind the folkloric stylization is concealed an authentic, primitive, mythic kernel, which has merely been clothed, dressed up with narrative motifs."

I should also like to recall that my own comparative Indo-European studies have produced evidence that seems to point in the same direction: the scene in which Skaði—in a veritable "svayamvara" in the Indian style—is provided with such limited clues on which to base her decision, can be linked with an homologous Indian story,[34] that of Sukanyā choosing Cyavana, her old—or rather rejuvenated—husband, in preference to the Aśvin who have taken on the same shape, simply by the divining of her own heart; and this story is in fact situated in the "Aśvin sector" of Indian mythology, which is homologous with the "Njörðr-Freyr" sector of Scandinavian mythology,[35] in other words, in what I term the "third function," the function of prosperity, fertility, health, and so on.

I should also like to add a last and purely Scandinavian consideration.[36] The representations of bare feet in cave paintings referred to by von der Leyen in his second essay are to be found in great numbers, and principally in two particular types of "context": near-schematic drawings representing cattle, which fits in well with von der Leyen's interpretation of the feet as fertility symbols; but also, with a regularity that has not been sufficiently noted, near pictures of boats and fleets, a fact that can be best interpreted if we place it side by side with the fact we are now considering, which is that Njörðr, a god doubly wealthy from his status as a Vane and also, independently, as the tutelary god of navigation and its profits, is chosen by Skaði

34. *Naissance d'Archanges* (1945), pp. 159–62; *Mahābhārata* 3: 123–25, śloka 10.345–10.409; *Mythe et épopée* 1 (1968): 285–87.

35. *Jupiter Mars Quirinus* (1941), pp. 155–69; *Mythe et épopée* (1958): 288.

36. One need only look through the 61 plates of "selected items" published by Arthur Nordén under the title *Felsbilder der Provinz Ostgotland in Auswahl* (Hagen i. W. and Darmstadt, 1923). There is a vast number of works available on this subject, and I prefer not to enter into a discussion of these drawings here.

solely from the aspect of his bare feet, which are the most beautiful feet in the entire divine world; perhaps those "footprints" on the Scandinavian rocks are already the symbol of a god who is at once the protector of flocks and ships.

These observations establish that every essential element in the story of the Njörðr-Skaði marriage—"svayaṃvara" in deliberately deceptive circumstances, choice of husband from bare feet, laughter induced by grotesque obscenity—is directly linked to the god's essential nature, and that we cannot therefore be dealing with a capricious and fortuitous aggregation of "narrative motifs," or with a corrupt "folk-tale prototype." They also establish, on this point, that not only the first of our theses—that of von der Leyen—but also the second (see above, p. 48) is untenable: neither the variant presented by the Hadingus saga nor any other purely literary composition could possibly be the source of the mythical story, whether directly or not.

In fact, one might even go so far as to think that on this point—that of the marriages—the resemblance between myth and saga is fortuitous: the differences are indeed considerable, and the saga variant has indisputably made use of a narrative motif that is fairly widespread (rather than the Cinderella story von der Leyen suggests), in which the girl, rescued from a monster, a dragon, and so forth, leaves a mark on her wounded rescuer's body so that she may be certain of recognizing him among the claimants for her hand and so marry him.[37]

What forces one in the end, even on this point, and despite their divergence, to accept that the saga is dependent upon the myth for at least the general sense of the episode is that this analogy—that of the marriages—is indissolubly linked in both saga and myth with yet another analogy, that which I demonstrated first, the duets (see p. 20): in both cases the marriage is the means to make the duet possible. And where the duet is concerned the interdependence of the two texts is not disputed (the presence in both of details as precise as "the wolves," "the sea-mew," are sufficient to establish it) and the dependence of the saga on the myth is indeed flagrant.

In the myth, the duet is fully justified: the couple have married in error, without mutual attraction; their conflicting tastes are a direct

---

37. One example is to be found in my *Contes Lazes, Travaux et Mémoires de l'Institut d'Ethnologie* (1937), p. 98.

result of their origins and their conflicting significances, since he is a sea god and she a skiing, hunting "giant of the interior," of that *Scandin-avia*[38] that no doubt provided her with her name as a result of a misinterpretation of its first element. A pact, alternately disagreeable to both parties, has been entered into in an effort to circumvent the incompatibility; so that the melancholy duet is an authentic and natural consequence of both marriage and pact. Moreover, it leads on to a no less natural result: the final separation of the ill-matched couple.[39] All the parts of the story are properly linked and motivated.

In the saga, however, there is nothing to prepare us for the duet: the marriage has taken place in joy and gratitude, with both partners fully aware of the other's identity; nothing in the preceding events has even so much as hinted at a preference on the part of Regnilda—who is merely the "average folktale princess"—for any one kind of landscape over another; nor do the couple make a pact to live alternately in two homes: they simply go to live "in Denmark," apparently always in the same place. And, lastly, the duet is as bereft of consequences as it is of causes: no separation ensues from it, and although Regnilda is never mentioned in the story again, the reason, as we learn quite incidentally later on, is not because she has gone home but because she is dead.

As for the details of the duet, in the myth everything is quite natural: the land where wolves howl to the horror of the sea-loving god

38. I do not believe that *Scadin-avia* is etymologically "the island of the goddess Skaði": the first term of the name must have, or have had, a more positive content, alluding to "darkness" or something else that we cannot be sure of. I believe that the name of the goddess Skaði was abstracted from the geographical name, which was no longer fully understood, and that she therefore stands in rather the same relation to the name of "her" country as *Ériu*, the Ireland personified in certain narratives, does to the geographical notion of Ireland: Ériu is the wife of one of the kings of Ireland at the time when the Tuatha Dé Danann arrive, she confers the sovereignty of the island, etc. (cf. Skaði's second marriage with the sovereign god Óðinn according to a tradition mentioned in *Ynglingasaga*, chap. 8); but the name of the island was not derived from the name of this female character, quite the contrary: Ireland, Latin *Hibernia*, Irish *Ériu*, Welsh *Iwerddon*, must be *Iweryen- (with normal fall of a *P-) "the fat," or cf. Greek *Pierios*, *Pieria* (Pedersen). On Skaði see Jan de Vries, *Altgermanische Religionsgeschichte* 2 (2d. ed.; 1957): 335–38.

39. It is generally admitted as being obvious that Snorri quoted no more than two fragments of two longer poems that Saxo or his source knew in their entire state (Paul Herrmann, *Kommentar*, pp. 121–22); is this probable? Saxo's verses have much more the feel of a verbose paraphrase. The duet of the two evil spirits, the *montanus* and the *marinus*, is different: Wettinus, *Vita Galli*, (= one of the companions of Columban), 6, quoted in Carl Clement, *Fontes religionis germanicae* (1928), pp. 54–55.

is the austere and genuinely wild mountain country of inland Norway. Whereas in the saga, how are we to reconcile the smiling landscape of Denmark with the expressions used by Hadingus: in *latebris opacis*, tristia sunt *juga vastitasque*, officiunt *scopuli rigentes difficilisque situs locorum, salebras, steriles* habitare *saltus*? Where are we, in fact: in the green land of Zealand or in the Scandinavian alps?

Lastly, in the myth the duet is beautifully balanced and homogeneous: we are given two and only two possible settings for human habitation, both on land: the seacoast and the mountains, each with its own particular animals, each complained of in turn by the husband and wife. In Saxo, Regnilda also limits herself to disparaging one habitat, *litus*, and praising another, *silvas*; but the antithesis that Hadingus expresses is between quite different things: the tedium of life on land on the one hand, and the sailor's or Viking's life aboard ship on the other.

Thus the saga variant appears from every point of view to be a somewhat clumsy literary adaptation of what in the myth was logically linked and harmoniously constructed. Though without sufficiently remarking upon this inevitable conclusion, Paul Herrmann in his commentary on Saxo[40] certainly indicated the principal weaknesses of the saga duet and more generally the evident difficulties that Regnilda caused the author:

> Saxo passes over Hadding and Regnild's conjugal life without comment: after Hadding has rescued her from the giant and she has recognized her rescuer thanks to the ring, she disappears from the saga. At the moment when the woman rises up from the underworld (viii, 14) her rôle is a strange one: is Hadding alone at dinner when the messenger from the supernatural world emerges from the hearth? If Regnild is not with him, why has she been eliminated in this way? When Hadding leaves Drontheim [viii, 15], it is certainly noted that she went with him, but nothing more. Later on we shall learn that she is dead solely from the fact that her ghost appears to her husband in a dream [viii, 23]. And, furthermore, how can Regnild when she is living among the beautiful Danish beech woods feel so nostalgic for the meager birch thickets of Drontheim fjord? How can the cries of the Danish seabirds be so surprising and hateful to her when we know she comes from Norway, a country that is jam-packed with noisy bird colonies? It is as

40. P. 121.

if Hadding had only been given a queen, Carl Rosenberg ironically remarks (*Nordboenes Andsliv fra Oldtiden til vore Dage* 1 [1878]: 213), so that he will be able to recite this poem.

A poem, let us remember, that in the mythical account in fact expresses the very essence of the two characters, explains the fragility of their union, and prepares their separation.

It is clear that this episode, linked to that of the marriage in both saga and myth—logically in the one and clumsily in the other, but nevertheless linked—makes it impossible to consider as purely fortuitous the rather looser analogy to be observed between the two versions during the marriage episode itself. We must simply recognize that the saga writer has taken the marriage episode from the myth and twisted it to make it fit in with a rather more banal narrative motif, or even that the saga writer has reworked the scene as presented in the myth in order to make it conform with a narrative motif that resembled it in several important features, but that seemed to him more serious and more suited to his literary form.

Thus it is now hardly necessary to insist on the third analogy, that between Hadingus's manifest gifts as a sailor and Njörðr's recognized position as the god of navigation. It would lead us to further reflections of the same kind, which may be summarized as follows:

This quality is fundamental in the god and even largely constitutes his essence; it cannot, therefore, in the myth, be a fortuitous folkloric allusion.

On the other hand, we should find that the theme of a supernatural gift for sailing is by no means the widespread commonplace in the saga literature that some seem to assume.[41]

Lastly, in the saga, this episode of magical sailing power, for which we have been in no way prepared, is presented framed between the marriage and the duet, in other words between the two interdependent episodes in which the two other analogies with the Njörðr myth have been noted, and it is the only other episode besides them that involves Regnilda, who in the two others is both the occasion and the instrument of the analogies.

It is not possible, therefore, to consider this concordance separately

41. See below, p. 106, nn. 1, 2 (10).

from the two others; it too must be interpreted—benefiting from the clear indication provided by our confrontation of the two duets—as a corrupt borrowing by the saga from the myth, as a literary adaptation of the functional definition of the god Njörðr.

If this is so, then we must investigate whether the homology of Hadingus and Njörðr is really limited to this partial list. I believe that it extends to other episodes, and above all—despite the Viking coloration it has received, as with all the borrowed material incorporated into Saxo's work, as for example that of the peace-loving Baldr—I believe that the career of Hadingus follows that of Njörðr in its general movement, in its characteristic division into two contrasting periods, one typically "Vane," the other controlled by Óðinn.

3

THE TWO LIVES OF HADINGUS

2) HADINGUS WITH THE ONE-EYED OLD MAN: THE ODINIC HERO, THE WINDS AND THE SEA

The life of Njörðr, who together with his son Freyr is the most representative of the Vane gods, is divided in the middle by a cæsura that is the equivalent of a metamorphosis.

The Vanes are the gods of fertility, of terrestrial and maritime wealth, and of sensual pleasures. They are thus distinct from the Ases, grouped around Óðinn their king and Ásaþórr their champion, whose strength lies in their knowledge, in their magic, or in their might in battle. The two groups were so distinct that in Snorri's[1] historicizing perspective as well as from the cosmological viewpoint of the *Völuspá*[2] they originally formed two neighboring but separate peoples, each with its own customs and morality. After a hard but inconclusive war, Snorri says, they came to an agreement: the principal Vanes, Njörðr at their head, came to live among the Ases, first as hostages but very soon as equal partners, received places of honor from Óðinn, and adopted the customs and morality of their new home. To be accurate, after this agreement we hardly hear anything more about the "Vane residue" that has remained aloof and separate, so that in practice the two societies, embodied in their chiefs, are from that point on amalgamated into one harmonious whole.

I have shown[3] that far from merely handing down to us the embellished memory of historical wars or invasions, of ethnic or cultural movements, this legend is simply the form taken in Northern religions by an old Indo-European myth whose occurrence is also attested in India and Rome, a myth that explained how the ideal

---

1. *Ynglingasaga*, chap. 4; *Skáldskaparmál*, 4 (= *Bragarœdur*, 1), p. 82.
2. Strophes 21–24.
3. See below, pp. 98–99 and 103, n. 16. On Njörðr, see above, p. 25, n. 19.

society was formed at the beginning of time, whether a society of ancestors (Rome) or of gods (India and Scandinavia): two groups or types of gods or men were first distinct and juxtaposed, the one embodying religious and legal sovereignty together with might in battle, the other embodying fertility and wealth; these two groups engaged in a severe but indecisive conflict that lasted until a pact between them finally incorporated representatives of the second group—or the second group in its entirety—once and for all into the society of the first group, which was thereby made complete and in consequence capable of a harmonious fulfillment of the three functions recognized as fundamental by the Indo-European ideology.

It is in the case of Njörðr, or at least with reference to him, that the few Scandinavian texts at our disposal make clearest the original conflict between the customs and moralities of the two groups of gods. Here is what happened, as recorded in the fourth chapter of the *Ynglingasaga*, when the major Vane gods came to live among the Ases and subordinated themselves to Óðinn:

> Óðinn established Njörðr and Freyr as sacrificial priests, and they were *Díar* among the Ases. The daughter of Njörðr was Freyja, she was a sacrificial priestess. It was she who taught the Ases for the first time the form of magic named *seiðr*, which was customary among the Vanes.
>
> While Njörðr was among the Vanes he had had his sister to wife, for that was the law with them, and their children were Freyr and Freyja. But among the Ases it was forbidden to marry with kin so close.

In fact, we know that once among the Ases, and freed from the "incest morality," Njörðr contracted a second and not very happy, albeit "normal," marriage with Skaði;[4] and one text will not even allow Freyr and Freyja to be born before this second union.[5]

As for *seiðr*, although it was taken up by the great Ase Óðinn and added to his own arsenal of magic, its use always remained tainted with a suggestion of infamy.[6]

But, needless to say, despite his becoming one of Óðinn's officers, Njörðr still retained his own particular mythological province, and in particular, as we have seen, his home in Nóatún, the "Enclosure of Ships," and control over the winds and navigation.[7]

4. See above, pp. 22–23.
5. *Gylfaginning*, p. 31.
6. *Ynglingasaga*, n. 9.
7. See above, p. 24.

In the humanized perspective of the *Ynglingasaga*, Njörðr outlived Óðinn and succeeded him as king when the latter rose up into heaven. Then he died of old age, after having seen most of the Díar disappear. Before dying he had himself marked with "Óðinn's sign," a lance wound, in order that he might join him in the invisible world, as the god had promised.[8]

His decisive meeting with the one-eyed old man, i.e., Óðinn, also bisects and transforms the life of Hadingus. Until then he has been living a strange existence with Harthgrepa. Henceforth he is the man with the one-eyed old helper, Óðinn. Let us first consider this second phase briefly.[9]

Saxo, needless to say, is unable to conceive of this second phase of his hero's career as being in any way different from the lives of all the other Odinic heroes of Viking epics. Since they are warriors and sea-rovers, naturally the aid they expect and receive from Óðinn is exclusively of a warlike kind.[10]

The aid begins with what is in fact an *initiation* episode (vi, 7–10). The old man takes the badly battered hero to his home, transporting him through the air on his horse,[11] over the sea; he then gives him mead to drink, thereby restoring his strength, reveals to him the means of escaping from his bonds in captivity, then sends him back to do battle with the raging lion and eat the beast's smoking heart,

8. *Ynglingasaga*, ṇ. 9.

9. I have not bothered overmuch with the points that have been sufficiently elucidated by the commentators and are not important for my purpose: wedge formation, the old man's *balista* in viii, 16, etc.—I am amazed that Paul Herrmann, *Kommentar*, p. 99, apparently trusting to Axel Olrik's *Kilderne til Sakses Oldhistorie* 2 (1894): 7, claims that Saxo is unaware that the one-eyed old man is Óðinn. How can we attribute such ignorance to Saxo when we find elsewhere, referring to another "Odinic hero" (7. x, 6): *Interea rex Sueonum Alverus . . . Danis bellum denuntiate. Cujus eventum Haraldo oraculis explorare cupienti senex praecipuae magnitudinis, sed orbus oculo, obvius exstitit, qui, hispido etiam amiculo circumactus, Othynum se dici bellorumque usu callere testatus utilissimum, ei centuriandi in acie exercitus documentum porrexit . . ."* And Paul Herrmann admits on p. 1 that the first book of the *Gesta Danorum*, as seems probable, was written after the seventh!

10. Paul Herrmann, *Kommentar*, pp. 99–100. On the "Odinshelden" (Haraldr Hildetan, Sigmundr, Sigurðr, in part Starkaðr . . .) see p. 421 et seq.; cf. on Hadingus as Odinsheld, Bugge, *Mythiske Sagen Arkiv för Nordisk Filologi* 16 (1900): 30.

11. These aerial journeys recall (particularly the phrase in para. 9) the Danish versions of the Wild Hunter: Hans Ellekilde, "Odinsjægeren paa Moen," in *Nordisk Folkminne, Studier till Carl-Wilhelm von Sydow* (1928), pp. 90 (and n. 2), 91, and 113; cf. Axel Olrik, "Odinsjægeren i Jylland," in *Dania* 8 (1901): 145: on the island of Anholt, in the middle of the Kattegat, all those who have seen him say that "One," i.e., Óðinn, "comes from the southwest," i.e., across the sea.

thus enabling him to become what he is destined to be, an almost invincible warrior:[12]

8. "*As thou farest hence, a foe, thinking thee a deserter, will assail thee, that he may keep thee bound and cast thee to be devoured by the mangling jaws of beasts. But fill thou the ears of the warders with divers tales, and when they have done the feast and deep sleep holds them, snap off the fetters upon thee and the loathly chains. Turn thy feet thence, and when a little space has fled, with all thy might rise up against a swift lion who is wont to toss the carcases of the prisoners, and strive with thy stout arms against his savage shoulders, and with naked sword search his heart-strings. Straightway put thy throat to him and drink the steaming blood, and devour with ravenous jaws the banquet of his body. Then renewed strength will come to thy limbs, then shall undreamed-of might enter thy sinews, and an accumulation of stout force shall bespread and nerve thy frame throughout. I myself will pave the path to thy prayers and will subdue the henchmen in sleep, and keep them snoring throughout the lingering night.*"

9. And as he spoke, he took back the young man on his horse, and set him where he had found him. Hadingus cowered trembling under his mantle; but so extreme was his wonder at the event that with keen vision he peered through its holes. And he saw that before the steps of the horse lay the sea; but was told not to steal a glimpse of the forbidden thing, and therefore turned aside his amazed eyes from the dread spectacle of the roads that he journeyed.

---

12. We may compare the "initiation" of Hialto (Höttr) by Biarco (Bjarki) in Saxo (2. vi, 5) and in the saga of Hrólfr Kraki (chap. 5): *Ursum quippe*, Saxo writes, *eximiae magnitudinis obvium sibi inter dumeta factum jaculo confecit* [Biarco] *comitemque suum Hialtonem, quo viribus major evaderet, applicato ore egestum beluae cruorem haurire jussit: creditum namque erat, hoc potionis genere corporei roboris incrementa praestari*. Similarly, in the *Ynglingasaga* (chap. 34), because the young Ingjaldr has proved inferior in warlike games, his tutor Svipdagr makes him eat a spit-roasted wolf's heart, as a result of which he becomes more ferocious. On this whole question of warrior initiations and warrior societies among the old Indo-European peoples, see the Introduction and third part of *Heur et malheur de guerrier* (1969), pp. 3 and 101–48 (= *The Destiny of the Warrior* [1970], pp. xi and 111–64); also all the vast Maryannu material, especially Roger T. O'Calaghan, "New Light on the Maryannu as 'Chariot-Warrior,'" in *Jahrbuch für kleinasiatische Forschung* 1 (1951): 309–24; Manfred Mayrhoffer, *Die Indo-Arier im alten Vorderasien* (1966), bibliography; Geo. Widengren, *Der Feudalismus im alten Iran* (1969), pp. 11–44, 45–63.
To ingest the blood or flesh of a savage beast may naturally produce different effects: In the case of Sigurdr (*Fáfnismál*, str. 31 and prose following), licking the dragon's blood from his finger enables him to understand the language of the seven birds, though a little later he drinks the blood of Reginn and the dragon, doubtless in order to give himself strength. On these practices throughout the world see James George Frazer, *The Golden Bough* 5 (*Spirits of the Corn and of the Wild*), 2 (1912): chap. 12, pp. 138–68 ("Homaeopathic magic of a flesh diet").
Lastly, for the *lion* in Denmark, in Courland, see above, p. 21, n. 10.

10. Then he was taken by Loker, and found by very sure experience that every point of the prophecy was fulfilled upon him . . .[13]

Later on (viii, 16), the old man has himself taken on board Hadingus's vessel just as he does, under the name and in the disguise of Hnikarr, in the legend of Sigurðr;[14] he explains the "wedge formation" to him[15] just as he does later, under his real name of "Othynus" to two more heroes, Haraldus Hyldetan (7. x, 6), then Ringo, Haraldus's opponent (8. iii, 8-9); he assists him on the field of battle against the "Byarmenses," not in the fray itself, which would not be in keeping with his customary mode of action, but from the rearmost rank, with the help of a magical piece of artillery,[16] and also by atmospheric counter-magic, dissipating the threatening cloud that the wizards of the "Byarmenses" have conjured up.[17] All this is typical matter in the careers of the "Odinshelden," Saxo's as well as those of the sagas.

Before leaving Hadingus, the old man makes one last intervention in his life consisting of a prophecy and a piece of advice (viii, 16). The advice is rather odd, as we have seen,[18] in that it is not followed in the narrative by any confirmation or effect. It consists of a warning "not

13. Paul Herrmann summarizes this initial episode by saying: "Óðinn rescues Hadingus from defeat. *Odin rettet ihn aus der Niederlage.*" But this is not quite true, since after carrying him off he brings him back to the same place, so that the hero is taken prisoner exactly as he would have been if the old man had not intervened. The intention is different: far from being saved from them, Hadingus *must go through* this series of perils to the end, he *must* attack and kill the most fearsome of wild beasts so that he can drink its blood; that is the necessary, preliminary service that the divine or human protector of a hero-candidate must render his protégé. Before sending him to face his terrible ordeal, Óðinn simply gives Hadingus the necessary store of strength and knowledge to confront it with success. In short, it is an initiation scene; cf. below, p. 45, n. 24.

14. *Reginsmál*, str. 16-18, and the accompanying prose passage.

15. Paul Herrmann, *Kommentar*, p. 103 and n. 2 (in particular bibliography of a polemic between Gustav Neckel and Finnur Jónsson, pp. 524-25).

16. The old one-eyed man's *balista* fires ten arrows at a time. The most similar incident to this occurs in a Faeroes ballad (cf. below, p. 139, n. 28), *Jústinjallskvæði*, str. 43, in which we find, referring to Óðinn in a battle: "An arrow flies from each of his fingers to strike down the grave warriors." Helmut de Boer, "Mythologisches aus den faeröischen Folkevisern," in *Göteborgs Högskolas Årsskrift* 26 (1920): 51-52.

17. These trials of magic between wizards attached to opposing armies are also a favored theme in Irish epic narratives: for example, "The siege of Druim Damhgaire," ed. and trans. by Marie-Louise Sjöstedt, *Revue celtique* 42 (1926): 1-123.—The *Byarmenses* are close kin to the *Finni*, the great master wizards known as such to Saxo: in III, ii, 8, he recalls Guso *Finnorum Byarmorumque* princeps. The *Bjarmir*, the *Bjarmaland* of the sagas, the *Biarmenses* and *Biarmi* of Saxo constituted for a long while a fairly powerful trading state on the shores of the White Sea, subjugated in the fifteenth century by Novgorod. On the *Biarmia* see lastly Alan S. C. Ross in *Virittäjä* (Helsinki, 1951), pp. 51-58 (in Finnish), summary, pp. 103-4 (in English).

18. See above, pp. 16-17.

to prefer obscure wars to glorious wars or near wars to distant ones." The prophecy, on the other hand, is completely fulfilled by the end of the saga: "But the old man, when he parted from him, foretold that the death whereby he would perish would be inflicted, not by the might of an enemy, but by his own hand." After that the old man does not reappear. But it is as though, from then on, Hadingus is expecting a sign. And he assumes he has received it when eventually, worn out by age and threatened by the plotting of his own kin, he learns also of the death of his Swedish friend Hundingus, drowned during a feast in his, Hadingus's, honor, given because Hundingus thought him already dead. And he is careful to choose the Odinic death par excellence,[19] that of the "god of the hanged," of the "hanged god": he hangs himself before his assembled subjects (viii, 27). This may be interpreted as a dilution on Saxo's part of a procedure exemplified in many sagas and Faeroe Island ballads:[20] the old man's prophecy may perhaps be a substitute for a true pact, the hero receiving Óðinn's protection on condition he gives himself to him wholly and is prepared to go and join him either at the expiration of a fixed period or when a certain sign is given.

At the same time, as I said earlier—following Much[21]—this Odinic death enabling the hero to join his *dominus et magister* Óðinn[22] recalls the death of Njörðr, who similarly, finding himself at the end of his long career, has the sign made on his body that Óðinn taught him and that will enable him to go to the god after death.

Except for the general fact of becoming Óðinn's man, and the correspondence between the two deaths—transposed into a warlike context, moreover—the relationship between Hadingus and Óðinn in this Odinic phase of his story is composed of "Viking" clichés in which it would be futile to look for any trace of the character of Njörðr and his relationship with Óðinn.

Two important facts, nevertheless, ought to be emphasized:

1. It is in this second phase—as with the unhappy union of Njörðr and Skaði—that the marriage of Hadingus and Regnilda occurs,

19. Jan de Vries, *Altgermanische Religionsgeschichte* 2 (2d ed.; 1957): 50.
20. Helmut de Boer, "Mythologisches aus den faeröischen Folkevisern" (see above, p. 43, n. 16), p. 53.
21. See above, p. 20, n. 5.
22. Paul Herrmann rightly comments (*Kommentar*, p. 105): "Ódin (*hangagoð*) ist sein Lehrmeister bis zum Tode"; cf. below, Appendix 1.

together with their disagreement and the duet expressing it (viii, 13, 18–19).[23]

2. In this second phase, aside from his relations with Óðinn, Hadingus manifests a particular relationship *with the winds and the sea* in which Óðinn is wholly uninvolved, and which play just as great a rôle in his victories and escapes from danger as the god.

This relationship also begins—in parallel with the initiation as a warrior devised by Óðinn—with a terrible ordeal that is equivalent to an initiation (viii, 11–19), since no power can be acquired without risk and pain, without having given rise in the first place to a sort of caricature of itself.[24] Having killed a sea-monster on the shore, Hadingus is condemned by an unknown woman to create terrible storms around him wherever he goes, whether on land or on sea:

23. See above, pp. 20–23.
24. See above, p. 43, n. 13. We recognize here an abundantly exemplified type of plot in three acts: glorious combat with catastrophic or excessive consequences to begin with; operation remedying the catastrophe; durable transformation of catastrophic or excessive consequences into a domesticated and beneficent *power*. It is one variety, "fictionalized" innumerable times in legends, of the initiation plot. Indra, Arjuna, and Cúchuclainn all became the invincible warriors they subsequently proved in just such a manner: Indra, having killed the monster Vr̥tra, was then reduced almost to nothingness and disappeared; the gods then recreated him, "blew him up again"; whereupon he then found himself, but only then, in enjoyment of his quality of Vr̥trahan with all the virtues that entailed and for the greater good of the universe. Arjuna was crushed, reduced to a bleeding lump, in his battle against the god Śiva, of whose identity he was unaware; he was then revived and cured by the god, and from then on he became invincible to demons and men alike. Cúchulainn emerges from his initiatory combat against the three Meic Nechtain literally inflamed, blind with fury, a danger to his own kin as well as to his enemies; he is plunged into vats of cold water; from then on he has control over his terrible power, together with the *delba*, the monstrous signs that are its manifestation, and is able to employ them at will. (See *Heur et malheur du guerrier* [1969], pp. 104–48; = *The Destiny of the Warrior* [1970], pp. 115–64).

More generally, and particularly in the Scandinavian area, every great specialist, whether man or god, must buy what is to be his province by means of an ordeal, and often by an initial misfortune. We have seen how this rule applies to Hadingus the warrior. Óðinn himself was forced to sacrifice one of his eyes in order to acquire his power to see the invisible, and thus to become a one-eyed god; and it was not until he had hanged himself and spent nine nights dying on a gibbet that he learned the secrets of the runes. Týr owes his power to the fact that he first lost his right hand in heroic circumstances, thereby consenting to become the one-armed god. Þórr returned from his first combat with a sliver of his adversary's weapon in his skull, a blemish that he was to retain from then onward, that was to become his distinctive sign, one that his worshipers, to judge by Lapp survivals, imitated by hammering a nail into the head of his statues (see below, p. 168, and n. 11).

The powers of the warriors Indra, Cúchulainn, etc. and that of the "master of the sea and winds," Hadingus, are not acquired by such mutilation but, as I have just explained, by a "reversed catastrophe"; but this is in fact only another expression of the same conception, which is the principle of so many initiatory plots (simulated deaths . . .) throughout the world. Basically, it is not so very far from the principle of vaccination, or from Musset's melancholy observation: man is an apprentice, pain is his master . . . .

11. As he boasted of his triumph, a woman came along and spoke to him in this manner: *Whether thou tread the fields afoot, or spread canvas overseas, thou shalt suffer the hate of the gods, and through all the world thou shalt behold the elements oppose thy purposes. Afield thou shalt fall, on sea thou shalt be tossed, an eternal tempest shall attend the steps of thy wandering, nor shall frost-bind ever quit thy sails; nor shall thy roof-tree roof thee, but if thou seekest it, it shall fall smitten by the hurricane; thy herd shall perish of bitter chill. All things shall be tainted, and shall lament that thy lot is there. Thou shalt be shunned like a pestilent tetter, nor shall any plague be fouler than thou. Such chastisement doth the power of heaven mete out to thee, for truly thy sacrilegious hands have slain one of the dwellers above, disguised in a shape that was not his: thus here art thou, the slayer of a benignant god! But when the sea receives thee, the wrath of the prison of Eolus shall be loosed upon thy head. The West and the furious North, the South wind shall beat thee down, shall league and send forth their blasts in rivalry; until with better prayers thou hast melted the sternness of heaven, and hast lifted with appeasement the punishment thou hast earned.*

12. So, when Hadingus went back, he suffered all things after this one fashion, and his coming brought disquiet upon all peaceful places. For when he was at sea a mighty storm arose and destroyed his fleet in a great tempest: and when, a shipwrecked man, he sought entertainment, he found a sudden downfall of that house. Nor was there any cure for his trouble, ere he atoned by sacrifice for his crime, and was able to return into favour with heaven. For, in order to appease the deities, he sacrificed dusky victims to the god Frö. This manner of propitiation by sacrifice he repeated as an annual feast, and left posterity to follow. This rite the Swedes call Fröblod [the sacrifice or feast of Frey].

After this sacrifice to Freyr, the other great Vane god, his redoubtable power over the winds and his familiarity with the sea are not eliminated but disciplined, or rather turned around the other way: that which at first persecuted him begins to provide him with magical assistance. This happens in two separate episodes:

a) First, the episode of his prodigious sailing powers (viii, 15) translated above[25] and used by Ferdinand Detter in 1894 for his

---

25. See above, pp. 23–24. There is no cause here to allude, as Paul Herrmann does, to the (H)oddo of whom Saxo writes (5, ii, 4) that he was *vir magicae artis doctus ita ut absque carina altum pererrans hostilia saepe navigia concitatis carmine procellis everteret.* Hadingus is not a wizard, either in this incident or at any other juncture. He is not a (H)oddo applying his magic by sea exactly as he would apply it anywhere else, capable of crossing the sea without a ship as other wizards fly through the air; he makes use of the sea, of his vessel, of the art of navigation, of the winds, supernaturally well, with perfection, and by virtue of a certain affinity, but with no further miracle than that perfection and that affinity.

assimilation of Hadingus into Njörðr in his rôle as a "Meergott": after having wedded Regnilda in Norway, Hadingus is taking his wife back to Denmark; their ship is pursued by searovers and, despite the equality of their sails and the seemingly identical winds filling them, he outstrips and escapes them. Detter has already pointed out, as I remarked earlier, that the narrator's intention is manifestly not to suggest that Hadingus's vessel is better constructed than the pirates', but to indicate some sort of protection or a "gift" for navigation that is independent of the prevailing physical and mechanical conditions.

b) Second, the episode of the war against Tosto, during which an extraordinary feat by Hadingus at sea nullifies his adversary's land victory (viii, 21):

> 21. Hadingus was conquered by this man in an affair by land; but in the midst of his flight he came on his enemy's fleet, and made it unseaworthy by boring the sides; then he got a skiff and steered it out to sea. Tosto thought he was slain, but though he sought long among the indiscriminate heaps of dead, could not find him, and came back to his fleet; then he saw from afar a light boat tossing on the ocean billows. Putting out some vessels, he resolved to give it chase, but was brought back by peril of shipwreck, and only just reached the shore. Then he quickly took some sound craft and accomplished the journey which he had begun before. Hadingus, seeing he was caught, proceeded to ask his companion whether he was a skilled and practiced swimmer; and when the other said he was not, Hadingus, despairing of flight, deliberately turned the vessel over and hid beneath it, thus making his pursuers think him dead. Then he attacked Toste, who, careless and unaware, was greedily watching over the remnants of his spoil; cut down his army, forced him to quit his plunder, and avenged his own rout by that of Tosto.

This last episode contains many commonplaces of Viking literature: the motif of the ships surreptitiously holed, which occurs seven times in Saxo, and also that of the feigned death, though admittedly in this precise form—that of apparent drowning—it occurs only here. The fact remains, however, that having been defeated on land it is on the sea, by the boldness and skill with which he sails his skiff, then turns it over and hides beneath it—an acrobatic feat that would have spelt destruction to anyone else—that Hadingus not only escapes but transforms his defeat on land into ultimate victory: on the water, in the sea, he finds success again, as the giant son of the Earth, in the Greek fable, replenished his strength by touching the earth.

Thus the "initiation" that first of all gave him such an unwelcome power over the winds and the waves has now been transformed to his advantage: he has become to them, as a hero, what Njörðr is to them as a god. As for the detail of the curse[26] that heralds his misfortunes—and in consequence his subsequent powers as well—it is

26. The source seekers have shown a great interest in this passage. According to some of them the scene and the animal designated by the really rather vague expression *inauditi generis beluam* were provided by the great Scandinavian and Anglo-Saxon texts. Paul Herrmann goes further. In his *Kommentar*, p. 116, under the heading "Classical Influences," we read an amazing parallel between what happened to Hadingus and what happened to Agamemnon at Aulis. Hadingus kills the divine *beluam* just as Agamemnon killed the doe of Artemis. The result of this unheard of, involuntary crime by the Greek leader— according to an author "that Saxo could have read and used although his style bears no trace of it"—according to Dictys, then, is a *lues*, a scourge; and in the verses of Saxo's imprecation we find: *nec taetrior ulla pestis erit . . .* , pests, lues, two synonyms. The *lues* consists in the fact that the winds refuse to allow the departure of the Greek fleet; and corresponding to these contrary winds in the saga, Herrmann says, we find the storms. He adds that in Dictys (chap. 19), it is a woman *deo plena* who informs Agamemnon of his punishment, just as it is a *femina* who *compellat* the hero. And so, Herrmann continues, we are faced with a series of correspondences so striking that it seems amazing that Bugge, with his "beispiellose Belesenheit," took no notice of them . . . We shan't take any notice of them either.

More realistic, but no more helpful when it comes to the matter involved—which is what is important—are the similarities of style that have been noted between the curse of Saxo's *femina* and the *Buslubœn* or "Busla's Request," a short poem occurring in the *Eddica minora*, and also the analogy drawn with famous threats or anathemata such as those Skírnir directs at Gerðr when she refuses to yield to Freyr's passion (*Skírnismál*, str. 26–37), or those of Sigrún against her brother, her husband's murderer (*Helgakviða Hundingsbana II*, str. 28). There certainly existed a literary convention of "verse curse," and it is this convention that gives the three Eddic or para-Eddic texts and the verse spoken by Saxo's *femina* an air of kinship. But the kinship is merely superficial. Not only are the circumstances of Saxo's curse very different, but so is its nature. The *Skírnismál* curse is not really worth considering: the curse is not a punishment at all; it is conditional, it is directed against a woman, and it heralds the murder of her father and herself, spinsterhood, rape, mockery, a fearsome draught . . . And it is easy to show that both in the *Buslubœn* and the curse of Sigrún quite different things are involved than in that of the *femina*.

With reference to the lines from *quatiere mari . . .* to *nec tegent* (ll. 4–6), Herrmann quotes one of the strophes spoken by Sigrún:

> Let it not sail, the ship that sails under you,
> even if the high wind blows in its sails!
> Let it not run, the horse that runs under you,
> even if the enemy is on your heels!
> Let it not cut, the sword held in your hand,
> but let it sing around your own head alone!

The threat in this case is quite clearly to *paralyze* the hero, on land and on sea, on his ship and on his horse, and to *disarm* him, just as it was said that Óðinn's magic immobilized men's bodies and blunted their weapons; it is, in short, exactly the opposite of the *unleashing of the elements* and the *perpetual tempest* that Hadingus will take with him wherever he wanders on land or sea.

instructive to compare it, outside the sphere of Scandinavian documents proper, with the Lapp beliefs of which we have such a well-circumstantiated account in the manuscript of Närö: the benefits and the ills brought by the wind over which Bieka-Galles, in other words Njörðr, has power—including its devastating effect on herds—are precisely those enumerated by the unknown woman and quoted above on pp. 24–25.

Thus everything has not been reduced to the commonplaces of "Viking" epic in the second, Odinic, period of Hadingus's career. We do find in well-developed form the two traits—and the only two—that mythology attributes to Njörðr in the second, Odinic, period of his career and that are in Njörðr's case interdependent: his ill-matched marriage with a mountain wife who loathes the sea; his power over the winds and navigation.

It is, however, the first period that provides us with the most instructive similarities between the hero and the god. I now hope to show that it is entirely constructed around the two traits that in mythology set the Vanes apart from other beings in a pejorative way: the morality of sensual pleasure and sexual freedom, including the practice of incest, and a reputedly shameful and culpable form of magic.

As for the much longer curse pronounced by Busla against King Hringr, that is at once more detailed and more general. It is true that it begins—like a sort of overture to the curse proper that will lend it greater weight—by announcing a worldwide earthquake (str. 3), but the detailed menaces that follow are quite different: poison in the breast, eyes turned outward, deaf ears (str. 4); "If you sail, let your oars break, let your sails tear or fly away, let the wood of your yard-arms snap!" (str. 5); "If you ride, let your reins break, let your mount stumble and fall, let your path lead you into the power of the trolls!" (str. 6); "Let it be in your bed as though you are forever burned by flaming straw, your throne as though tossed by high waves! And worse yet: if you wish to enjoy a girl, failure!" (str. 7); "Let the dwarfs, giants, wizards, and mountain trolls burn your house! Let the frost giants hate you, let stallions kick you, let straw prick you, let the storm make you lose your way!" (str. 8).

In Saxo, the curse is no less terrible, but it is limited to one precise gift: *by his mere presence, as though it were his special power, Hadingus will unleash a tempest* [*perpetuum turbinem*], *which by sea will engulf his vessel and on land will blow down any house in which he tries to take refuge after his shipwreck*. There is a predominance of marine elements, as is natural in the punishment of a crime committed on the *seashore*, against a *belua* that apparently came out of the sea: in fact, in the fulfillment of this threat, the shipwreck occurs first, and, though the first lines of the threat itself suggest an equality between misfortunes on sea and those on land, the latter (to be precise, ll. 13–16), in fact, put all the emphasis on storm by sea (*sed cum te exceperit aequo*, etc.). It is exactly as if Hadingus has contracted some uncontrollable, catastrophic power over the *wind* in general, but a power whose origin and principal applications lie at *sea*.

4

THE TWO LIVES OF HADINGUS

(CONTINUED):

1) HADINGUS WITH HARTHGREPA

a) Legitimate Incest among the Vanes

Among the Vanes, as we know, Njörðr lived with his sister as his legitimate wife.

Many brilliant constructions have been built upon Snorri's terse statement of fact. Claiming that the Scandinavian god Njörðr was known to Tacitus, in northern Germany, as the goddess Nerthus, instancing analogies between the rites of Nerthus and those of Freyr as described in a much-quoted passage from the *Flateyjarbók*, rites in both of which a *hiéros gamos* occurs, Kaarle Krohn and other authors have argued that the god couple Njörðr-Freyr—who are indeed closely associated in all the Nordic documents—had originally been, not a "father-son" couple, but a "mother-son" or "brother-sister" couple linked by an incestuous relationship. It is a theory incapable of proof: there is no authority whatever for assuming that among the Germanii of Tacitus, on the continent, it was a god and son—or brother—of Nerthus being represented by the priest of whom it is merely said that he was the only one with the right to touch the goddess's chariot, that he could sense the moment at which she became present in the sanctuary, and that he accompanied her in her cow-drawn vehicle.[1]

No less gratuitous are the conclusions that have been drawn since the work of Magnus Olsen both from such Scandinavian place names as indicate occasional proximity between Njörðr and the god Ullr

---

1. Franz-Rolf Schröder, *Ingunar-Freyr* (1941), p. 41, also says: "*Ingwanaz* ist der männliche Partner, der Sohn und Gemahl der *Nerþuz-*Ingwanō, der mütterlichen Erd- und Eibengöttin." The theory has sometimes been presented differently; for example, Paul Herrmann, *Nordische Mythologie* (1903), pp 202–3, posits an original male-Njörðr/female-Njörðr couple parallel to the known Freyr-Freyja couple. See below, Appendix 6.

and also from the two successive names of the Norwegian island of
Tysnesœ, formerly Njarðarlög:[2] this scholar accepts that the former
Scandinavian pantheon included a *female* Njörðr, like the continental
Nerthus who lived as the wife either of the god Ullr or of the god Týr,
in the rôle of god of heaven. But the conclusion exceeds the data:
the information provided by toponymy bears solely upon the *fact*
of the religious association of the two divinities (and even so we should
not be too quick to deduce an association from simple proximity),
not on the mythical *nature* of the relationship between them.

But in any case, why resort to games of this kind, to contrived
refinements that merely add a burden of irrelevant hypotheses to a
situation whose principle alone has any real importance? Snorri is
categorical: as long as he remained among the Vanes, Njörðr was his
sister's husband. In the *Lokasenna*, Loki reminds the god—now one of
the Ases—of his past in the following jibing words:

> 36. *Enough, Njörðr, leave your arrogance,*
> *I shall not remain silent either:*
> *with your sister you engendered a son,*
> *and that is exactly what we might have expected!*

Whether it was a law, as Snorri says, or mere looseness of morals,
as Loki implies, such was in any case the Vane practice. Freyr and
Freyja, who were brother and sister, also lay together, and in the same
poem Loki reminds Freyja of her past shame. Though it is true that
he prefaces the accusation with another one:

> 30. *Silence, Freyja! I know your very heart,*
> *and there is no lack of blame to lay at your door!*
> *Of the Ases and the Alfes now in this hall,*
> *every one has been your lover!*

In which Loki is in agreement with another malicious tongue at
work in the *Edda*, that of the witch Hyndla, who says to the goddess
(*Hyndluljóð*, 46–47):

> *You run nightlong, my pretty dear,*
> *Like the she-goat with footloose males.*

Freyja could at least have hesitated on the threshold of the nearest
kinship of all. But Loki knows she did not:

2. See above, p. 25, n. 19.

> 32. *Silence, Freyja! You are an evildoer*
> *and filled full with shame:*
> *they caught you with your brother, the kindly gods,*
> *and you were made to fart for it!*

And it is not in order to deny these facts, it is in order to excuse them and to claim legality for them that Njörðr, the family patriarch, intervenes and draws down on his own head, among other insults, the accusatory strophe 36, quoted first. The justification Njörðr offers is both amusing and instructive, since his excuses summarize one whole liberal approach to sexual morality:

> 33. *It is but trifling harm,*
> *if women take themselves a husband,*
> *a lover, or both at once . . .*

And let us note in passing that in all these eddic incest stories, in this morality of laxity that Njörðr contemplates with such serenity, it is the woman who takes the initiative, who debauches men, and even her own brother. And indeed, a little further on in the *Lokasenna*, the god Týr, rising in his turn to defend not the sister but the brother, says of Freyr:

> 37. *Freyr is the best of all the heroes*
> *in the hall of the Ases:*
> *he molests neither maiden*
> *nor wife of man*
> *and strikes off the shackles of all!*

Thus it was Freyja who took the first step, with him as with the others, like the Yamī who in a famous hymn from the RigVeda[3] seeks in vain to seduce her brother.

The interpretation of these incestuous relationships among the Vane gods, and that of Njörðr in particular, is a delicate matter. The sexual freedom, the sensuality, all the things imputed to Freyja are easily understood: their totality closely resembles all that is said of Aphrodite, of love goddesses in general, and is associated with the "third function"; similarly, the Fricco of Upsala, which is to say Freyr, the god whom Adam de Brême saw as endowed *ingenti priapo*, presided *paci et voluptati*. But incest is something quite different, a violation of a society's most fundamental statute; or else, when it is

---

3. *R̥gVeda*, 10, 10. Cf. Pūṣan, his sister and his mother (*R̥gVeda*, 6, 55, 4–5, etc.).

found legally instituted in a society, it is not at the level of the third function, applicable to the entire population, but at the level of the first function and applicable solely to an aristocracy or ruling dynasty (Egypt, Iran . . .). Frazer has collected from all over the world[4] a vast number of ethnographic facts that combine to demonstrate the disastrous consequences of incest on agriculture, on the fertility of nature: Oceania, Africa, ancient Greece, Ireland, even ancient Rome all provide evidence on this score. So what ought we to conclude?[5]

4. *The Golden Bough* 1 (*The Magic Art and the Evolution of the King*): 2, pp. 110–19.

5. Classifying the themes involving incest in the ancient literatures of Europe, particularly among the Celts and German tribes, is a vast and important study. Where the German tribes are concerned the essential points have been made, with reference to the incest of Sigmundr and Sign´y, in the second part of a work by Franz-Rolf Schröder published in 1935: *Germanische Heldendichtung, ein Vortrag nebst einer Studie zur Heroisirung des Mythos* (*Philosophie und Geschichte* 55). The usual forms of incest are generally quite different from what one finds among the Vanes: whether knowingly or not, a father lies *once* with his daughter, or a brother with his sister, and a great hero is born from this exceptional coupling.

In Ireland, Cengus Tuirnech gets his daughter with child when he is drunk; he sets the newly born infant afloat on the sea in a boat also containing tokens of its rank: purple cloak and golden cup; after being taken in by fisherfolk and named Fiacha Fer Mara, "Fiacha Man of the Sea," the child becomes a king of Ireland and Britain, and his sons after him (*Cóir Anmann* 55, in the *Irische Texte* of Ernst Windisch and Whitley Stokes [3, 2 (1897): 312]). The son of this Fiacha, Eterscél Mór, couples with his adopted daughter one day when she is guarding his sheep, and this incident produces Conaire Mór, later king of Ireland, on whom the interdiction, the *geis*, is laid that he must never see the sun rise or set at Tara ("De síl Chonairi Moir," in *Ériu* 6 [1912]: 134–35, 138, translation). Cairbre Musc couples with his sister Duibfind and engenders Corc Duibne, known by his mother's name as Corc Duibfinde (*Cóir Anmann*, 62, 66). The triplet brothers Find-Emain get their sister Clothru with child, at her instigation, and the child is Lugaid, another great hero (*Dindsenchas de Rennes* 140, in the *Revue celtique* 16 [1895]: 148–50. Cf. also *Tucait Indarba na nDessi* [*Anecdota from Irish Manuscripts*] 1, 19, 2; *Revue celtique* 50 [1933]: 103); cf. in Wales the legend of Vortigern. Among the Irish Celts incest is the *col*, the sin par excellence: O'Donovan's lexicon defines the adjective derived from it, *cullach*, *colach*, "incestuous, because of the greatness of his sin, *col*. [because] he is [i.e., has relations] with his mother and his sister" (see the note by Joseph Loth, *Zeitschrift für celtische Philologie* 17 [1917]: 147–52).

Among the German tribes the union of Sigmundr and his sister Sign´y produces Sinfjötli, a glory of the race of Völsungar, and they couple *in order* to engender him (*Völsungasaga*, chap. 7). In Saxo, apart from the attenuated example we are dealing with here, there is the story of another incest (IV, v, 4): Rolvo (the very great prince and hero Hrólfr Kraki) owes his birth to the incestuous and (as far as the father was concerned) involuntary union of the Viking Helgo and his daughter Ursa (Helgi and Yrsa); this error is directly attributable to the machinations of Ursa's own mother, Thora, who wishes to punish Helgo for having once abandoned her after getting her with child; when he knows he has slept with his daughter he sets out on an expedition and gets himself killed.

In all these cases, Celtic and Germanic alike, it will be seen that the incest is either accidental or seen as an exceptional event, and has the intention (either in the minds of the characters or at least in the plot of the story) of giving birth to a hero who is similarly exceptional.

It seems to me very striking that Njörðr practices incest only so long as the complete divine society has not yet been formed, in other words in a sort of presocial chaos; but as soon as he and his family have been introduced among the Ases, thus forming the third stratum of the perfected hierarchical society, as soon, in other words, as it has become his and his family's duty to provide that precise, functional service that their faithful expect of them (bestowal of fertility and prosperity), he gives up his incest. In short, the incest practiced by the Vanes, by Njörðr, seems to me to stand in a definite relation to their function, but not a positive relationship, a negative one rather, representing a temporary state of development prior to social organization and doomed to disappear as soon as that organization has taken place, so that, within the total resulting system, once sexuality has been placed under restraint and corrected—and corrected in exemplary fashion in the persons of the great Vanes—the safeguarding of the right sort of fertility will be guaranteed.

But here again, whatever its *meaning* may be, the *fact* is beyond dispute. Moreover, it has immediate parallels on the other side of the Baltic: I refer the reader to a famous article by Kaarle Krohn[6] in which the Helsinki scholar made only one mistake[7]—because of the incest attached on the one hand to Njörðr and Freyr and on the other to a *homologous* Finnish mythological figure—of concluding from the *identity* of that figure and the two gods that a Finnish *borrowing* from the Vane mythology had occurred. We should be rather more guarded, I believe, and limit ourselves to the information contained in the Finnish texts, which is interesting enough in itself: it is to a minor god of spring and fertility that the incest theme is linked.

This character, who is mentioned only twice in the *Kalevala*[8] but to

---

6. "Sämpsä Pellervoinen < Njörðr, Freyr?" in *Finnisch-Ugrische Forschungen* 4 (1904): 231–78.

7. See justifiable criticisms of Axel Olrik, *Danske Studier* (1907), pp. 62–64, and *Danmarks Heltedigtning* 2 (1910): 252–54, pointing out that Osiris is the brother of Isis as well as her husband, and that one marginal tradition has Atys being Cybele's son as well as lover.

8. In *runo* 2 it is "Pellervoinen, the son of the earth, Sämpsä, the young lad," who on old Väinämöinen's behalf peoples the "continent without greenery" with the trees (only the oak has a separate, miraculous origin); in *runo* 16 it is he who, after the refusal of the aspen, goes to cut down the oak that Väinämöinen needs to finish his boat. It is also for cutting wood in the forest that the genie Pellervoinen (i.e., Sämpsä beyond question) is

whom an entire epic poem transmitted in several versions was devoted, is named Sämpsä. Krohn distributed a questionnaire, a "Rundfrage," throughout the various Finnish provinces and was able to establish from the replies that the peasants give the name *sämpsä* —or more usually today *sämpsykkä* (*sämpsä-heinä, sämpsykkä-heinä*) to a plant—*scirpus silvaticus*—that is the first to appear when the snow thaws and that they keep an eye out for it in the spring in order to pick it and give it to the cattle. Moreover, the word appears to have been borrowed from a Germanic language and is akin to the dialect German *Simse, Semse*, a name for the reed. In the Finnish song, of which Krohn has collated the variants, this personified *sämpsä* is generally referred to as *Sämpsä Pellervoinen* (Sämpsä, son of Pellervo), the latter name, in the speech of Ingermanland, being a synonym for *pellava* (hemp), though it is also employed on the Karelian borders in the sense of *pelto* (field; genitive *pellon*; borrowed from the germanic: cf. German *Feld*).[9]

The subject of the poems is as follows: upon the arrival of spring, as the ice melts, the sea god Ahti sends a series of messengers to an island, or to the fearful land of Pohjola, to persuade Sämpsä—who is hiding, or hidden, or asleep there—to come and bring fertility to the fields and also, according to one version that refers to "young women full of blood" (*neitoiset verelliseksi*), to the women. He sends him the son of winter (or sometimes the wolf or the wind), and Sämpsä refuses. He sends him the son of the summer (or sometimes the sun), and Sämpsä accepts. And then, one version says:

> He comes to scatter seed,
> to sow thickly in the fields.
> He sowed the bogs, the heather sprouted,

---

employed in a Finnish tale used by Eugène Cosquin in his *Contes populaires de Lorraine* 1 (1886): 11–12 (in the commentary to "Jean de l'Ours"; following Reinhold Köhler, *Jahrbuch für romanische und englische Literatur* 7: 26). On Sämpsä since Krohn see also Uno Holmberg, "Doppelfrucht im Volksglauben," in *Mémoires de la Société finno-ougrienne* 51 (1924): 63–64, n. 1; Oscar Almgren, *Hellristiningar och kultbruk* (1927), pp. 293–94; Nils Lid, "Vegetations-gudinne og vaarplantar," in *Skrifter, utgitt av det Norske videnskapsacademi, Historisk-filoso-fiske Klasse* 4 (1928): 211, who quotes (cf. Emil Nestor Setälä, *Sanastaja* [1927], p. 48) the evidence provided by the Finn Christfrid Ganander who in his *Mythologica Fennica* (1789) parallels *runo* 2 of the *Kalevala*: Sämsä is the mythic sower who sows the seed of trees everywhere; in his dictionary, still in ms. form, he presents Sämpsä as the god of the forests and trees, and quotes a folksong—reminiscent of Njörðr—in which Sämsä pushes a boat out to sea and "hoists the sails to the tree."

9. See below, pp. 132–33.

he sowed the marshes, the birches sprouted,
he sowed the hills, the pines sprouted,
the cool earth for the cherry trees with their clusters,
the cold earth for the junipers,
for the alder woods the pleasant places.
Ahti lacked land
before Sämpsä lacked seed.
To the south he scattered it first,
then he threw it to the east,
toward the north he sent it flying
and finished toward the west.

In short, these are the actions and gestures of the annual, vernal, regenerator of nature: whether god or hero, Sämpsä behaves exactly like a model *Wald-und Feldgeist*, like a character adhering strictly to all the Mannhardt and Frazer rules. But why did he begin by leaving the vegetable kingdom to wither and perish, for it is indisputable that he is the culprit? One variant from Ingermanland attributes the lack of growth quite simply to the fact that he is asleep:

Why doesn't it sprout, our oats,
and why doesn't the barley show
or grow on the land cleared with fire,
or rise in the valley,
or on Sämpsä's meadow,
or on Pellervo's hill?
This is why our oats don't sprout
and why the barley doesn't [etc.—]
Sämpsä lay in his bed
on his back with seven crosses,
on his side with ten buttons,
you could see his legs on the bed
and his red stockings on the straw . . .

Other versions give a different reason. Sämpsä had run away; he had been forced to run away. A variant from northern Karelia begins:

Sämpsä, the son of Pellervo,
lay with his sister,
slept with his mother's child.
Because he knew destruction was on the way,

that the day of misfortune was at hand,
he went away
toward the dark country of Pohjola,
to live with the creatures that devour
to shake off the scent,
with the sturdy men that swallow you up . . .

In the Ilomantsi region, it is his stepmother rather than his sister:

Sämpsä, son of Pellervo,
slept with his stepmother,
on the heap of seed.
He took six seeds,
he took some of Sämpsä's seed
from the black tail of a winter weasel . . .

Or again:

An old woman, from under the firm earth,
a boy, from the earth of the field:
he slept with his stepmother
on the heap of seeds,
in the womb of the seed ship.
He took six seeds . . .

In the fragments collected in the Vuonninen district, in which the name of Sämpsä is not actually mentioned even though they are certainly concerned with him, the incest is committed with his own mother:

You have slept with your own mother,
On her breast you have rolled,
beside the rocky sea . . .

Or else:

Because you abused your own mother
when you were going over the hill,
behind the multicolored sled . . .

Once again, despite the persistent association of the sea with fertility and incest, these facts do not in any way prove that Sämpsä *is* Njörðr, or even, despite the Germanic origin of the word *sämpsä*, that he constitutes a borrowing by the Finns from a Germanic fertility cult. They prove simply that the Finnish fertility cults and myths, like the homologous Germanic cult and myths, and like the myths of the Vanes and Njörðr, contained an incest theme, and more precisely, the theme of an initial incest subsequently punished and eliminated.

Let us go back to the beginning of the Hadingus saga. The boy-child is brought up in the home of the giant Vagnophthus (v, 1), and as soon as he is an adolescent he "is granted the prime of manhood"; he has no taste for anything other than the exercise of arms, *omisso voluptatis studio* (vi, 1). That does not sound very much like a Vane; but anything else was unthinkable from Saxo's Viking point of view for a character who is later to be a great warrior, an "Odinic hero." But now what follows (in vi, 2)? This martial instinct is most efficaciously opposed, neutralized, suspended, until his encounter with the one-eyed old man:

> Harthgrepa, daughter of Wagnhophthus, tried to enfeeble his firm spirit with her lures of love, contending and constantly averring that he ought to offer the first dues of the marriage bed in wedlock with her, who had proffered to his childhood most zealous and careful fostering and had furnished him with his first rattle. Nor was she content with admonishing in plain words, but began a strain of song as follows:
>
> *"Why doth thy life thus waste and wander? Why does thou pass thy years unwed, following arms, thirsting for throats? Nor does my beauty draw thy vows. Carried away by excess of frenzy, thou art little prone to love. Steeped in blood and slaughter, thou judgest wars better than the bed, nor refreshest thy soul with incitements. Thy fierceness finds no leisure; dalliance is far from thee, and savagery fostered. Nor is thy hand free from blasphemy while thou loathest the rites of love. Let this hateful strictness pass away, let that loving warmth approach . . ."*

We are in the presence of a sort of Nordic Hippolytus, subjected not merely to the exhortations of a prudent pedagogue but also to those of a gigantic Aphrodite who happens to be the pedagogue's daughter. Her propaganda is wholly Aphrodisian in that she decries his warrior's vocation as *impietas* and advocates the pleasures of love and sensual gratification as *pius*, an attitude, let us not forget, that constitutes the fundamental nature and one of the reasons for the existence of the Vane gods. But what follows is even more interesting: "Let this hateful strictness pass away," Harthgrepa has just said (*cedat odibilis iste rigor*), "let that loving warmth approach" (*adveniat pius ille calor*) . . .

> "*and plight the troth of love to me, who gave thee the first breasts of milk in childhood, and helped thee, playing a mother's part, duteous to thy needs.*"

Let us not forgo the pleasure of reading these curious notions in their Latin form:

> *et Veneris mihi necte fidem,*
> *quae puero tibi prima dedi*
> *ubera lactis opemque tuli,*
> *officium genetricis agens,*
> *usibus officiosa tuis.*

These are the words with which she concludes her exhortations, as though the purpose of the entire poem was to lead up to them. Freud would doubtless have found useful material here for his *Leonardo da Vinci*, but from the simple point of view of narrative plotting the argument is an astounding one: "I am the woman you ought to lie with and marry because I gave you my breast as a mother!" Paul Herrmann in his commentary[10] cannot get over his amazement. He summarizes this *ganz unheroisch und nur in einem Heldenroman denkbar* poem as follows: "Astonishment that Hadding thinks solely of war and killing and never of the pleasures and feminine values; misplaced reminder of the fact that she suckled him and brought him up." *Unpassend* (misplaced, unsuitable in such circumstances) is how he describes this reminder of their relationship as wet nurse and suckled child—almost of mother and son . . . And in his German verse translation—an extremely good one, be it said—Herrmann felt that he ought to soften this impropriety:[11]

> *Weiche der Sinn, der kalte, Dir schnell,*
> *Lass Du die Brust Dir erglühen in Dank,*
> *Flicht mir der Liebe erfreuenden Bund,*
> *Die ich als Kind Dir zuerst ja die Brust*
> *Reichte mit Milch und in sorglichem Sinn*
> *Pflegte Dich liebend, das hülflose Kind . . .*

In his desire to uphold morality, however, Herrmann seems not to have noticed that he was committing an error of taste of which Saxo

10. P. 117.
11. P. 26.

himself is innocent, since what he says more or less is: "Let your breast warm with gratitude toward me, since I first gave you my breast with my milk . . ." In the circumstances, was it really worth softening the line *officium genetricis agens* further on into "Die ich . . . in sorglichem Sinn pflegte dich liebend . . ."?

The fact is inescapable. An improper fact, if you wish. But if so, then all the more improper in that it is by no means merely an *unpassende Erinnerung* but an argument, a piece of reasoning: "You sucked my milk, I acted as your mother, and *therefore* you ought to unite yourself to me with the bonds of Venus." And no less curious is the fact that Hadingus does not protest at this argument. He does not display the swift and constantly maintained reaction of the Vedic Yama to the arguments of his sister Yamī. His sole counter-argument is one concerned with the difficulty of executing what she asks, the vast size of this amorous wet nurse, the physical disproportion between their two bodies, *ejus magnitudinem humanis inhabilem amplexibus*. And he yields totally as soon as Harthgrepa has revealed to him—at great length (vii, 3)—that she has two sizes at her disposal, each corresponding to one aspect of her character, and that she can change from one to the other at will:

> "*I dart out my ingathered limbs, and presently, while they are strained, I wrinkle them up, dividing my countenance between shapes twain, and adopting two forms; with the greater of these I daunt the fierce, while with the shorter I seek the embraces of men.*"

Saxo is no blunderer. He was extremely well lettered. He possessed a delicacy of touch that was at least the equal of that found in any of his contemporaries. We can therefore be certain that the presence here of this *unpassende Erinnerung*, of this odd argument, is not to be attributed to a piece of grotesque clumsiness but to the fact that it already existed in his model and was expressed in an earlier poem making the same point. If Saxo had taken it upon himself to make any changes we may be sure that they would have been directed at toning down the oddness of the original.

And the fact is that in the domain of Nordic fable there is only one area in which the bonds of close kinship, of a relationship between an almost-mother and an almost-son, as with that between mother and son, stepmother and stepson, or brother and sister, could be used as an argument for the legitimacy, for the desirability of a marriage: the world of the Vanes. And the god who provides the typical proof of this practice is Njörðr.

It seems to me hardly feasible to attribute to mere chance the fact that this particular morality, specific to Njörðr's early career—during the whole period of his life within his tribe and according to the customs of his tribe—should be so explicitly expressed in the early career of a character whose later adventures present so many remarkable affinities with the god. In this first book of Saxo's work, so deeply imbued with mythology—or in the Icelandic model he followed, which comes to the same thing—it can only be an underlying intention of presenting the stories relating to Njörðr and the initial incest of the Vanes in another, "historical" form that leads the hero's foster mother to say to him, this time in prose, *oportere eum primum genialis tori munus suis erogare connubiis, quae infantiae eius exactioris curae fomenta perrexerit primaque subministrarit crepundia.*

5

THE TWO LIVES OF HADINGUS

(CONCLUDED):

1) HADINGUS AND HARTHGREPA

b) The "Bad Magic" of the Vanes

Before their reconciliation and fusion to form a perfected divine society, the Ases on the one hand and the major Vanes on the other were not distinguished solely by their matrimonial customs but also by the variations in their knowledge and sacred powers: in the *Ynglingasaga* (chap. 4), as we have already seen,[1] Snorri says that after the amalgamation it was Freyja who taught the Ases for the first time the magic known as *seiðr*, which among the Vanes, on the other hand, had always been customary; he also says that after the amalgamation Óðinn established Njörðr and Freyr as sacrificial priests (*blótgoðar*) and that they were *díar* among the Ases, while Freyja became a sacrificial priestess (*blótgyðja*). Though the little-used word *díar*—obviously derived from the old Irish *día* or god[2]—tells us nothing, Freyja's position as *blótgyðja* and her knowledge of *seiðr* are both characteristic of the Vane "functions."

In chapter 9 of his fine book *Farms and Fanes of Ancient Norway*,[3] Magnus Olsen has made a study of the available information relating to the *gyðjur*, the priestesses of pagan Scandinavia. The information is scanty, admittedly, but its lesson is nonetheless clear: wherever the facts are reasonably circumstantiated *we find that these priestesses were linked to the worship of Freyr, one of the two great Vane gods.*

The famous story of Gunnar Helmingr, a *hiéros gamos*, as we have

1. See above, p. 40.
2. On *díar*, an Irish word, see Maurice Cahen, *Le mot "dieu" en vieux-scandinave* (1921), p. 23.
3. Magnus Olsen, *Ættegaard og helligdom* (1926), pp. 243–56; pp. 282–97 in the English edition (1928), *Farms and Fanes of Ancient Norway, the place-names of a country discussed in their bearings on social and religious story* (Institutet for sammenlingnende kulturforskning, series A, 9).

already seen—which has been justifiably linked with what Tacitus says in *Germania* (40) with regard to Nerthus and her priest—makes it clear the Swedes looked upon the image of Freyr as a living being, and that the priestess assigned to him, who was even regarded as his wife (*kona*), was a young woman; this young priestess, apart from looking after the temple also took the god round from district to district, in a chariot, for an annual visit, and the couple were everywhere received with cordiality and lavish hospitality.[4]

In Iceland, the ancient literature mentions a woman, þuríðr, whose cognomen was *hofgyðja*, which is to say "priestess of the temple,"[5] and this cognomen points in the direction of Freyr in two ways: first, þuríðr was half-sister to þórðr Ossursson, in turn called *Freys-goði* or "priest of Freyr"; second, her family, the Freysgyðlingar, lived on a farm close to which there was a place known as *Freysnes* "Freyr cape."[6]

Finally, Magnus Olsen's investigations show[7] that whenever a woman in Iceland is designated *gyðja* or *hofgyðja*, examination of her genealogy invariably shows that her family originated in one of the districts in Norway where we know, particularly from their place names, that the dominant cults were those of Freyr or Njörðr (Tröndelagen, Namdalen, Hevne).[8]

4. *Flateyjarbók* 1 (ed. of 1860): p. 335–39; cf. Paul Herrmann, *Nordische Mythologie* (1903), pp. 198–200. On these journeys by gods of the Freyr type see below, Appendixes 3, p. 189, and 5, pp. 207–8.
5. *Landnamabók*, p. 276.
6. Magnus Olsen, *Ættegaard og helligdom*, p. 248 (Eng. ed., p. 288).
7. Ibid., p. 251 (Eng. ed., pp. 291–92).
8. Magnus Olsen has confirmed this opinion with another argument. The Old Scandinavian word signifying the oldest form of sanctuary is *hörgr*: this was at first a simple pile of stones, in all probability, covered later on, under the influence of the *hof*, with a building. And an examination of the most important mythological texts tells us two things: on the one hand that the *hörgr* was specifically the sanctuary of a Vane god; on the other that the *hörgr* belonged to the priestess, the *gyðjur*. Here are the texts:
(1) In the *Vafþruðnismál*, str. 38, Gangaðr, i.e., Óðinn, who has gone to consult the giant Vafþruðnir under that name, says of Njörðr:

> He reigns over hof and hörgr by the hundred,
> and he was not born of the Ases.

In the *Grimnismál*, str. 16, of Njörðr again, referring to a characteristic feature of his abode (*Nóatún*, see above, p. 22): ... *He rules over a high-built* hörgr.
In the *Hyndluljóð*, str. 10, Freyja says of her worshiper and protégé Óttarr:

> He has made a hörgr [here = stone altar] for me;
> now the rock shines like glass,
> he has reddened it with so much bullock blood:
> Óttarr has ever been a devoted worshipper of goddesses.

It is therefore natural and significant to find Óðinn establishing Freyja, the great Vane goddess—and Freyja alone—in the feminine priesthood that seems to have been especially attached, in mortal eyes, to the Vane gods.

As for the second indication provided by the *Ynglingasaga*, it is important in that it establishes an *original* distinction between a "Vane magic" and an "Ase magic," but it is also obscure: what is this *seiðr*? In 1903, in his *Nordische Mythologie*,[9] Paul Herrman reduces the dis-

---

(2) The *Gylfaginning*, p. 20, describing the mythical abode of the gods and employing words that denote the "sanctuaries," says that Óðinn first had built in the center of the enclosure, for the seats of the *stjórnamenn* gods (i.e., "directors, supreme judges of destinies") a magnificent building that he named *hof*, which is the name of the most developed form of pagan temple. Later, another hall was built, also very fine, which was a *hörgr* and belonged to the *gyðjur*. Here the latter word is clearly no longer used in the sense of "priestesses" but in that of "goddesses" (a secondary meaning, produced by a later extension: Maurice Cahen, *Le mot "dieu" en vieux-scandinave*, p. 46 and n. 1); but it is clear that Snorri is transposing the customs of this world into that of the gods, and that if he gives the celestial *gyðjur* this fabled *hörgr* to live in as their specific home it is because the real *hörgar* were in fact, or had been in the still recent past, the dwellings of the earthly *gyðjur* or priestesses.

These early examples, drawn from the two *Eddas* (neither of which contradicts them elsewhere, incidentally), are in rough agreement with the information to be derived from toponymy. "Rough" agreement because we must take into account the fact that the *hof* (which never occurs in the Eddic poems except in the phrase "*hörgr* and *hof*") later acquired an ever-growing importance in western Scandinavia, so that we find the name *Fröy(ju)hof* in Norway; whereas in Sweden, on the contrary, the notion of *hof* took root less well, so that we find a place near Uppsala named *Óðinshargher* (the present *Odensala*), and in Södermanland a *Thorshargher* (the present *Torshälla*). But such overlappings are adequately explained historically and do not contradict the evidence of Snorri's poems. Thus this double characteristic of the *hörgar*—sanctuaries of the Vane gods and houses of the *gyðjur*—establishes yet another link between the office of priestess and worship of the Vanes, a specific link that illustrates and confirms that asserted, in the person of Freyja, by the end of chapter 4 of the *Ynglingasaga*.

The word *hörgr* is common Germanic (**harugaz*): Old High German, *harug, haruc, haruh*, Anglo-Saxon, *hearg, hearh*, all denote a pagan sanctuary (*nemus, lucus, sacellum, fanum, delubrum, idolum*). Hjalmar Falk and Alf Torp distinguish it from Latin *carcer* and link it to the Irish *carn*, "a heap of stones (particularly one made with a religious intention)," and *carric* (from **karsekki-*), "rock." See on *hörgr* the arguments summarized in Hugo Gering and Barend Sijmons, *Kommentar zu den Liedern der Edda*, 1: (*Götterlieder*) (1927): 9–10 (to *Völuspa*, 7b), and in J. de Vries, *Altgermanische Religiongeschichte*, 1 (2d ed.; 1956): 378–81; the toponomastic study of Magnus Olsen, "Hedenske kultminder i norske stedsnavne," in the *Skrifter* of the Society of Sciences of Kristiania (1914), pp. 285–300 (chap. 25: "*Hörgr* in Norwegian and Icelandic names"); lastly, in Germany, the work of Edward Schröder, "Harug, Harah in Ortsnamen," in the *Festschrift Schuhmacher* (1930), pp. 84–87.

9. P. 566. This text contains an error. Chap. 7 of the *Ynglingasaga* does not present Óðinn as the inventor of *seiðr* and is therefore not in contradiction with the end of chap. 4. Herrmann is also wrong in underestimating *Lokasenna*, str. 24: Loki is not making a "tendentious interpretation," he accuses Óðinn roundly and openly of having dishonored himself by practicing *seiðr* at Sámsey. Moreover, the translation of the third *Völuspa* line

tinction between the two magics to a simple opposition between "black magic" and "white magic":

It is hardly surprising, in those early days when the influence of Christianity led to the interpretation of the pagan gods as devilish spirits, if the two magics became confused: Snorri Sturluson equates the magical powers of the gods with *galdr* and *seiðr*, making Óðinn and the Ases into *seiðmenn*, and Saxo represents them as wizards. Snorri even mentions Óðinn in one passage (*Ynglingasaga*, chap. 7) as being the inventor of *seiðr*; though elsewhere (chap. 4) he had with more accuracy put on record the fact that Freyja first taught the Ases this form of magic that had hitherto been particular to the Vanes. Óðinn is never presented in the *Edda*, or in any other source worthy of credence, as being a *seiðmaðr*, but rather as the inventor of the magic of chants and runes. Though in the *Lokasenna* (strophe 24) Loki accuses Óðinn of having practiced *seiðr* at Sámsey by going from house to house like a wizard, it is an accusation that must be considered, along with the others that accompany it, as being a "tendentious interpretation." On the other hand it is with evident horror that the *Völuspá* attributes the practice of *seiðr* to the Vane Gullveig: by her practices she is said to have stirred spirits to movement, and just as men burned wizards and cut them to pieces if they "came back from the dead," so the Vane goddess is rent with spears by the Ases and burned three times to prevent her resurrection. All this being so, there is nothing very bold in thinking that the inverse measures of esteem granted to white and black magic today date back to the days when worshippers of Óðinn and worshippers of the Vanes existed side by side: the adherents of Óðinn condemned not just the voluptuous, sensual way of life of the Vanes but also the *seiðr* that flourished among them. In the tenth century this contrast was still obscurely perceived, but it soon vanished altogether when the powerful magic of the Lapps swept down from the north and subjugated the great mass of the people. When that happened, both church and lay legislature rose as one to institute the severest measures against the exercise of "magic" in general.

Although undoubtedly oversimplified, this view of the matter is by no means entirely inexact; even today, the basic argument is still as satisfying—neither more nor less so—than anything put forward

---

in str. 22 ("set spirits in movement") is unlikely. Lastly, toward the end of the passage quoted, Herrmann seems to be contrasting the Vane worshipers and the faithful of Óðinn's religion as though they were two different *peoples* in conflict, a view that is certainly false: see below, pp. 98–99.

since. The difficulties subsist because they are inherent in the available information itself. First—whether because the ancient authors presupposed a basic knowledge of such matters in their readers, whether because some regrettable sense of propriety prevented them from telling what they knew, or whether they themselves had an insufficient tradition to draw upon—there is the lack of precision found in all the mentions, descriptions, or definitions given by Nordic texts of the various types of magical techniques, and in particular that of *seiðr*. Second, there is the fact that the initial distribution between Ases and Vanes of the various magical techniques is presented in the mythological texts as belonging to *prehistory*, relegated to a time, hardly ever dwelt upon, when the Ases and the Vanes, when Óðinn and Njörðr, together with Freyr and Freyja, were still not in alliance, whereas after that alliance, and thanks to the teaching of Freyja, the Ases and Óðinn in particular took over *all* the provinces, *all* the varieties of the magic art: with the result that none of the texts specifically and explicitly concerned with Óðinn's powers—such as chapter 7 of the *Ynglingasaga*—provides us with the *differential* information that is needed. Thus we find Óðinn endowed not only with the power of calming the winds and fire, which in the prose *Edda* comes within Njörðr's province, but also with ownership of the magic vessel *Skíðblaðnir*, which is one of the customary appurtenances of the god Freyr.

In 1935, a very distinguished book on *seiðr* was published in Stockholm by Dag Strömbäck, who is now a professor at the University of Uppsala.[10] After an exhaustive review of the material, whose inadequacy he stresses as clearly as did his predecessors, Strömbäck turns to the shamanism of the Lapps and Siberian tribes in search of indirect, comparative enlightenment. The method is certainly interesting, and one that produces interesting results, even though it is here pushed a little too far.

It is only in two passages occurring in very late romance-sagas (fifteenth and seventeenth centuries)[11]—in which the word is prob-

10. *Sejd, Textstudier i nordisk religionshistoria (Nordiska Texter och Undersökningar utg. i Uppsala av B. Hesselman* 5, 1935). It is one of the books that led to a general interest in shamanism.

11. *Hrólfs saga Kraka*, chaps. 32–33 (Strömbäck, pp. 85–86), and *Friðþjófs saga*, 6, 14. (Strömbäck, pp. 90–91). The other texts alluded to on p. 160 at the beginning of chap. 4 ("*Seiðr* and Animal Metamorphoses") are on the author's own admission external to the problem. Lastly, it is excessive to see an allusion to ecstatic phenomena in the third line of *Völuspá*, str. 22.

ably no longer employed with any differential value but merely as a vague synonym of "magic"—that we find *seiðr* mentioned as being associated with the fundamental practice of the Siberian wizards, which is the achievement of an ecstatic state, a separation of the body, which remains inert, and the soul, which then wanders abroad. Not that this practice is absent from the older Scandinavian texts better informed about paganism: among others, there is a very clear case in the admirable piece of psychological observation constituted by the story of the "suggested emigration" of the Norwegian Ingimundr to Iceland, at the beginning of the *Vatnsdœlasaga*;[12] but this in fact strengthens my case, since the liberation of the wizard's soul is not classified here by the narrator as a feat of *seiðr*: the three "Finns" whom Ingimundr, again in Norway, sends out in this way on their exploration to Iceland (three journeys there and back) perform their ceremonies in secret, without their being designated by any descriptive name, whereas the initial prophecy of the *völva*, the witch, which put the idea into Ingimundr's head that his emigration was inevitable, took place during a feat of *seiðr*, and it is plain from the text that the *völva* was present during this feat, in soul as well as in body, and even in mind, fully capable of argument, polemic, and dialectics.

It is similarly impermissible to ascribe to feats of *seiðr* the "absences," the cataleptic states described as occurring to Óðinn at the beginning of chapter 7 of the *Ynglingasaga*: These do indeed amount to shamanism (in which, it should be added, the emphasis is much more on animal transformations and displacements in the physical world than upon journeys in the spirit world), but far from naming it as *seiðr* Snorri treats this talent separately, at the start of the chapter, then goes on to speak of the god's power over fire and wind, of his magic vessel, of the head of Mímir, of his relations with the dead and hanged, of the animal spies at his disposal, and generally of the magic of chants and runes in which he excelled, and it is only after all this that he mentions *seiðr*, considering it quite manifestly as something distinct from *everything* previously mentioned. Here are the last lines

---

12. Chaps. 10 (*seiðr* séance), and 15 (settlement in Iceland); cf. Paul Herrmann, *Nordische Mythologie* (1903), pp. 548–50 (German translation). It will be seen that the sign given to Ingimundr by the *seiðkona* to prove the truth of her prophecy is this: a silver amulet he possesses, *representing the god Freyr*, has already been miraculously transported to that very spot in Iceland where he himself is to settle later (a claim later made good by events); a further connection between *seiðr* and the Vane gods suggests Magnus Olsen, *Ættegaard og helligdom*, (see above, p. 62, n. 3), p. 251 (English ed., p. 292).

of this passage, one of the most important we possess on the nature
and aims of *seiðr*:[13]

> Óðinn knew and himself practiced the method that has the most
> powerful effects and that is named *seiðr*. It was by this means that he
> could fathom the fate of men and of events still to come, and also to
> speak to men of their deaths or misfortunes or illnesses, and also to take
> away from men their intelligence or strength in order to give it to
> others. But the use of this magic is accompanied by so great a degree of
> effemination [*ergi*][14] that men ["viri," *karlmönnum*] were of the opinion
> that they could not give themselves up to it without shame, so that it
> was to the priestesses [*gyðjunum*] that it was taught.

(And I must recall here that the *gyðjur* seem to have been closely
linked with the worship of the great Vane gods, and that Freyja,
according to chapter 4 of the same book, was given the rank of
blótgyðja by Óðinn as soon as she had in her turn revealed the secrets
of *seiðr* to him.)

It is therefore by no means sure that *seiðr* is associated with the
customary forms of shamanism that have occasioned so much interest
in the West during the last fifteen years or so, and which Mircea Eliade
has so completely covered in his two masterly studies.[15]

Whatever the position on this point, it is evident from the compilations and commentary of Strömbäck that *seiðr*, practiced mostly by
seiðkonur but also by *seiðmenn*, involved an accompanying chorus, that
it generally took place in a house (in contrast to the magic known as
útiseta),[16] and that it was prepared for the previous evening or night.
The *seiðkona* sometimes sat on a special platform or *seiðhjallr*. There

13. The final comment has been justly linked with what Saxo says of the *effeminate*
character of the ceremonies of the Vane god Frö (Freyr) at Uppsala (6. v, 10); see below,
pp. 115–116.

14. On *ergi*, "effemination," *ragr*, "effeminate," see my *Loki*, p. 271, and Josef Weis-
weiler, "Beiträge zur Bedeutungsentwickelung germanischer Wörter für sittliche Be-
griffen," in *Indogermanische Forschungen* 41 (1933): 16–29 (1: "germ. *arga-, Old Icelandic
ragr").

15. "Le problème du chamanisme," in the *Revue de l'Histoire des Religions* 131 (1946):
5–52; followed by his great work, *Le Chamanisme* (1968), in which the Germanic data are
dealt with on pp. 299 et seq.

16. The attempt to combine *seiðr* and *útiseta* made by Robert Höckert in his strange
book, *Völuspá och Vanakulten* I (1926): 40–41, is not a happy one, any more than the author's
argument on this subject against the work of Elias Wessén (2: 100–101); Hugo Gering,
Über Weissagung und Zauber im nordischen Alterthum (1902), p. 6, used by Höckert as cor-
roboration (2: 101, n. 1), is clearly mistaken: *seiðr* cannot be reduced merely to a sacrifice
accompanying *útiseta*.

is also mention of a *seiðstafr*, a wand of undefined function. But no trace of a drum, unless we follow Strömbäck in making more than seems wholly justified of the gibe Loki hurls at Óðinn (*Lokasenna*, str. 24, in which *vétt* is unfortunately a "hapax": *draptu á vétt sem völor*, "you have struck upon the *vétt* like witches"). The purposes of the operation, or operations, were apparently extremely various. We have already noted Snorri's account of the diverse uses to which Óðinn put his *seiðr*: seeing into the future (*spá*), inflicting a whole gamut of woes on his enemies. The sagas, both "family sagas" and "narrative sagas," confirm these two aims with many variations and also indicate a few rare cases in which *seiðr* may be declared of public utility, which enables Strömbäck to make a distinction between "black *seiðr*" and "white *seiðr*."[17] We must be careful not to go too far in this direction, however: it is clear that the narrative sagas employ the word *seiðr* in an approximate sense, so that the *seiðkonur* and *spákonur* they depict as traveling around from farm to farm are without doubt frequently no more than fortune-tellers comparable to today's fairground gypsies. But this extended use of the word does not weaken the evidence provided by Snorri: in all its forms, benignant and malignant alike, *seiðr* was looked upon as distinct from all other forms of magic in that it was debasing and above all unworthy of use by males. Later, with the advent of Christianity, when such reprobation spread to cover the practice of witchcraft in its entirety, this distinction no doubt became blurred, but it is still made very clear indeed in chapter 7 of the *Ynglingasaga*, which speaks with admiration of Óðinn's gifts and powers, making an unfavorable exception of this one alone, the one that in chapter 4 of the same book we are told was characteristic of the Vanes, had originated among them and had been spread by the great Vane goddess Freyja.

Snorri does not seem to have known very much about the actual content of *seiðr*, since he says nothing more about it and refers solely to its effects, but he takes care to emphasize this external characteristic, this almost moral inferiority. Rather than following Paul Herrmann's rather too precise distinction and speaking of a "black magic" as opposed to a "white magic," it would therefore be preferable to speak of a "low magic"—looked upon as shameful and reprehensible

---

17. Chap. 2: "Sejdterminologi och sejdrekvisita"; and chap. 3: "Vit och svart sejd."

—as opposed to the "noble magic" that was alone practiced by Óðinn before he had been instructed in the other and thus contaminated, as it were, by Freyja.[18] But having said that, it must immediately be recognized that in the mind of a scholarly medieval Christian such as Saxo, more at home with the conceptual categories of the classical, Western world in which he lived than in those of the already vanished world of Scandinavian paganism, to which he had access only by hearsay, the distinction "low-magic—noble magic" would have been only too easily reduced to the more familiar distinction "black magic —white magic" in his attempts to make sense of it, with the result that he would tend to incorporate into the realm of "low magic," into *seiðr*, a number of "black magic" practices that earlier Nordic peoples did not connect with it at all.

Let us return now to the saga of Hadingus, to that first, pre-Odinic period in which the hero is indoctrinated and governed by the pleasure-loving Harthgrepa and in which we have already noted, in an adapted and attenuated form, the first great characteristic of the Vanes: legitimate incest.

The background and general life-style of Hadingus and Harthgrepa as a couple recall what we know of the life-style of those semi-divine households in which the divine element is a Vane god or goddess and the human element a priestess or priest (or a worshiper). I am thinking not only of Nerthus being looked after and driven

18. Strömbäck concludes his study with reflections on similar lines (p. 192): "Everything points to the fact that *sejd* was looked upon among the Nordic peoples with fear and revulsion. It is true that those who practised 'white *sejd*' [see previous note] were treated with honor, but there is no doubt that this was was the result of fear than of trust and esteem. As for those who dealt in black *sejd*, society punished them with the harshest and most humiliating means at its disposal. The extreme attitude of the authorities with regard to *sejd* practitioners is particularly well illustrated by what we are told in the *Heimskringla* about the *sejd* of Ragnvald Rettilbeini and his companions: Haraldr of the Shining Locks, who certainly lacked neither understanding nor tolerance with regard to the superstitions and practices of his time, acts in this case with staggering severity against his son and the latter's *sejdmenn*, even though there is no evidence at all to indicate that the *sejd* used in this case was particularly ill-intentioned." The episode here referred to is in the *Heimskringla* 34, ed. F. Jónsson (1893), 1: 149–51: Rögnvaldr Rettilbeini, bastard of Haraldr and a Lapp woman, is administrating Haðaland in his father's name; hearing that his son has become *seiðmaðr*, Haraldr sends his legitimate son Eiríkr Blóðœx against him; the latter "burned his brother Rögnvaldr together with eighty *seiðmenn*, and this action was much praised." On this extreme blame already attaching to certain forms of magic, notably *seiðr*, in pagan times see also Helge Ljungberg, *Den nordiska religionen och kristendomen, Studier över det nordiska religionsskiftet under Vikingatiden* (1938), p. 304.

around by her priest, or of Freyja protecting her devoted worshiper Ottarr and taking him with her when she goes to conjure up Hyndla and questions her about Óttarr's fate (*Hyndluljód*), but also, and above all, of the couple formed, in Sweden, by Freyr (for whom Gunnarr Helmingr so boldly substitutes himself) and his priestess, his "wife": they live at first in the fane where their love is consummated, then they set out on an annual tour of visits, the priestess driving, protecting, literally "keeping the god out of trouble," moving on together from district to district, from farm to farm, being welcomed and feasted by the inhabitants. Similarly, Hadingus lives for a while in Harthgrepa's home, then, when he wishes to leave, she goes with him. On their journey, the two of them alone visit the house of *hospites*, while Harthgrepa attempts to continue her protection of Hadingus, even though she is not wholly successful.

Added to the already numerous features that we have found to be common to the hero Hadingus and the great Vane god Njörðr, this analogy with the Vane god-human couples, and particularly with that of the Swedish Freyr and his priestess, in a journey episode that has no parallel in the saga literature to my knowledge (other than a passage from the *Örvar Odds saga* that seems to derive from the same source as our text), becomes particularly striking: if the god Njörðr did indeed serve as a model to the writer who first devised the character and adventures of the human Hadingus, then there can be no doubt that we have here a fictionalized vestige indicating the importance of the *hieros gamos* in the Vane myths and cult, and in particular of the character of the priestess, the *gyðja* taking care of and escorting the god.

The analogy provided by setting and general behavior is strengthened by a more specific similarity. In both phases of his life, first with Harthgrepa, then with the one-eyed old man, Hadingus is the occasion and beneficiary of magic operations. But of how different a kind! In the first phase, after the point when the giant nurse has achieved her ends, *Hadingi concubitu potita*, and while she is accompanying him on his travels, the narrator records only one adventure in three episodes (vi, 4–6):

> 4. While upon the journey she had undertaken, she chanced to enter in his company, in order to pass the night, a dwelling, the funeral of

whose dead master was being conducted with melancholy rites. Here, desiring to pry into the purposes of heaven by the help of a magical espial, she graved on wood some very dreadful spells, and caused Hadingus to put them under the dead man's tongue; thus forcing him to utter, with the voice so given, a strain terrible to hear.

5. *"Perish accursed he who hath dragged me back from those below, let him be punished for calling a spirit out of bale!*

" Whoso hath called me, who am lifeless and dead, back from the abode below, and hath brought me again into upper air, let him pay full penalty with his own death in the dreary shades beneath livid Styx. Behold, counter to my will and purpose, I must declare some bitter tidings. For as ye go away from this house ye will come to the narrow path of a grove, and will be a prey to demons all about. Then she who hath brought our death back from out the void, and has given us a sight of this light once more, by her prayers wondrously drawing forth the ghost and casting it into the bonds of the body shall bitterly bewail her rash enterprise.

"Perish accursed he who hath dragged me back from those below, let him be punished for calling a spirit out of bale!

"For when the black pestilence of the blast that engenders monsters has crushed out the inmost entrails with stern effort, and when their hand has swept away the living with cruel nail, tearing off limbs and rending ravished bodies; then, Hadingus, thy life shall survive, nor shall the nether realms bear off thy ghost, nor thy spirit pass heavily to the waters of Styx; but the woman who hath made the wretched ghost come back hither, crushed by her own guilt, shall appease our dust; she shall be dust herself.

"Perish accursed he who hath dragged me back from those below, let him be punished for calling a spirit out of bale!"

6. So, while they were passing the night in the forest foretold them, in a shelter framed of twigs, a hand of extraordinary size was seen to wander over the inside of the dwelling. Terrified at this portent, Hadingus entreated the aid of his nurse. Then Harthgrepa, expanding her limbs and swelling to a mighty bigness, gripped the hand fast and held it to her foster-child to hew off. What flowed from the noisome wounds he dealt was not so much blood as corrupt matter. But she paid the penalty of this act, presently being torn in pieces by her kindred of the same stock; nor did her constitution or her bodily size help her against feeling the attacks of her foes' claws.

It is at this point, without transition, as though Óðinn had been waiting for just this incident to manifest himself—in order to repair the damage to the hero's warlike vocation done by the wiles of his sensual nurse—that the decisive articulation in the career of Hadingus occurs:

> 7. Hadingus, thus bereft of his foster-mother, chanced to be made an ally in a solemn covenant to a rover, Lysir, by a certain man of great age who had lost an eye, who took pity on his loneliness . . .

We have already examined the interventions of this "old man" on Hadingus's behalf in this second phase of the hero's life. They are supernatural, magical. During a Viking expedition he carries him off through the air on his horse, gives him a draught that will give him added strength, and reveals to him the means of escaping from his coming captivity as well as that of rendering himself invincible by eating a lion's heart (vi, 7–10). Later, not only does he teach him the most efficacious battle formation for his ships, but during the battle he also puts a magic *balista* at his disposal, and by means of a counter-cloud dissipates the cloud conjured up by the wizards on the side of his enemies; and lastly he foretells the way Hadingus will die (viii, 16).

It is clear, then, how great the gulf is, within the domain of "magic," between the undertakings of the old man and Harthgrepa's imprudent consultation of the dead. Óðinn communicates the secret formulas for success with assurance and without hesitation; his knowledge, his horse, his draught, his magical machines, and his prophecies all safeguard and enlighten his protégé surely and swiftly; moreover, all these things can be openly admitted to, increase the stature of both performer and beneficiary, and are successful. Harthgrepa, on the other hand, undertakes a feat shadowed by darkness, conjures up a wrathful spirit from the dead, and suffers one of the shameful punishments that await all captured *seiðkonur*. For Paul Herrmann has justly observed[19] that early on during the war between Ases and Vanes, when the Ases are visited by a strange female figure named Gullveig or "Gold-Madness"—probably a spy on behalf of the Vanes —she is presented—not surprisingly, coming from the Vanes—as a witch who in particular practices *seiðr* (the madness for gold being metaphorically assimilated, in its effects, to the worst kind of magic), and once unmasked she is dealt with as such (*Völuspa*, str. 21–22):[20]

19. *Nordische Mythologie*, p. 557.
20. These two strophes, in which there are some slight textual and syntactical cruxes are examined in Strömbäck, *Sejd* . . . pp. 17–21; together with the two following strophes they have also been employed in my essay *Tarpeia* (1948), pp. 253–74.

21. *I remember* [*the völva said*] *the war of the armies, the first time in the*
     world:
     when they [= the Ases] *pierced Gullveig with spears*
     and, in the hall of Hárr [= Óðinn], *burned her,*
     burned three times the thrice-born,
     often and not rarely—yet she lives still.

22. *Witch they called her in all the houses she visited,*
     the völva who saw true; she practiced charms [*vitte ganda*],
     she bewitched [*seið*] *wherever she could,*
     she bewitched [*seið*] *the troubled spirit,*
     always she was the pleasure of the ill-living woman . . .

(We should also note in passing that over and above *seiðr* this
female Vane agent also practices other varieties of minor magic
[*vitte ganda*] that[21] she is *also* believed to have introduced into the
world of the Ases, which had till then been innocent of all such
things.)

Thus Gullveig, the Vane witch, is "pierced with spears" before
being burned,[22] without result. Harthgrepa is merely torn to bits,
but irrevocably.[23] In both cases it is the woman's *bad* magical activity
that brings about her condemnation and cruel punishment.

This is not the moment to dwell upon certain details of the incident that have been used elsewhere to draw a number of grave and
futile consequences, such as the huge hand that gropes around in the
hut and is cut off by the hero,[24] or upon the fact—unique in Scandinavian fable, I believe—that it is a giantess, not a woman or a goddess,

21. On *gandr* and the "gandium" observed among the Lapps, cf. Kaarle Krohn in
Finnisch-Ugrische Forschungen 6 (1906): 158–59.
22. Burned: cf. the punishment of Rögnvaldr and his eighty *seiðmenn* referred to in
n. 18, above. Rudolf W. Fischer, reworking an old idea in the light of new research, has
interpreted the triple combustion of Gullveig as an alchemical ritual for the purification
of gold, Gullveigswandlung, *Antaios* 4 (1963): 581–95. Heino Gehrts has applied his own very
personal method of exegesis to Gullveig as well, in "Die Gullveig-mythe der Völuspá,"
Zeitschrift für deutsche Philologie 88 (1969): 321–78. Cf. below, p. 101, nn. 12, 13.
23. There is nothing in Saxo's text that will allow Harthgrepa's terrible death to be
construed as anything other than a punishment for her necromantic feat. Axel Olrik
would like it to be the result of the giants' anger at seeing Harthgrepa enter into an alliance, or rather a liaison, with Hadingus (*Kilderne til Sakses Oldhistorie* 2 [1894]: 6). We should
not try to extract too much from Saxo's turn of phrase: the *originis suae consortes* (i.e.,
giants) of para. 6 are clearly the same beings referred to in para. 5 of the poem as *daemones*
(l. 12) and *monstra* (l. 20) and which, again in para. 6, produced *plus tabi quam cruoris* when
wounded; the narrator thus merely wishes to convey that Harthgrepa's punishment is
the work of supernatural and terrible beings.
24. See below, pp. 108–9, nn. 3, 5 (2).

who conjures up the dead man, a fact that I shall soon return to in greater detail in another context,[25] since what I mainly want to stress here is the manifest intention of the saga's author in this incident: Harthgrepa's feat is one of repulsive, reprehensible, punishable, and punished magic, whereas the male feats of the one-eyed old man are the products of a high and noble form of knowledge. As with the opposition between the two moralities and sexual codes, this opposition also lends the first phase of Hadingus's career—dominated, moreover, by a woman—a "Vane" coloration in contradistinction to the Odinic coloration of the second phase.

No objection can be drawn from the fact that Harthgrepa's feat of magic, that of conjuring up the dead,[26] is not one of those classed as belonging to the category of *seiðr* by Scandinavian mythology; or from the fact that this very feat is looked upon, in chapter 7 of the *Ynglingasaga*[27] and elsewhere,[28] as being a special power of Óðinn's and as such is free from evil and excluded from the reprehension that Snorri reserves for *seiðr* alone.

I do not indeed think that Saxo's source, or Saxo himself, was reproducing or had the intention of reproducing, in the first phase of Hadingus's career, the exact *content* of that variety of magic which in the days of pagan orthodoxy characterized the "pure Vanes," the

25. See the following chapter.

26. It is the use of *valgaldr*, analogous to the Old High German *hellirun(a)* (cf. Rudolf Koegel, *Geschichte der deutschen Literatur* I [1894]: 51–55). It will be noted that Harthgrepa's feat is not what is termed in Old Scandinavian *útiseta*: the witch conjuring the spirit does not "take up her seat . . . outside," she operates *inside* a house, *ingressa penatibus*. On the conjuring of the dead cf. Åke Ohlmarks, "Totenerweckungen in Eddaliedern," in *Arkiv för Nordisk Filologi* 52 (1936): 264–97.

27. "And sometimes he awakened dead men from the ground."

28. In the Eddic poem *Baldrs draumar* (Balder's dreams), Óðinn rides on a horse into the country of the dead and there, by chant and spell, conjures up a dead *völva* to comment on the dreams that are justifiably causing Baldr such concern. But that is a relatively late poem and rather clumsily put together: cf. my *Loki* (1948), p. 140. The other "early" cases in which a dead person is conjured up by incantation concern human characters only: in the *Edda*, at the beginning of the *Grógaldr*, Svipdagr goes to ask his dead mother for magic chants to protect him (a theme carried on in many a Scandinavian ballad); in the *Hervararkviða*, incorporated into the *Hervararsaga*, the bellicose heroine Hervör forces her father Angantýr to rise from his tomb, hand over to her the sword with which he has been buried, and predict the future for her (ed. Christopher Tolkien, *The Saga of King Heidrek the Wise* [1960], p. 14–19). In several passages in his *Nordische Mythologie* (pp. 544, 559), Paul Herrmann has included the expedition of Freyja and Óttarr to consult the witch Hyndla (*Hyndluljóð*) among the examples of conjuration of the dead; this is an error; there is a sort of *evocatio* involved, but the witch is by no means dead.

Vanes during the first part of their history: first, because he probably knew nothing more concrete about it, and, second, because it was not what he found important; what mattered to him was the expression in dramatized incident, clear to the minds of his age, of this opposition between a "low magic" and a "noble magic," the former worthy of every sort of reprobation, the latter acceptable and worthy of admiring wonder in the way that the magic feats in our fairy stories are to us. And what could be more representative of that "low magic" than the extreme and repulsive example of the soul drawn back from hell and forced to speak through the lips of its corse? It was of little importance that this practice, far from exciting blame, was actually looked upon as one of Óðinn's more impressive feats in the age of true paganism: the writer took it as it was, together with—or even because of—the unfavorable connotation put upon it by the entire Western medieval world, since the literal anachronism did nothing to weaken, and even emphasized, the antithesis that had to be expressed between a shameful action and a series of noble feats.

6

THE FIRST MYTHOLOGICAL
DIGRESSION:

GIANTS, ASE GODS, AND VANE GODS

The preceding analyses have made clear the singularity of the rôle played by Harthgrepa. Let us now summarize them from the point of view of this curious figure.

First, though Hadingus is not the only saga hero to enter into a sexual liaison with a giantess,[1] nevertheless he is the only one in whom such a liaison involves any hint of incest, allowing himself to be won over by Harthgrepa's strange argument that she has served him in the office of *genetrix* (vi, 2). In this respect, insofar as the fictional requirements of the saga form allow, the saga reproduces in this first part of Hadingus's life the conscious and explicitly justified incest practiced in normal conditions by a Vane god with a Vane goddess.

Second, when seducing Hadingus Harthgrepa plays the part of advocate, of propagandist on behalf of love and sensual gratification as opposed to warlike ardor (vi, 2, again):

> *. . . nec manus impietate vacat*
> *dum Venerem coluisse piget.*
> *Cedat odibilis iste rigor,*
> *adveniat pius ille calor . . .*

The Nordic Venus, the goddess whom Hyndla compares to a nanny goat cavorting from billy goat to billy goat, whom Loki accuses of having lain with all the gods, including her brother, the Vane Freyja, could not have expressed it better: it is the Vane morality in a nutshell.

Third, Harthgrepa performs a magical operation of the "low,"

---

1. Paul Herrmann, *Kommentar*, pp. 98, 99, 113.

repugnant, reprehensible kind, and in a context, moreover, specifically opposing it to a nobler kind of magic, just as in authentic Scandinavian mythology the despised and condemned form of magic named *seiðr* was originally connected with the Vane gods, with Freyja, in contrast to the other forms of magic characteristic of the leader of the Ases.

Lastly, in a general way, Harthgrepa shares the career of Hadingus with Óðinn. She has all the early part. Then, as soon as she has vanished from the scene, Óðinn takes delivery of the hero and becomes his protector. And it is then that Hadingus weds his second wife, Regnilda, with whom he has neither blood nor milk tie. This diptych form corresponds to that found in the career of Njörðr: as long as he remains a pure Vane he knows nothing of Óðinn or the Ases, and lives in legal incest with his sister, also a Vane; then he is accepted among the Ases, honored and promoted in rank by Óðinn, and marries a second wife who is no kin to him.

Thus from any point of view we take, in every sphere in which precise analogies between the saga of Hadingus and the Njörðr or Vane myths are to be found, it is Harthgrepa, the giantess, whose presence activates or emphasizes the "Vane analogies" and who in particular takes the place in the saga of the female Vane characters in the myths. In other words, it is as though this giantess has been used by the author to give explicit expression *to what in mythology constituted the original essence, in direct contrast to that of the Ase gods, not of the giants, but of the Vane gods.* However we explain this, and even if we could find no explanation for it at all, it is a fact that needed to be formulated.

As it happens, however, there are two different sets of considerations that do seem to explain it, one drawn from Saxo's own text, the other from Scandinavian fable. And at the same time they lead us to an understanding of the two amazing mythological *excursus* that Saxo, or his source, either placed or left, like apparently useless irrelevancies, in the saga of Hadingus. Let us take the first one first.

Saxo knew that apart from and opposed to the giants—a notion he found clear enough and identified with the *gigantes* of classical antiquity—the Scandinavian pantheon included not one but two kinds of gods. Only he was not at all sure what the distinction was between them.

In all the remainder of the *Gesta Danorum* this vagueness has no importance, since he never has any occasion to dwell on or even to mention the difference between the two groups: his "Frö deus," for example, is never confronted with Othinus, and Saxo's Balderus stories avoid any classification of the gods as entirely as the corresponding pages in Snorri's *Edda*.

Here, however, things are quite different, unless all the similarities we have observed between Hadingus and Njörðr have totally misled us. It is in effect in the Njörðr myths, with the "Vane phase" and the "Ase phase" of his career separated by the war and the eventual pact between Vanes and Ases, that the original distinction between the two groups of gods was most vividly expressed; thus if the author of our saga did in fact draw his inspiration from the mythical Njörðr story, reproducing in particular the contrast between the two halves of his career, he could not avoid having to give Hadingus as a partner in the first part of his life, not a "goddess of the Óðinn group," but a female being constitutionally different from the divine type of being he was to marry in the second. And it was here that he could have been, and was, hampered by the fog obscuring the true distinction between Vane and Ase gods in his mind.

Nor is this mere hypothetical reconstruction. The proof of this embarrassment and of the effort made by the author to introduce some semblance of order into his fragmentary conception of this subject is provided by a passage whose presence, at the very start of the work, has always appeared enigmatic.

Saxo has just told us that after their father's murder Hadingus and Guthormus, Gram's two sons (the second of whom is to play no rôle in the rest of the story), were taken by their tutor Brache to Sweden, where they were put into the care of the two giants Vagnophthus and Haphlius. Then, when his saga is scarcely even begun, Saxo interrupts himself (v, 2–6):

> 2. As I shall have briefly to relate doings of these folk, and would fain not seem to fabricate what conflicts with common belief or outsteps the faithful truth, it is worth the knowing that there were in old times three kinds of magicians [*mathematici*] who by diverse sleights practiced extraordinary marvels.

3. The first of these were men of monstrous stock, termed by antiquity giants [*gigantes*]; these by their exceeding great bodily stature surpassed the size natural to mankind.

4. Those who came after these were the first who gained skill in divination from entrails, and attained the Pythonic art [*primam physiculandi sollertiam obtinentes* and *artem possedere Pythonicam*]. These surpassed the former in briskness of mental parts as much as they fell behind them in bodily condition. Constant wars for the supremacy were waged between these and the giants; till at last the sorcerers [*magi*] prevailed, subdued the tribe of giants [*giganteum genus*] by force of arms, and acquired not merely the privilege of ruling but also the repute of being divine [*divinitatis opinionem*]. Both of these kinds [i.e., *gigantes* and *magi*] had extreme skill in deluding the eyesight, knowing how to obscure their own faces and those of others with divers semblances, and to darken the true aspects of things with beguiling shapes.

5. But the third kind of men, springing from the mutual union of the first two [*ex alterna superiorum copula pullulantes*], did not answer to the nature of their parents either in bodily size or in practice of magic arts; yet these gained credit for divinity with minds that were befooled by their jugglings [*divinitatis accessit opinio*].

And then, after a paragraph exhorting the reader to show tolerance of the simplicity of barbarians, since it was quite normal in one sense, for even the *prudentia* of the Latin race had been taken in once by impostures of the same kind, Saxo returns to the story of his saga and goes on to recount the strange love affair between Hadingus and Harthgrepa.

This "Gottertheorie," often commented upon,[2] has still not yielded up its two mysteries: the parent-offspring relation it establishes between the first and second categories of beings and the third has no equivalent in the Scandinavian texts that have come down to us; moreover, it does not at first glance seem to have any application to the Hadingus saga, to which it is nonetheless presented as a necessary preface.

It is true, of course, that, in the main, Saxo's theory reproduces beliefs attested to elsewhere: the contrast and conflicts between giants and gods, and the seniority of the giants are all traditional enough. In fact, they form the background to all Scandinavian mythology, as they do for many European folk stories, such as the epic of the Narts

2. Bibliography in Paul Herrmann, *Kommentar*, p. 85.

among the Ossetians and the Circassians of the Caucasus. The division of the gods into two main groups is no less authentic. I am aware that the issue has sometimes been confused by taking Saxo's third category to represent either the dwarfs or the Elves, but these are frivolous interpretations only too easily dismissed: it would be odd indeed if the dwarfs were the offspring of the giants, and in any case there is no question of their fitting the expression in paragraph 5 (*auctorum suorum naturae nec corporum magnitudine nec artium exercitio respondebant*, etc.) which implies a *lesser* stature than that of the giants and a *lesser* ability in magic than that of the first category of gods, but both a considerable stature and a considerable ability all the same; as for the Elves, often linked with the gods, they are not in fact gods properly speaking but rather the souls of the dead, or of a certain section of the dead, and cannot by any means be considered as important enough to be balanced against the Ases in a classification that included no other divine category but these two. The only distinction made by Scandinavian mythology among the gods of the first rank remains that with which we have been dealing up till now, that between Ases and Vanes, and it must therefore be this distinction that is involved in Saxo's division of the gods into his two categories. But it is precisely at this point that the difficulty occurs, for though he is correct in dividing the gods into two categories, the contents of his two categories are very different from those of the authentic tradition.

In fact, in Scandinavian mythology the distinction between Ases and Vanes is a double one. There is first a *difference of function* between them, the first possessing the overall, royal, magical, juridical, and armigerous direction of the world (Óðinn, Týr, Þórr), the second being the patron gods of prosperity, fertility, sensual pleasure, even obscenity (Njörðr, Freyr, Freyja). Second, and as a consequence of the first difference, there is an *inequality of rank*, since as early as Indo-European times the functions had been hierarchized, and fertility (etc.) was merely the third and least important of them, ranking below high magic and martial strength.[3] Saxo does, of course, retain a difference of activity and an inequality of rank, but he no longer formulates them in the same way as the original pagan theory.

He reduces the difference in activity to that between a greater power and a lesser power, that between a more powerful or dexterous

3. See *Mythe et épopée* 1 (1958): 288.

magic and a less efficacious or less dexterous magic. Without doubt the first category of his gods, defined both by *physiculandi sollertia* and by its bellicose nature, answers satisfactorily to the mythological Ases; but the second category, the one that ought to correspond to the Vanes, is defined from the point of view of its activity, like the first, in terms of a very generalized kind of magic (*artium exercitio, praestigiis*), and differentiated merely by the inferior quality or efficacy of that magic (*nec . . . respondebant*); thus only the lack of any bellicose tendency—a lack not specifically stressed, moreover—can be said to correspond to any essentially Vane characteristic. The difference in the activities of the two groups is thus assimilated into the inequality of their status, and to Saxo this latter is merely the effect and outward sign of a process of degenerescence: the second kind of gods was produced by crossbreeding either between giants and goddesses or between gods and giantesses (*ex alterna copula*).

There is no point in wasting time in attempting to justify this theory: there is not a single passage or allusion anywhere in early Scandinavian literature that suggests anything of the sort.[4] This means that this mythological digression, whether influenced or not by classical or biblical traditions (such as the marriages of Angels and Daughters of Men in Genesis), is simply an artifice employed by an intelligent author—Saxo or his model—ill-informed as to the real categories of the divinities in the early religion, as a way of accounting as best he could for what in his eyes was nothing more than a kind of degenerescence among one section of the gods. But, that said, we must go on to record and stress what for our purpose—that of explaining the ambiguous nature of Harthgrepa—is essential: *in Saxo's Göttertheorie there exists not merely an affinity but kinship, consanguinity, between the giants and the gods who stand in place of the Vanes, whereas there is no kinship or even affinity between the giants and the gods who stand in the place of the Ases; the beings who stand in place of the Vanes, and they alone, are both giants and gods.* This makes it understandable that an author who knew that there were two kinds of gods, but not that

4. On the contrary, it is Óðinn who is on one occasion (*Gylfaginning*, 5, p. 14) said to be son of Bestla, daughter of the giant Bölorn—names never met with elsewhere. But this fact offered by Snorri at the end of the Ymir myth is doubtless merely intended to link Óðinn with the oldest known beings in the world (Ymir begets Buri, who begets Borr, who by Bestla begets Óðinn and his two brothers Vili and Vé); these are not giants in the same sense as the others but rather gigantic characters in a cosmogony.

the distinction between them was founded upon a radical difference in their functions and status, believing on the contrary that it was all just a matter of "more" or "less" power, should have allotted to a giantess, Harthgrepa, the function of displaying the typical Vane characteristics in a fiction whose plot was dependent upon those characteristics and made it necessary for him to leave them clearly in evidence. And such a shift becomes even more explicable when we realize that once conceived in such terms Hadingus's liaison with a superhuman partner would immediately fit into a familiar type of saga episode, would merge, despite the retention of the incest theme in attenuated form, into a commonplace of the saga literature: the temporary union of a hero with a giantess who loves and protects him.

If we examine Saxo's *Göttertheorie* in detail, along with the Harthgrepa episode that the author himself has told us the theory should help to justify, we do encounter features that seem to prove that the giantess Harthgrepa is in fact standing in for a being of Saxo's third category. How does Saxo specify the differentiating characteristics (*discretis praestigiis*: 2, end) of the three categories?

1. He begins by including all three within the general term *mathematici*, i.e., wizards; nevertheless, only the second two categories have acquired *divinitatis opinionem* (4 and 5). Why?

2. It would seem that he does not recognize the giants as possessing anything in the way of *praestigia*—their size apart—other than the one faculty—which is spontaneous and organic rather than truly magical and the result of knowledge—of metamorphosing themselves (4, end), a faculty also possessed, moreover, by the second category (ibid.), and therefore also, though the text does not actually say so, by the third category, since it is a product of crossbreeding between the other two.

3. The beings in the second category, on the contrary, are technically skilled in, and even the initiators of, physical magic (*primam physiculandi sollertiam obtinentes*, 4), and later of divinatory practices (*artem pythonicam*, ibid.); the war they declare on the giants is in no way a war of wizards against wizards: they and they alone are given the differential title (ibid.) of *magi* at the time when they subjugated the *giganteum genus*; so that what we are witnessing is simply the familiar

conflict of *ingenium* aided by the *arma* it invents with *habitus corporeus* of vast size (ibid.), notations confirmed, moreover, in the next paragraph dealing with the double heredity of the offspring produced by the crossbreeding: it is clearly *corporum magnitudo* that refers to the giants and *artium exercitium* that indicates the beings of the second category, whom for simplicity's sake we will refer to as Ases.

4. The beings in the third category share these same *artes* but to a lesser degree; even though their powers are more limited, they too are therefore *magi*, which the giants are not.

Now if we turn our attention back to the saga story it is clear that Harthgrepa's actions answer much more to the characteristics given for the third category of beings than to those of the giants. She does not merely change her shape by dilation and contraction—a non-differential characteristic according to the end of paragraph 4—she also undertakes a specific magical operation (*magicae speculationis officio*: vi, 4), using *carmina dira ligno insculpta* (ibid.), and with the intention of finding out the future (*superum mentem rimari cupiens*, ibid.): this implies that she possesses the *ars pythonica* (v, 4) that the theory does not attribute to the giants but does assign to its equivalent of the Ases, and therefore also, though to an inferior degree, to the beings of the third category who take the place of the Vanes. And in Harthegrepa's case the magical operation involved is certainly of an inferior kind, and even doubly so: first, on grounds of worth, since it lies in the province of the repugnant and reprehensible necromancy, and, second, on grounds of skill, since she fails, and like the sorcerer's apprentice falls victim to the forces she has raised.

Thus although Harthgrepa is actually described as a giantess, in fact there is nothing giant-like about her except for her size. Apart from that she behaves as though she is a "goddess" of the second rank, like a Vane, or one of the beings who replace the Vanes in Saxo's *Göttertheorie*, and in a way that no pure giantess ought to or could behave according to the tenets of that same theory. This confirms that her prototype was a Vane and that she is the artificial product of an author's transposition.

There is another cause that might have favored this shift in Harthgrepa from "Vane" to giantess. Though the blood kinship that Saxo or his source establishes between the two is without foundation in the true Scandinavian tradition, it is nevertheless true that this same tradition does recognize and stress a number of important features that are common to giants and Vanes and distinguish them both from the Ases.

1. The giants and the Vanes are essentially and equivalently rich.[5] There are numerous poetic metaphors presenting the giants as "possessors of gold."[6] Snorri (*Bragarœður*, 2 = *Skáldskaparmál*, 4, pp. 81–82) tells how the giant Þjazi—father of Njörðr's second wife Skaði—was the son of a giant named Œlvadi who was so "rich in gold," *gullauðigr*, that his three sons, after his death, when it came to measuring out and distributing what they had inherited equally, decided that they would all fill their mouths with gold an equal number of times until there was none left. Hence, according to Snorri, the many Scaldic periphrases for designating gold: "the mouth count, the language, the word, the discourse of these giants." In the *Þrymskviða* (str. 25), another giant, Þrymr, complacently enumerates his riches, which he feels achieve total perfection. And the Vanes too are prodigiously rich. Not only does the phrase "Freyja's tears" signify gold, but Njörðr too, Snorri says, is so rich and fortunate in his possessions, *svá auðigr ok fésæll*, that he is able to give riches derived from the land and chattels to all those who invoke him for that purpose (*Gylfaginning*, 11, p. 31); and similarly, of Freyr, he says that he also presides over mankind's wealth of possessions, *fésæla manna* (ibid., 13, p. 31). Under Njörðr's rule, Snorri also says in his other book (*Ynglingasaga* chap. 9), together with peace there were also such good harvests that the Swedes believed that it was he who presided over agricultural prosperity and man's wealth in possessions, *fyrir ári ok fyrir fésælu manna*. Of a wealthy Icelander, one saga says that he was "as rich as Njörðr," *auðigr sem Njörðr* (*Vatnsdælasaga*, chap. 7), and of the no less wealthy Arinbjörn, the bard Egill said that it was Freyr and Njörðr who gave him such abundance of riches (*Egilssaga Skallagrímcsonar*, chap. 78). Óðinn's attitude toward gold is very different; he feels neither need nor desire to hoard wealth; by means of his magical knowledge he knows where treasure is hidden, and by means of his incantations he can open up the hoards, neutralize their owners, and take whatever he wants (*Ynglingasaga*, chap. 7).

2. There is no need to insist any further here on the lubricity, the

5. *Tarpeia* (1947), pp. 266–69.
6. Rudolf Meissner, *Die Kenningar der Skalden*, pp. 227–28.

taste for sensual pleasures, that is part of the very definition of the Vane gods: we have already seen how well Freyja lives up to this definition;[7] as for Freyr, he is the god that Adam Bremensis says figured in the temple of Old-Uppsala *cum ingenti priapo*,[8] and it was Freyr again, euhemerized into a king of Sweden, who after his conquest of Norway, according to Saxo, publicly offered its princesses for prostitution (9. iii, 4).[9] And we also find these predilections as a constantly recurring characteristic of the giants. Their principal conflicts with the gods were the result of their sexual appetite: þrymr, Hrungnir, the mason in the story of Sleipnir's birth,[10] all at one time or another demand or kidnap the gods' most desirable womenfolk, which in most cases means Freyja.

3. Though it does sometimes happen that the Ases enter into sexual relationships with giantesses (Óðinn and Gunnlöð: *Hávamál*, str. 13–14, etc.; inversely, Gefjon going to a giant for the begetting of the four son-oxen she needs for her great plowing: *Ynglingasaga*, chap. 5, and beginning of *Gylfaginning*), it is noteworthy that it is exclusively between Vanes and giantesses that stable, conjugal unions are entered into: Njörðr marries the giantess Skaði;[11] Freyr, after a great deal of

7. See above, pp. 40, 51.

8. "Fricco," i.e., Freyr, is defined *pacem largiens mortalibus voluptatemque* (a good summary of Harthgrepa's double doctrine in her poem, 6., 2) and sacrifices are made to him *si nuptiae celebrandae sunt*: Adam Bremensis, *Gesta Hammaburgensis ecclesiae pontificum*, ed. Schmeidler (4, 26).

9. *Quo tempore rex Suetiae Frö, interfecto Norvagiensium rege Sywardo, conjuges necessariorum ejus prostibulo relegatas publice constuprandas exhibuit.* A local tradition in the Trondheim district, if we are to believe Axel Olrik, *Kilderne til Sakses Oldhistorie* 2 (1894): 102–3. The saga in question is that of Regnerus Lothbrok, which is certainly related to the adventure of Freyr and Gerdr (*Skírnismál*; cf. n. 12, below).

10. *Þrymskviða*, str. 7, 22, 23. 27; *Skáldskaparmál* 25, p. 101; *Gylfaginning* 25, p. 45.

11. One of Njörðr's two wives, the second (the first having been his sister) is thus a giantess, and one of Hadingus's two wives, the first, his pleasure-loving wetnurse (the second being Regnilda), is also a giantess. It is therefore as though the myth situation has simply been reversed in the saga from this point of view: it is certainly the second marriages of both (with Skaði and Regnilda) that correspond on the plot level (nonincestuous marriage, *svayamvara*, identification by leg or feet, followed by duet for and against seashore life); but the respective *places* of the giantess and the human woman in the two successive marriages have been reversed. The fact that one of Njörðr's two wives was in the myth a giantess may have contributed, together with the other reasons given in the text, to the decision to make one of Hadingus's two wives—though the first one in his case— a giantess too. The *Ynglingasaga* (chap. 8) records what is according to the bard Eyvindr Skáldaspillir (late tenth century) an erroneous and doubtless fictional tradition (a genealogical invention in honor of the járl Hákon inn Ríki): after her break with her husband Njörðr, Skaði is supposed to have married Óðinn in Sweden and borne his numerous children, among them Sæmingr, from whom Hákon claimed descent. On Skaði and *Scandin-avia* see above, p. 35, n. 38.

plotting involving Njörðr, Skaði, and her servant Skírnir, succeeds in winning the giantess Gerðr in official marriage, *brullaupinu*.[12]

These are all features[13] that even in circles where mythology was still recognized and understood—and even more so in those where its classifications were becoming blurred—may well have struck a methodical mind and led it to establish blood-relationships and kinship between giants and Vanes, and even to treat them with a certain equivalence in the domain of fictional narrative and plot.

We are now in a position to correct the first impression these paragraphs of *Göttertheorie* give of being unconnected insertions, an impression that led Paul Herrmann to say in his commentary:[14] "This presentation [of the three categories of superhuman beings], which is in appearance rigid and systematic, is eventually far from clear *and above all is not subsequently made use of in the story that Saxo goes on to tell.*"

But we can now see that this judgment is not correct, that there is no lack of cohesion in fact. The Hadingus saga centers around a hero of the *Vane type*, a human reworking of the great *Vane* Njörðr; entrusted first of all to a being *of the first category*, a *giant*, the hero lives during one phase of his career with that giant's daughter, a being who in fact presents all the characteristics of beings *of the third category*; then, in the remaining phase of his career, he comes under the

---

12. *Gylfaginning* 23, pp. 40–41; *Skírnismál*, opening prose (in which it has long been thought that Skaði as Freyr's mother cannot be an original element: Sophus Bugge, *Sæmundar Edda*, p. 90, n.; Barend Sijmons and Hugo Gering, *Kommentar*, pp. 217–18; etc.) and str. 19, 39, 40; in str. 38, Gerðr, who yields to the urgings of the messenger only under the influence of magic threats, says that she never thought she would have to love a member of the *Vaningjar* race, a Vane.

13. Another convergence between Vanes and giants may be noted. The Vanes, as we have seen in the previous chapter, were the specialists in *seiðr*; and *seiðr* together with other analogous practices were felt early on to be "Finnish," which is to say Lapp (so much so that the name *finnar* became a synonym for "wizard," just as "Chaldean" did in the early Mediterranean world, and a fabulous monster could be termed *finngálkn*). On the other hand, though the giants are not endowed, apart from their faculty of metamorphosis, with magic powers (they know more than others, they are *hundvíss*, "endowed with vast knowledge," and even Óðinn has difficulty matching the giant Vafþúðnir in erudition: the reason, quite simply, being that they have been in the world longer than all the other beings), they too, for other reasons, have been placed by those speculating in mythological localization in the "rime-covered" north: *Hrímþursar*, *Hrímnir*, *Hrímgrímir* are all giant names—one generic the others of individuals—derived from *hrím* "rime"; other giants in Norway are called *Jökull* (glacier), *Fönn* (fresh snow), *Drífa* (pile of snow), *Mjöll* (powdery snow), *Snjór* (snow). The *skiing* giantess Skaði evokes similar landscapes.

14. P. 86.

mentorship of Óðinn, the representative par excellence *of the second category of beings*. It cannot therefore be truly said that this theoretical excursus that begins the saga, this prefaced general mythology, is not subsequently made use of: it governs and clarifies the saga's plot by providing differential definitions of the three types of character occurring in the various episodes.[15]

Such obscurity as it contains lies in the insufficient distinction made between the three categories of supernatural beings: the functions and powers of the "Ases" and the "Vanes" are contrasted solely in terms of the greater and lesser; the affinity of the "giants" and the "Vanes" becomes a kinship sufficiently close for the "Vane" goddess of the saga to be represented by Harthgrepa, who is a "giantess," though in fact one of a very distinctive kind.

This interpretation, derived from close scrutiny of a number of convergent facts, is incompatible with that put forward by Axel Olrik in 1894[16] and that popularized in his commentary of 1922 by Paul Herrmann.[17]

According to the Danish scholar, the Hadingus saga presents us with a definite problem, or rather with a religious conflict that accompanied the death-throes of Scandinavian paganism; not the head-on conflict between the old religion and Christianity we find reflected in other texts, in the *Örvar Odds saga*, in the *Friðþjófssaga*, or, in Saxo himself, at the end of book 8, in the story of Thorkillus Aðalfari; but as it were internal convulsions within the dying religion itself, of which Saxo, needless to say, would have been unable to grasp either the meaning or the extent, but that we today are in a position to reconstruct.

Toward the end of the pagan era, Olrik's theory goes, when many people had ceased believing in the old gods, the majority continued nevertheless to believe in the giants, and this belief eventually increased to such an extent that it produced a sort of religion. This in turn led to a reaction among the remaining believers in the old religion, including the author of this saga: this writer, therefore, "hurled himself into the burning religious debate of his era, vindi-

---

15. This justification of Saxo's *Göttertheorie* preface will be completed in the next chapter dealing with the Mithothyn episode.

16. *Kilderne til Sakses Oldhistorie* 2 (1894): 6–9.

17. Pp. 97–98, 105–6.

cating the doctrine of the Ases in its struggle against the giant-worship that was developing in the vacuum of unbelief. This is why he so insistently attributed to the giants all actions of a barbaric nature, including this evocation of the dead that traditional Scandinavian lore in fact attributes to Óðinn. Around Óðinn, on the other hand, we find the world of the Ases depicted in all its majesty, with its promise of eternal life, in a succession of fairytale tableaux well calculated to win wavering spirits back to the faith of their ancestors." Paul Herrmann went even further: "Götter und Riesen ringen um Hadding . . ."; he sees the hero as the stake in a tournament or struggle between two opposing influences defined in the same terms as those used by Axel Olrik, *jættetro* against *asatro*, *Riesenglaube* against *Götterglaube*.

This eloquent and romantic construction is unhappily built in air. The facts that ought to support it condemn it, and the religious state it presupposes is literally unthinkable.

If Axel Olrik is correct, if the writer is concerned with demonstrating the superiority of the Ase religion over that of the giants, if it is true that giants and Ases "are engaged in a struggle for Hadding," are fighting over him, then in view of the Nordic tradition as a whole, certainly not lacking in direct and resounding victories of Ases over giants, we would expect at least once in the saga to see Ases and giants, Óðinn (or some other god) and a giant, confront one another and "ringen" in earnest: nothing of the sort occurs. Harthgrepa does not succumb to the gods but to the vengeance of the dead man she has conjured up and of the "kindred of the same stock"[18] as the owner of the severed hand, angry at the mutilation of one of their number (vi, 5 and 6). We would expect to see the giants abandon Hadingus once and for all, if not actually persecute him, after he has been taken under the protection of their perpetual rival Óðinn: but quite the contrary is true, since the giant Vagnophthus, his foster-father, appears at his side during a difficult battle (viii, 1) and provides him with useful assistance, just as the one-eyed old man has already done (vi, 7–10) and is to do again later (viii, 16). We would also expect the saga writer, being so enthusiastic an advocate of the Ases's cause, to employ the ordinary weapon of the advocate and to decry the opposing party, to demonstrate to those on the brink of defecting from *asatro*

---

18. See above, pp. 71–75, particularly p. 74, n. 23.

to join *jættetro*, using Hadingus as an example, that the aid of giants is useless or harmful: but Hadingus is in fact raised very well by Vagnophthus and Harthgrepa (vi, 1); moreover, Harthgrepa does in fact save him from the threatening hand; and though she does commit a grave blunder in conjuring up the dead, it is nevertheless she alone who pays the penalty, not Hadingus, who remains unhurt (vi, 6).

Indeed, so much are the facts against him on this point that Axel Olrik was forced to retouch some of the texts slightly in order to malign the giants.[19] He would have us believe, for instance, that the sea monster Hadingus kills and the woman who hurls such a terrible curse upon the hero as a result of this ill-judged exploit are both giants, *en jætte i dyreham, en jættekvinde*. But that is not at all what Saxo's Latin says (viii, 11): the sea monster, *inauditi generis belua*, is a *god* in disguised form (*quippe unum e superis alieno corpore tectum*, the woman tells him, *sacrilegae necuere manus: sic numinis almi interfector ades*), and the "woman" herself is introduced with no other qualification (*quem facto ovantem obvia femina hac voce compellat*).

Do we at least find Óðinn's help presented at its maximum of efficacity, total and without eclipse? By no means: under "Óðinn's rule" Hadingus sometimes experiences reverses, and it seems—we know why—that Óðinn is unable to do very much to help him by sea: during Hadingus's great ordeal, when he can no longer stir without unleashing tempests, Óðinn does nothing for him at all, and it is a sacrifice to a Vane, the "Fröblót," that finally cancels the curse incurred by his murder of the sea monster (viii, 12).

All these numerous and not unweighty facts run counter to the thesis of the great Danish "philologischer Dichter."[20] Taken all together, they give the impression, not of any special pleading, not of any polemic intention, nor of a conflict between two beliefs and two forms of worship, but simply of a romantic story, a romance that we now realize was conceived and oriented in accordance with the career of the god Njörðr and that, like that career, introduces several differ-

19. P. 7. Paul Herrmann also, *Kommentar*, p. 119, 1.6, says: "... der Fluch der Unheil verkündenden *Riesin*." However, in his translation, p. 36, 1.12 from bottom, he had correctly written: "da trat ein *Weib* in seinem Weg ...".

20. The expression is taken from Paul Herrmann, *Kommentar*, p. 97, who qualifies the interpretation in question: "eines der glänzendsten Verdienste und einer der glücklichsten Funde des philologischen Dichters Axel Olrik."

ent categories of beings and mythical actions without any controversial intention.

Moreover, the very concept of a conflict between *asatro* and *jættedyr-kelse* during the last days of paganism is in itself inadmissible. Neither in Germania, nor in the Caucasus, nor in any other part of Europe has there ever been such a thing as "giant-worship": the giants are mythical and folkstory characters, but no one ever makes sacrifices to them, or prays to them, or summons their aid—unless they happen to know one of them intimately, which happens only in the romances.

How is it possible to imagine that at the very moment when Christianity was bringing the old religion down in ruins a "religion of giant-worship" could have come into existence and rivaled the new one as a somehow healthier form of paganism more fit to survive than the old? How is it conceivable that there existed for the last of the pagans such "eine brennende Streitfrage," "et religiöst problem"? We are told that there was a period when, as the old beliefs grew weaker, "Aberglaube aller Art emporwuchert und in seinem Gefolge die Verehrung der Riesen aufkommt," provoking a reaction among the traditionalist pagans; but where, anywhere in the rest of the world where Christianity has supplanted other pagan religious systems, can we find any analogous process? A blossoming of superstitions certainly, but within the old framework, not in opposition to it, debasement of the existing gods, myths, and even forms of worship, but never, based on something as early, as mediocre, and as imperfectible as a belief in giants, the genesis of another paganism to threaten the first.

The "spiritual conflicts" thought to have tormented the souls of an élite during the last days of Nordic paganism have been abused generally. There have been attempts, for example, to explain the *Lokasenna* as antipagan or antimythological polemic, though it is a work of an entirely different kind and one springing from a quite different source. The savage beauty of the *Völuspá* stands to gain nothing whatever from the burden of vindicatory and romantic intentions it has had imputed to it. And even then, in those two poems the supposed conflict is at least between two forces—paganism and Christianity—that did actually exist, that we are familiar with, that could have and must have in fact—though not in the Eddic poems—attacked one another and been forced to defend themselves. But in this case Axel Olrik is in fact inventing with his *jættedyrkelse* a *tertius gaudens* of which one would be hard put to find any evidence elsewhere and that is rendered quite improbable by an examination of other religious movements analogous to the Christianization of Norway and Iceland.[21]

21. The most recent research has completed the ruin of Axel Olrik's reconstruction of a supposed *jættetro-asatro* conflict. In an article in the *Arkiv för Nordisk Filologi* 62 (1947): 151–71, under the title "*Trúa*, en ordhistorisk undersökning till den nordiske religionshistorien," Helge Ljungberg has examined the uses of the verb *trúa* (cf. German *treu*, English *true*) in Old Icelandic and has shown, contrary to the claims of Walter Heinrich Vogt (*Arkiv för Nordisk Filologi* 35 [1938]: 9), that they never went beyond the meaning of "rely upon, trust in." Here are a few lines of the conclusion: "In short it would seem that any more adequate speculation upon faith (*tro*, in the Christian sense of the word) was foreign to our ancestors. . . . The Nordic religion was centred on the forms of worship not on faith. The adjective *goðlauss*, or 'without-god.' was not applied to someone who no longer believed in the gods but to the man who refused to sacrifice to them." Moreover, this study is merely a confirmation and development of a point Ljungberg had already clearly made in his great book *Den nordiska religionen och kristendomen* (1938), in particular pp. 307–8. The author is certainly correct, with the reservation that we must surely admit, for notions such as that of "trust," and according to individuals and circumstances, a certain elasticity that may take them beyond their point of normal balance as far as a "faith" approximate to the Christian interpretation of that word; cf. my work, mitigating the rigidity of Sylvain Lévi's excellent analyses, on the Sanskrit *śraddhā* and the Latin *fides* in *Mitra-Varuna* (2d ed.; 1948), pp. 65–71, and *Idées Romaines*, 1969, pp. 47–69; also Hans Werbin Köhler, "Śraddhā in der vedischen und altbuddhistischen Literatur," Göttingen dissertation, 1948.

7

THE SECOND MYTHOLOGICAL DIGRESSION:

THE WAR BETWEEN THE ASES AND THE VANES

We are now also in a position to understand and justify the second mythological excursus with which the saga of Hadingus has been filled out: the episode of Othinus and Mithothyn.

Although Saxo, or his *auctor*, remodeled the life of Njörðr in order to compose that of Hadingus, although he placed or left at the beginning of his narrative a *Göttertheorie* that still contains, in however corrupt a form, certain insights into the distinction between the typical Vane and the typical Ase, although he went on to divide his hero's life into a pre-Odinic phase governed by Vane characteristics (sensuality, incest, low magic) and an Odinic phase (warlike exploits, noble magic, normal marriage), nonetheless he was embarrassed when it came to coping with what in mythology constitutes the articulating link between the two phases of Njörðr's life: he has eliminated "the war between the Ases and the Vanes," which, as a result of the pact that concluded it, introduced Njörðr and the other great Vanes into Óðinn's society.

He has eliminated it completely, and several considerations give one to think that he could not have done otherwise.

His Hadingus is a man and no more than a man. He is not therefore on the same level as either of his two protectors, since Harthgrepa is a giantess and the one-eyed old man a god. A conflict opposing Hadingus to the latter, concluded by a pact making him the god's ally and quasi equal, was thus inconceivable.

Moreover, apart from being a mere man, Hadingus is also a mere individual and not, as with Njörðr and the Vanes, the most typical representative of a species. And the one-eyed old man is a similarly isolated being. Saxo is well aware, for he says so elsewhere—for

93

example, in the saga of Haraldus Hyldetan—that the one-eyed old man is Othinus, but the model, the general blueprint as it were for the careers of "Odinic heroes," eliminates all the other gods, leaving just the protecting god and the protected man face to face, each the only one of his kind. Hadingus's career could not diverge from this model. It was thus impossible to burden it with a "war of species" of which the understanding between the one-eyed old man and Hadingus would have been a partial conclusion, a fragment of a more general "social" treaty.

Thus Saxo or his source had no choice but to articulate the two halves of his character's career in the simplest way possible, the one most in conformity with the life of the typical Odinic hero: it is the one-eyed old man who without cause or preparation, at a moment that he arbitrarily fixes (the most one can say is that he waits for the "Harthgrepa phase" to reach its own conclusion without interfering), *elects* his protégé. Thus of the war between Ases and Vanes, in this biography of Hadingus, there is no longer the slightest trace.

Saxo or his source, however, has not let it go to waste for all that. In more or less the place where we would expect to find an account of the war,[1] that is to say at the beginning of the Odinic phase, at the moment of the old one-eyed man's first intervention, there occurs a digression that is absolutely unrelated to the plot, a veritable foreign body, in which there is no further mention of Hadingus, or of his interests, or of Denmark,[2] but simply an account of a conflict that "at this time" brought Othinus, a so-called god and king of the gods, into opposition with other divine characters and ultimately with the wizard Mithothyn (vii, 1–3).

> 1. At this time there was one Othinus, who was credited over all Europe with the honor, which was false, of godhead, but used more continually to sojourn at Uppsala; and in this spot, either from the

1. A little later. This slight shift is doubtless to be explained by the fact that in the writer's conception of his plot it was essential to show the tragic end of Harthgrepa being followed immediately by the one-eyed old man's adoption of Hadingus, in other words by the scene (Liserus, Lokerus, initiation) in which it is expressed.

2. There is even an odd contradiction. Othinus, presented as a false god, as a mighty earthly leader who passes himself off as a god, resides for preference at Uppsala, the capital of the Swedish king. Yet at that time, according to Saxo's own writings, there was already a powerful and very much alive king on the Swedish throne—Suipdagerus.

sloth of the inhabitants[3] or from its own pleasantness, he vouchsafed to dwell with somewhat especial constancy. The kings of the North desiring more zealously to worship his deity, embounded his likeness in a golden image; and this statue, which betokened their homage, they transmitted with much show of worship to Byzantium, fettering even the effigied arms with a serried mass of bracelets. Othinus was overjoyed at such notoriety, and greeted warmly the devotion of the senders. But his queen Frigga, desiring to go forth more beautified, called smiths and had the gold stripped from the statue. Othinus hanged them, and mounted the statue upon a pedestal, which by the marvelous skill of his art he made to speak when a mortal touched it. But still Frigga preferred the splendor of her own apparel to the divine honors of her husband, and submitted herself to the embraces of one of her servants; and it was by this man's device that she broke down the image, and turned to the service of her private wantonness that gold which had been devoted to public idolatry. Little thought she of practicing unchastity, that she might the easier satisfy her greed, this woman so unworthy to be the consort of a god; but what should I here add, save that such a godhead was worthy of such a wife? So great was the error that of old befooled the minds of men. Thus Othinus, wounded by the double trespass of his wife, resented the outrage to his image as keenly as that to his bed; and, ruffled by these two stinging dishonors, took to an exile overflowing with noble shame, imagining so to wipe the slur of his ignominy.

2. When he had retired, one Mithothyn, who was famous for his juggling tricks, was likewise quickened, as though by inspiration from on high, to seize the opportunity of feigning to be a god; and, wrapping the minds of the barbarians in fresh darkness, he led them by the renown of his jugglings to pay holy observance to his name. He said that the wrath of the gods could never be appeased nor the outrage to their deity expiated by mixed and indiscriminate sacrifices, and therefore forbade that prayers for this end should be put up without distinction, appointing to each of those above his especial drink-offering. But when Othinus was returning, he cast away all help of jugglings, went to Phaeonia[4] to hide himself, and was there attacked and slain by the inhabitants. Even in his death his abominations were made manifest, for those who came nigh his barrow were cut off by a kind of sudden death; and after his end, he spread such pestilence that he seemed almost

---

3. A passing shot at the Swedes, whom Saxo disliked.

4. The Danish island of Fyen, not the land of the *Finni*, despite Henrik Schück and a number of others.

to leave a filthier record in his death than in his life: it was as though he would extort from the guilty a punishment for his slaughter. The inhabitants, being in this trouble, took the body out of the mound, beheaded it, and impaled it through the breast with a sharp stake; and herein that people found relief.

3. The death of Othinus's wife revived the ancient splendor of his name, and seemed to wipe out the disgrace upon his deity; so, returning from exile, he forced all those, who had used his absence to assume the honors of divine rank, to resign them as usurped; and the gangs of sorcerers that had arisen he scattered like a darkness before the advancing glory of his godhead. And he forced them by his power not only to lay down their divinity, but further to quit the country, deeming that they, who tried to foist themselves so iniquitously into the skies, ought to be outcasts from the earth.[5]

This episode has been the occasion of much commentary and argument. At the time when the summary—and in principle correct —equation Njörðr = Hadingus was accepted, the means was available to explain the presence of this singular digression. But that means was lost by the subsequent—and no less summary—rejection of that equation.

Here is the explanation put forward by Ferdinand Detter in 1894.[6] The argument is somewhat complicated and needs simplification, but the basis is sound.

After Saxo has given a very brief account of several of Hadingus's warlike exploits, suddenly, without any link to what has gone before, and introduced simply by the words *ea tempestate cum Othinus quidam* . . . there occurs the story of Othinus and his wife Frigga, which is a singular amalgam of three originally distinct myths:

a) We first recognize the myth of the necklace, in which the *Brísingamen* has been replaced by the statue of Óðinn;[7]

b) But when we read of this statue that Óðinn, *mira artis industria*, rendered it *ad humanos tactus vocalem*, then we are dealing, as P. E.

---

5. This passage is typical of the cleric Saxo's attitude with regard to the pagan myths. He disapproves of them yet is fascinated by them, and even takes sides: despite a number of harsh phrases he is "for" Óðinn and "against" Mithothyn.

6. *Zur Ynglingasaga*, in the *Beiträge zur Geschichte der deutschen Sprache und Literatur* 18 (1894): 74–75; see above, p. 20, n. 3.

7. *Flateyjarbók* 1 (edition of 1850): p. 275; cf. my *Loki*, pp. 48–49.

Müller has already noted in *Notae uberiores*, 63,[8] with the myth of Mímir's head. The *septentrionis reges* who send that statue to Byzantium correspond to the Vanes, who sent back the head of the slain Mímir to the Ases. The myth has undergone a transformation: the speaking head of Mímir has become a statue that speaks when it is touched;

c) Lastly, introduced as a third element in the story, we find the story of Mithothyn.

The next section is of particular interest:

It is clearly not an accident that the Mímir myth [to be precise, the myth of Mímir's speaking head] occurs linked to the story of Hadingus and that they both figure in Saxo's book one. In the *Ynglingasaga* it is perfectly clear why the account of the Ases versus Vanes war figures in the introduction: the intention there is to show how Njörðr, the ancestor of the Ynglingar dynasty, came to be allied with the Ases. In Saxo's model, although this original interdependence had already been blurred and lost, the two myths nevertheless remained in juxtaposition; and since Saxo wished to follow his source faithfully he had no other recourse but to link them together with the vague synchronism of an *ea tempestate* ...

In the *Ynglingasaga*, chapter 4, dealing with the war of the Ases and the Vanes, is preceded by a chapter 3 containing the story of Óðinn's brothers Vili and Vé, who during Óðinn's absence shared out his heritage between them and took his wife Frigg. This fact again enables us to understand why the Mímir myth is linked in Saxo with the Mithothyn story. True, there is no question of an adulterous liaison between Frigga and Mithothyn, but there is at least mention of a second infidelity on Frigga's part, this time with one of her *familiares*. The analogy with the necklace myth, which also involves infidelity on Frigg's part, then further facilitated the introduction into the present amalgam of the myth of Óðinn's brothers (V. Carl Müllenhoff, *Zeitschrift für deutsches Alterthum* 30: 220).

I have quoted this laborious exegesis at length, first because it is clearly argued and nearer to the point than the illusions indulged in by the "Märchenmotive" adherents, but also and above all because it explains so simply and clearly why this episode appears in this particular place in Hadingus's biography.

8. In the edition of Saxo begun by Petrus Erasmus Müller, bishop of Zealand, and completed by Hans Mathias Velschow, professor of history in the University of Copenhagen, there is a body of *Notae uberiores*, a very valuable addition made in 1858, the first attempt at disentangling Danish sources from Norwegian ones.

The Mithothyn episode undoubtedly contains, he says in essence, an adaptation of the mythical episode of Mímir's talking head, which forms part of the Ases versus Vanes war; moreover, in mythology, in Snorri, the principal result of that war was to remove Njörðr, together with Freyr and Freyja, from a Vane society and to install them in the Ases society, the society of Óðinn; it was therefore natural, in the biography of a hero manifestly conceived on the model of Njörðr in several of his adventures, that something of the Vane war should still be apparent, should have been retained in perceptible form, at the point where the hero becomes Óðinn's man. And this is the very solution to which we are led by a more complete comparison of the careers of Njörðr and Hadingus.

With the exception that instead of being a complicated amalgam of three myths as Detter would have it, only one of which belongs to the Ases and Vanes war, it may be that the entire excursus in Saxo's chapter 7 is a memory—a rather distorted one, I agree, but still coherent—of the various episodes of that war, and of that war alone. This would increase the elegance of a solution that is in any case already established in principle. Without discussing Detter's work[9] or lingering over questions as insignificant and as simple to clear up—despite the most amazing controversies over them[10]—as the occurrence of the name *Byzantium* in this text, I shall put forward an argument that seems to me to make such a simplification possible. This argument is, of course, hypothetical in character and therefore cannot be looked upon as being more than a "model" that will facilitate future discussions.

I have already given a brief summary of the results of my research into the Ase-Vane war. This episode is the extention in Scandinavian fable of a tradition also to be observed in the case of Rome, incorporated into the nation's history as the legend of first the war, then the fusion of Romulus's "protoromans" with the Sabines, and, similarly, in India, as the myth of the violent opposition, then the consent of Indra to the admission of the Açvin among the gods: in all these

9. Nor any other author. A clear exposition of the solutions put forward will be found in Jan de Vries, *Altgermanische Religionsgeschichte* 2 (2d ed.; 1957): 208–14.

10. I am thinking of, for example, that of Sune Ambrosiani, then *amanuens* at the Nordic Museum in Stockholm, *Odinskultens härkomst* (1907), p. 10.

forms what is involved is a myth explaining the formation in the past of a complete, trifunctional society—divine or human according to the individual case—of the type customary among the Indo-Europeans, a formation that was achieved by the entry of the group representing the third function (fertility, prosperity, etc.) into the hitherto incomplete society composed of men or gods who claimed to exercise solely the two higher functions (magical and juridical sovereignty, and might in battle.)

And there are passages in the *Völuspá* and in Snorri, given the insight provided by such extra-Germanic parallels, that enable us to formulate a fairly accurate notion of what this initial war, this "war of armies for the first time in the world" as the *Völuspá* puts it, must have been like. I have dealt with this subject both in *Jupiter/Mars Quirinus* (chap 5, pp. 155–78) and in *Tarpeia* (essay 5, pp. 249–74), and also made a synthesis of these studies, though principally from the Roman point of view, in *L'Héritage indo-européen à Rome* (chap. 3, pp. 125–42), material reworked in *La religion romaine archaïque* [1966], pp. 78–84). Here is a summary of the events involved:

A) The war proper forms a diptych comprising two episodes each of which gives pride of place to the major trump card of each side: *the corruption by gold*, used by the wealthy Vanes, and *the high magic*, used by the Ases in the person of their leader, the sovereign Óðinn. Each side in turn plays its trump and entertains hope of victory, but in the event no decisive outcome is achieved:

a) The episode of the gold consists (str. 21–22 of the *Völuspá*) in the dispatch by the Vanes to the Ases of a being named Gullveig, "Drunkenness or Power of Gold," a terrible scourge that turns the heads of the women especially, bewitching them and causing them to commit innumerable foolish acts. The Ases attempt to kill this being, apparently itself made of gold, by piercing it with stakes and subjecting it to a triple metallurgical operation (*brent gull*: "Three times burned the three times born"), which unfortunately fails of its effect;

b) The episode of the high magic occurs (str. 24) at the moment when the Vanes are beating back the Ases and are about to penetrate their very fortress. It consists in the spear that Óðinn hurls at the enemies, a gesture that as we know from analogous scenes in several sagas usually results in victory for Óðinn's side. But this time, it must be assumed, this sovereign magic does not have its usual definitive effect, since the two sides make up their minds to come to terms.

B) Then follows the treaty of reconciliation, and even, with regard to the Vane leaders, the fusion of the two opposed groups:

a) Njörðr, Freyr, and Freyja go to live among the Ases, first as hostages, then before long as completely naturalized members of Ase society, changing their sexual morality and teaching the Ases the lesser, lower magic characteristic of the Vanes.

b) The Ases give the Vanes, or send to live with them, two characters, one of whom, Mímir, though extremely intelligent, is killed by the Vanes in the belief that they have been tricked; when the Vanes send Mímir's head back to Óðinn he treats it with magic so that the head is preserved, talks to him, and gives him good advice;

c) In specific exchange for the Ase Mímir, according to one tradition (*Ynglingasaga*, 4), the Vanes also give the Ases a certain Kvàsir (who according to another tradition is born from the mingled spittle of Ases and Vanes as they conclude the treaty: *Skáldskaparmál*, 4). This Kvásir, Snorri says (*Skáldsk.*, l.c.), was so wise that there was no question to which he could not reply. He went abroad through the world in order to teach mankind wisdom. But one day two dwarfs killed him, drained his blood into three vessels, and explained to the Ases that "Kvásir had choked in his intelligence because there was no one clever enough to drain his knowledge away quickly enough with questions." His blood, mixed with honey, became *mjöðr*, the hydromel of poetry and wisdom that was then appropriated by Óðinn.[11]

Such is the account, or a different but analogous version, that the author of the Hadingus saga, Saxo or his source, must have had before him while writing the biography of Hadingus modeled on that of Njörðr. He decided to retain this episode, not by transposing it into Hadingus's life in human terms, as with the others—a process scarcely possible for the reasons given earlier—but as a parenthesis, as a divine or pseudo-divine story contemporary with the human story he was telling and unconnected to it by any other link than that contemporaneity. My view, then, is that he retained it while also telescoping it, condensing it to the greatest possible extent even, since it was no longer anything more than a digression instead of being, as in the myth, the element that controls the course of the entire narrative. Here is an account of how we may envisage this hypothetical procedure:

11. On the myth of Kvásir and its partially Indo-European origins see my *Loki* (1948), pp. 97–106.

1. The conflict between the "gods" is left in: it takes the form of a rivalry between Óðinn on the one hand and Mithothyn and his wizards on the other for the *caelestium honorum tituli* (vii, 3).

2. Also left in is the alternation of successes and defeats. But one of the two sides ultimately achieves total victory, and the story no longer ends with a pact of reconciliation but with the re-establishment, absolutely intact, of "the rule of Othinus," and instead of naturalizations we have exiles. Saxo or his source cannot conceive of a compromise between the gods because he cannot conceive of two kinds of gods (or wizards who have persuaded people that they are gods) being sufficiently different to be complementary.

3. The episode of the golden being (A, a) sent by the Vanes to the Ases who has an especially corrupting effect on their women and brings them to harm, whom smiths attempt without success to destroy in Óðinn's hall and who endangers the Ases to the benefit of the Vanes, this episode also subsists in the following form:

> A statue of gold has been sent to Othinus, a statue that the text no longer presents as a trap, as a device sent to Othinus by his enemies, but on the contrary as a token of homage from the northern kings.
>
> The effect of this gift, though not its intention, is the same as that produced by the sending of the "power of gold" in the myth: the gold on the statue turns the head of Othinus's wife and leads her, via the path of cupidity, to theft, sacrilege, and adultery.[12]
>
> Moreover, though it is no longer Othinus and his Ases who attempt the metallurgical destruction of the golden being, the corrupting object (on the contrary, Othinus attaches great value to it), nevertheless the statue is attacked and partially destroyed by smiths[13] (a coincidence of detail that is even, when one thinks about it, rather astonishing), then by a servant; only in doing so they are obeying not Othinus but the woman who has been corrupted by her lust for gold, his wife Frigga.
>
> The result of this episode is Othinus's defeat, since he goes into exile and eclipse, losing his *pristina claritas*, which has been besmirched, and leaving his *divinitatis titulus* unfilled for a time.

12. I do not think it necessary to bring Óðinn's brothers Vili and Vé into it here (the gold corrupted the wife and involved her in adultery, in *stuprum* generally), or the necklace (*Brísingamen*) either.

13. On the ideology of the smith see Mircea Eliade, "Metallurgy, Magic and Alchemy," in *Zalmoxis* 1 (1938): 85–129; *Forgerons et alchimistes* (1956; *The Forge and the Crucible*, 1962); "The Forge and the Crucible: A Postscript," *History of Religions* 8 (1968): 74–88; Atsuhiko Yoshida, "Mythe d'Orion et de Cédalion," *Collection Latomus* 102 (= *Hommages à Marcel Renard* 2, 1969): 828–44.

4. The high magic episode (A, b) is here the return of Othinus: he reappears, in glory, and needs do no more than reappear in order to put to flight the principal wizard—who in Othinus's absence, believing himself safe, *occasionem et ipse fingendae divinitatis arripuerat*—and to humble and remind of their human condition all those whom Mithothyn had made into "gods"; as for the "gangs of sorcerers" who had arisen—the expression is finely conceived and expresses the immediate, irresistible action of this epiphany on the part of the sovereign god very vividly—*subortos magorum coetus veluti tenebras quasdam superveniente numinis sui fulgore discussit*. It is clear what has been made of the Ases' revenge in the saga: it goes beyond the limited success it enjoyed in the myth: success, since Óðinn's high magic succeeded in re-establishing the Ase position weakened by the "Power of Gold" episode, but limited success because there was no absolute victor and the two sides were thus led to conclude a peace.

Between the inadequate sorcery of Mithothyn and his *magi* and Othinus's triumphant *numinis fulgor* there exists the same difference of degree, of perfection, that Saxo employed in his *Göttertheorie* earlier on [v, 4–5] to distinguish between the magic powers of the two categories of gods, or in other words, as we have seen, between the old Ases and the old Vanes.

It is possible that the conflict of the two liturgical doctrines that in Saxo reinforces this opposition between the two types of magic activity has a similar meaning. Óðinn, the sovereign god, presides from on high over a religion in which he is omnipresent, whatever the other god being specifically honored; he carries within him that tendency toward the *one*, that totalitarian character that in Rome, too, and in India, characterizes the first cosmic and social level, the function of magico-religious sovereignty. Whereas the third level, the level of fertility, of prosperity, of wealth, tends to multiplicity, to fragmented specialization:[14] this becomes particularly obvious, for example, when after the reconciliation and fusion of the two groups of enemies to form a complete, tripartite society, the Rome of the three tribes, each of the two erstwhile enemy chiefs, henceforward co-kings, establishes a form of worship: Romulus, eponym of the Ramnes, or in other words, in this story, the representative of the sovereign function, establishes one form of worship and only one, that of Jupiter the sovereign god; whereas Titus Tatius, eponym of the Tities, commander of the rich Sabine peasants, creates

14. Lastly, *La religion romaine archaïque* (1966), pp. 161–66, 173–79, 266–71.

a great number of specialized cults relating to his function, though each with its well-defined boundaries: Varron, taking the Annals as evidence,[15] says that Tatius *vovit Opi, Florae, *Vediovi Saturnoque, Sobli, Lunae, Volcano et Summano, itemque Larundae, Termino, Quirino, Vortumno, Laribus, Dianae Lucinaeque.* The contrast between the unitary liturgical doctrine of Othinus and the statement of the wizard Mithothyn that the people should not *diis vota communiter nuncupari,* but on the contrary *discreta superum cuique libamenta constituere,* this antithesis between *communiter* and *discreta quique,* if we are in fact faced with a complex derived from the primitive myth opposing Ases and Vanes—and in consequence superimposable upon the conflict between Romulus and Tatius—must express the same teachings as those of the two types of religion founded by the two "functional" Roman kings.[16]

5. This is apparently not all, however. Saxo or his source has not merely retained the two main episodes of the struggle between Ases and Vanes proper—by turning them into the two phases of the rivalry between Othinus and Mithothyn. He has also retained something of the two principal episodes—that of the speaking head of Mímir and that of the murdered and mutilated Kvásir—that the myth placed after the compromise treaty and presented as ensuing from that treaty. Except that in Saxo, since there is no treaty, since the conflict ends in the total revenge of Othinus, he seems to have incorporated these two episodes into the two preceding ones, and indeed used them in his saga as the denouements of those episodes.

The episode of Mímir's head (B, b)—Mímir slain and leaving a head that speaks to Óðinn—is stuck on, to put it crudely, to the outcome of the Gullveig episode (A, a): it is not a new character but the golden statue itself, between its two mutilations, that Othinus endows by magic with the power of speech, *vocalem reddidit.*

The episode of the Vane Kvásir, murdered and drained of his blood while journeying through the world (B, c), is joined to the episode of Óðinn's feat of high magic, to the dazzling return of Othinus (A, b): it is not a new character, it is the wizard Mithothyn himself, Othinus's

---

15. *De lingua latina* 5: 74; cf. Dionysius of Halicarnassus 2: 50. See *La religion romaine archaïque* (1966), pp. 174–75; *Mythe et épopée* I (1968): 298.

16. What I have just said partly nullifies chap. 8 of my *Mitra-Varuṇa* (2d ed., pp. 148–62), in particular sect. 3 ("Totalitarian Economy and Distributive Economy"): it is one of the joys of research to be able to correct an erroneous or inadequate solution. What still stands of my previous interpretation of Mithothyn (cf. *Mythes et dieux des Germains* [1939], pp. 35–37) is that the writer of the saga has cast the conflict of the two opposing sides, and of their leaders, in the "temporary king" mold.

principal adversary and rival, who flees abroad when Othinus returns and who, in his flight, is first killed by the people, then mutilated and pierced, as was customary with inveterate wizards and the bodies of ghosts;[17] the very wise, the too wise and sympathetic Kvásir is here represented by the particularly skillful and antipathetic Mithothyn, but these are simply alternative subjective colorations of their common characteristic, great knowledge—in one case bad spells, in the other beneficial learning.[18] Lastly, the use of Kvásir's blood (the *mjöðr* or hydromel of poetry and wisdom), which was fundamental to that character, has no counterpart in the Mithothyn episode.[19]

Thus Saxo's chapter 7, taken in its entirety, may be no more than a telescoped form of the mythical story of the war between Ases and Vanes. It is simply that the most important moment of that war, the reason for which the myth exists, which is to say its end, the treaty, together with the entry of the principal Vanes into the Ase society and the constitution of a complete social administrative board, no longer appears in the saga. We are left solely with the conflict between Othinus and the wizards, which ends like all wars—in Saxo at least—in a decisive outcome, with a victor, Othinus, and a vanquished, Mithothyn. Here then is the situation we now face:

1. The saga of Hadingus proper, all those episodes in the career of Njörðr that have been fictionally transposed into that of Hadingus, clearly shows Hadingus exchanging the protection and instruction of Harthgrepa for the protection and instruction of the one-eyed old

17. Examples in Paul Herrmann, *Kommentar*, p. 110.

18. The corresponding being to Kvásir in Indian lore, *Mada*, the personification of "drunkenness," whose birth brings the conflict of the higher gods (notably Indra) and the Aśvin to an end—like Mithothyn, and unlike Snorri's Kvásir—is dangerous and antipathetic; Mada's slaying and dismembering are a blessing to the universe: *Loki*, pp. 102–4.

19. Except perhaps in the wizard's name. Properly treated, Kvásir's blood becomes the "mjöðr of Óðinn." Perhaps this is an explanation of the name *Mith-othyn*? The edition princeps of Basel (1534), and the Frankfurt edition (1576) both have *Mithotyn*, and it was only later that it was printed as either *Mitothin* or *Mithothyn*; the first element must therefore undoubtedly be *mith-*, which in Saxo's usage would be the correct rendering of *mjöð-*. In which case Mithot(h)yn would be either "the Othin(us) of the mjöðr" (Saxo sometimes writes *Othin* for *Othinus* or *Othynus*) or an approximation for a badly understood expression, "the mjöðr of Óðinn." It is noteworthy that the name occurs just after the one-eyed old man's first intervention (vi, 7) in which the *mjöðr* of that character is involved, since the *suavissima quaedam potio* that he takes Hadingus *ad penates suos* to drink, in order to give him added strength, *vegetior corporis firmitas*, is certainly "Óðinn's mjöðr," that drunk by the eternal warriors, the Einherjar, in Óðinn's abode, Valhöll. The reinvigorating effect of *mjöðr* is undoubted: in the *Njáls saga*, chap. 30, a weary warrior breaks off in the middle of a battle to take a cup brimming with hydromel, drinks, then rushes back into the fray.

man (of Óðinn, though he is not named), which is to say that the saga undoubtedly presents everything in the myth that ensued from the conclusion of the conflict between the prototypes of Hadingus and Harthgrepa on the one hand (i.e., Njörðr and the Vanes) and the prototype of the one-eyed old man (i.e., Óðinn, the Ase leader) on the other; but the saga does not give any account of the conflict: the transition from the first part of Hadingus's career to the second takes place not without violence, it is true—since Harthgrepa is torn to pieces by her own kind—but without any conflict between the protagonists; in particular, the one-eyed old man takes Hadingus under his wing simply at the moment he chooses to do so, in friendship, pacifically, because he takes pity on his solitude after Harthgrepa's death.

2. Inversely, the digression concerned with Othinus and his enemies the wizards, which is still mythology—historicized mythology but nevertheless still superhuman, in which the characters are still "false gods," which is to say gods—and in which Othinus, unlike the one-eyed old man in the rest of the saga, is presented under his true name, this unprepared for, unjustified digression narrates that expected conflict in precisely the expected place, but shorn of its conclusion, shorn of Óðinn's adoption of some of his adversaries.

It is clear, therefore, what the editing process involved must have been. All that could not be transposed into human terms and given a place in the saga as such, in the fictionalized biography of Hadingus, was inserted by the writer as a parenthesis still in mythological form, involving not just the realm of Denmark but *totam Europam*, and not just ordinary mortals but the wizards of various kinds who were the possessors or usurpers of *tituli divinitatis*. But he inserted this digression in almost exactly that place where he needed to fill in the gap left by his fictionalized transposition, and he edited the digression in such a way that it would fill that gap without leaving any untidy edges, without duplication of his material.

It is a fairly extraordinary piece of work, but the result is there in front of our eyes, with the clear implication that the writer knew just what he was doing. It is always fascinating, though unfortunately rare, to be able to grasp so clearly, in a transposition of myth into history, both the intention and the plan, the difficulties and the solutions.

8

THE HADDINJAR

I hope that the preceding analyses have coherently demonstrated my thesis: that the homology of Njörðr and Hadingus is not restricted solely to the four episodes or characteristics pointed out in the nineteenth century; that it extends to other episodes, and above all to the division and the double meaning of both careers; and that it also takes into account the two mythological digressions with which Saxo has burdened his story.

Needless to say, everything has not been explained.[1] But then everything does not need to be explained. The saga's author, consciously writing a "Viking's biography," may have enriched his hero's life either with the usual clichés of that type of literature or with episodes drawn from other biographies,[2] other epic cycles.[3] Saxo may also have

1. In particular, the long episodes of the old bald men fighting remains unexplained (viii, 7–10).—The descent into the underworld (viii, 14; which there is no reason to describe as "Celtic" since early Scandinavian literature includes several analogous stories, some linked with the very Germanic feast of *jól*, and even here the afterlife described is specifically Germanic) is no doubt to be justified by the "Odinic hero" character of Hadingus from then on: the sight of the happiness of Óðinn's chosen in the other world (the eternally fighting warriors, the Einherjar) can only encourage him to follow the god's urgings in this one, and later on, at the end of his career, to hang himself in order to return to Óðinn. —The episode of the stolen treasure (viii, 6), a recurrent folklore theme, is perhaps a reference to the fact that the hero's prototype, Njörðr, like all Vanes, is a god of wealth: see above, p. 85; but good Viking that he is (cf. my *Mythes et dieux des Germains*, last chapter: "census iners"), Hadingus spends what he has conquered and does not leave any wealth to his son (2. i, 1).

2. Even so, we must not forget that the borrowings may have occurred in the opposite direction. Paul Herrmann made a systematic study (*Kommentar*, pp. 112–14) of the comparison often made sketchily before him between "Hadding" and Örvar Oddr, and concluded that the latter's saga is the basis for the romance we are now studying. Nine of his ten listed reasons are illusory. Here they are, with the refutations bracketed in italics:

(1) Both are trained to the pursuit of arms in early youth (*too banal to count*);

(3) Hadingus's father Gram kills an enemy with a wooden mallet; Oddr's grandfather and sometimes Oddr himself kills foes with a mallet (*The saga of Gram is in Saxo independent*

of that of his "son" Hadingus [see below, Appendix 2]; besides, such a characteristic is only too easily transferred from one hero to another);

(4) The episode of the two bald old men (see above, p. 106, n. 1) may be linked with a scene in which Oddr explains three great noises by the collision of two winds called up by Finnish magicians (*The whole analogy depends solely on the number "two" and the atmospheric character of the phenomenon*);

(5) Frotho I, son of Hadingus, is given a garment by his sister that no iron can pierce; Oddr receives a shirt from a king's daughter in which he cannot be wounded (*The theme is too common; besides, Frotho I is not Hadingus and their sagas are independent*);

(6) Oddr, like Hadingus, is wounded in the leg (*So are numbers of other heroes!*);

(7) Oddr and Hadingus both free themselves from captivity by telling stories or singing to their jailers until the latter fall asleep (*A frequent theme of which Herrmann himself gives many other examples; in the case of Hadingus, given the magical intervention and advice of the one-eyed old man, it is probable, despite Herrmann, that the hero is using a disguised form of the leysigaldr, the "unbinding spell" specific to Óðinn*);

(8) Hadingus, when still a baby, is cared for by a giantess who persuades him to sleep with her when he grows up; Oddr, captured by a giant, is taken by his captor for a baby and given into the care of his daughter, whom the hero wastes no time in getting with child (*Two quite different themes within an abundantly represented genre: sexual relations between men and giantesses*);

(9) Just as the one-eyed old man causes Hadingus to enter into a pact of brotherhood with a Viking, a man in a blue cloak (certainly Óðinn) causes Oddr to enter into a pact of brotherhood with himself and two Vikings (*An easily transferable Odinic theme: such brotherhood is part of Óðinn's province [cf. Lokasenna, str. 9]; moreover, this episode only occurs in the later version of the Oddr saga: if it was transferred from one hero to the other, then it must have been from Hadingus to Oddr and not vice versa*). This man persuades Oddr to abandon an expedition against his foe Ögmundr just as the one-eyed old man foretells his captivity to Hadingus (*The two incidents are quite different: in this same episode, Herrmann also compares fights against monsters that it is easy to show have nothing in common with our saga*);

(10) Oddr lives to be three hundred; Hadingus ends up an old man aged at least one hundred (*Herrmann himself recognizes that this last calculation is contrived; Hadingus's lifespan is undoubtedly long, but only normally so; there can be no link with Oddr's three hundred years, which are directly linked to the subject, to the general trend of the saga, both quite different from what we know of Hadingus*).

This leaves one argument of some weight, the second: "Just as Hadingus escapes from the Vikings thanks to a magically swift feat of sailing," Herrmann says, "so Oddr's father always has a good wind no matter which direction he wishes to sail in, and Oddr himself has inherited this family privilege." This theme is indeed rare in Scandinavia in this form, and it recurs persistently through Oddr's—doubtless artificial—family: his grandfather Ketill as well as his father Grímr both enjoyed this gift before him (cf. the texts quoted by Richard Constant Boer in his edition of the *Altnordische Sagabibliothek* [1892], p. 11, n. on l. 26 = chap. 4, 4; cf. p. 60, n. on l. 9 = chap. 30, 9); and such was also the case, one text says, "with other men of Hrafnista," the island off the Norwegian coast from which Oddr's family originated (today Ramstad, in Namdalen). This similarity, though important, is not sufficient to prove either that Hadingus relies upon Oddr or the contrary. This privilege natural in a hero modeled on Njörðr, could also have been laid claim to, with or without reference to Njörðr, the patron of islands (cf. above, p. 26), by one or several families of *sailors* living on an *island*.

Thus Herrmann's arguments are reduced to nil. And if we consider the *spirit* of the two sagas, in particular their relation with paganism, they are seen to be not merely different but directly opposed to one another; a fact pointed out by Axel Olrik, Herrmann himself, and above all Gustav Neckel in his article "Hamalt fylkja" (*Arkiv för Nordisk Filologi* 34 [1918]: 322–46), unfortunately, in connection with the extravagant Celtic exegesis dealt with in n. 5, below.

Lastly, the Oddr saga occurs in two versions, one that was certainly not written before

drawn inspiration, as he often did elsewhere, from himself, and re-modeled earlier passages in his own work.[4] More generally, he may have gleaned material freely from here and there, according to the whim of the moment.[5] But none of these other possible elements has

---

the end of the thirteenth century, the other before the end of the fourteenth (Boer, preface to edition cited above, pp. x–xi); Saxo's story dates from the early thirteenth century. If influences are to be admitted, it is therefore more likely that they would have been transmitted from Saxo or his lost source to the authors of the Oddr saga.

3. I am thinking of the Handwanus, "king of the Hellespont," episode. Whatever Paul Herrmann may say (*Kommentar*, p. 93), it seems difficult to make an absolute distinction between this *Handwanus*, who buys back his liberty with his weight in gold (*Handwanum cepit (Hadingus) eique redemptionis nomine corpus suum auro rependendi potestatem fecit*), from the *Andvari* who has to give Loki as a ransom all his gold, which then serves to fill exactly and cover—another ransom—the skin of Otr (prose beginning of the *Reginsmál* and *Skáldskaparmál* 47: 126–28. The link is all the more probable in that the same (*H*)*andwanus* reappears in Saxo (2. i, 89) where having been defeated by Frotho I, son of Hadingus, he hurls all his riches into the deep, reproducing the gesture made by Högni (*Atlakviða*, str. 26 and 27) that causes the gold of Andvari to become the fatal "Rhine Gold": *Andwanus cum patriae res perditas eversasque conspiceret, regias opes navibus impositas, ut undas potius quam hostem ditaret, in altum demersit.* From the presence together of these two motifs it seems evident that Saxo or his source knew and utilized *fragments* of the Scandinavian Nibelungen saga.

4. For example, the fire-bearing birds of 1. vi, 10, in the war against Handwanus (see previous note), which Saxo also used in his book 4 (v, 4); cf. the parallels in the sagas mentioned by Paul Herrmann (*Kommentar*, p. 93).

5. Here again circumspection is necessary. Neckel (see above, p. 106, n. 1) claimed to have established that the saga of Hadingus (whom he identifies as we have seen—p. 15, n. 6—with the Viking Hasting, an unwelcome guest of the French and British coasts) was constructed artificially with motifs borrowed from Celtic literature. He accumulated—I cannot honestly say grouped—seven arguments of which the majority are amazing and of which not one is telling: the sexual liaison between Hadingus and Harthgrepa, and in general love affairs between heroes and giantesses, being foreign to the spirit of early Germanic poetry, must derive, as do liaisons between heroes and fairies in Western literature, from the love affairs of Celtic heroes with the women of the *sidhe*; more generally still, the familiarity of mortals with supernatural beings, with gods, even with Óðinn, and in particular the search for a human husband by a girl from the other world—*Harthgrepa*, "*ein werbendes Mädchen*"!) all betray a Celtic influence; Harthgrepa, since she is Hadingus's foster mother, corresponds to Scáthach teaching Cúchulainn and Fer Diad (*but Scáthach teaches those heroes swordsmanship, nothing else, whereas Harthgrepa teaches Hadingus quite different things and dissuades him from a warrior's career!*); as Hadingus's protectress she corresponds to the Welsh Rhiannon, the protectress of Pwyll. All these arguments, subjective, or forced, or inconsistent, do not even offer ground for discussion.

Hence we find Neckel himself stressing three coincidences as being of particular importance to him because, according to him, they eliminate chance: the journey to the underworld (viii, 14), the clawed hand in the hut that Hadingus cuts off (vi, 6), and Harthgrepa's faculty of contracting and dilating her limbs (vi, 3).

(1) The first motif, without being as frequent in Scandinavian literature as in Celtic literature, is nevertheless well represented in it, as Alfred Nutt showed in 1895 in the essay he added as an appendix to Kuno Meyer's edition of *The Voyage of Bran, son of Febal* (chap. 12, 1: 295–309); in the case of the underground journey taken by Hadingus, the entire atmosphere of the otherworld is specifically Germanic; lastly, the scholarly Saxo was familiar with his Vergil and the sixth book of the *Aeneid* in which Aeneas carrying the

resulted in a dislocation of the structure that we have unearthed and found sufficiently intact, beneath the ample layers of Saxo's Latin style, for us to recognize its articulations in the light of the Njörðr myths on which it was originally modeled.

There does remain one point, however, that cannot be considered as secondary but that may be expressed in two differing forms between which we are as yet unable to choose: why, when reworking the mythical career of Njörðr, did the writer name his hero Hadingus; or inversely, why, when he came to write the biography of a character named Hadingus, did he take his material from the Njörðr myths?

Hadingus, as we established in an earlier chapter,[6] is not Hasting. His name, despite its undoubled -d-, is identical to that of a pair of brothers several times mentioned in the Eddic poems and the sagas. Saxo himself (5. xiii, 4) is aware of these *duo Haddingi*, which is to say the *Haddingjar*, the two youngest of the twelve sons of Arngrimr, all formidable *berserkir*, the list of whom is to be found in the *Hyndluljóð*,

---

golden twig accompanies the Sybil down into Hades: another model just as acceptable as the other, if foreign model there must be;

(2) The second motif does indeed occur in Pwyll's *Mabinogi*, but it is also met a great deal elsewhere, particularly in folktales. And one even becomes doubtful of the seriousness of the argument when one finds Neckel referring the reader to Friedrich Wilhelm Panzer's *Beowulf* and ignoring all but the variants marked as being "in the Celtic tradition or influenced by the Celts: Chluas Guillin, Perceval, Beowulf," without mentioning either Panzer's general theory about *Beowulf* (*Beowulf* as a variant of the tale of the "Bärensohn") or, above all, the fact that the motif of the gigantic hand wounded or severed by the hero (as with Pwyll, as with Hadingus)—a motif often linked with that of the forest hut (as with Hadingus but not with Pwyll)—is a common motif in one of the two principal forms of this tale and that variants of it can be found in Iceland, in Flanders, in the Auvergne, in Sicily, in Venetia, in Bohemia, in Greece, in India, and analogues of it in Poland, in Russia, in Kabylia . . . ;

(3) The third motif is familiar in the *Märchen* (no. D 55 in the classification by Stith Thompson; cf. D–631) and in local folklore (Ludwig Laistner, *Nebelsagen* [1879], p. 154); moreover, the two Celtic examples quoted by Neckel cannot be construed in the way he attempts to construe them: the voluntary corporeal distortions of the Irish Cúchulainn are terrible, monstrous, but lacking in precisely this particular feature, while the purely martial circumstances in which they occur have no relation whatever with Harthgrepa's transformations; as for Evnyssien in Branwen's Mabinogi (Joseph Loth, *Les Mabinogion* [2d ed.; 1913] 1: 143–44; cf. my *Loki*, p. 265), he arches himself, stretches himself (*ym-estynnu idaw ynteu yn y peir*: the verb *estynnu*, with the reflexive *ym-*, is taken from the Latin *extendo*) in the Cauldron of Resurrection, and bursts it, but he nevertheless remains the same *size*, and moreover the *effort* of his stretching bursts his own breast; there is therefore no question of a supernatural physical gift.

In short, one stands aghast in the face of such irresponsibility in the handling of comparison.

6. See above, pp. 15–18.

str. 23, in the Örvar Odds saga, chapter 29,[7] and in the *Hervararsaga*, chapter 3, (ed. Sophus Bugge [1873], p. 206).[8] According to this last source the two brothers are so closely united by their twinship that together they have the strength of only one man, whereas the eldest of the twelve, Angantýr, on the contrary has the strength of two.

But this presence of the *tveir Haddingjar* at the naval battle of Sámsey, in the Örvar Oddr saga (Saxo's Arvaroddus), is merely a secondary use of a hero's name: in the same way we find Heracles on the Argonauts' vessel, we find the Dioscuri fighting beside Jason, two or even three different legend cycles having been made to overlap, each increasing its stature by such associations in a sort of mythological gala performance. It has been pointed out, moreover, that among the names of the twelve sons of Arngrímr listed there also occur a Hervardr and a Hjörvarðr, alliterating names of which the second also appears in another and much more important context in which the name of the Haddingjar also figures. It looks very much as though the list of Arngrímr's sons, and their doughty ship, has been filled out with names borrowed from a variety of legends, and in particular the epic complex I am about to deal with.

This complex is one of the most tangled and diversely interpreted to be found in early Scandinavian literature, and even in Germanic literature as a whole, and certainly whatever side one takes the implications are very far-reaching. Restricting ourselves to Scandinavia, this complex consists of the varying traditions involving the heroes named *Helgi*: three of the *Edda* poems,[9] a romance saga,[10] and one episode[11] and two lines[12] in the second book of Saxo.

7. *Örvar Oddr saga*, chaps. 28–31, contains the account of the famous battle of the isle of Sámsey (Denmark): the twelve sons of Arngrímr attack the ships of the two great sea-rovers Örvar Oddr and Hjálmarr (Saxo: Arvaroddus and Hialmerus) while the latter are ashore on the island, and kill their crews. The two friends return, Oddr takes on seven of the brothers, Hjálmar five, among them Angantýr. The brothers perish, but Hjálmar too succumbs to the wounds inflicted on him by Angantýr. Oddr takes his corse back to Sweden, where Ingebjörg, the king's daughter, dies on hearing of the death of the hero (whom she had known in chap. 20).

8. The other edition, that of Chrstopher Tolkien (1960), chap. 2, p. 3, names only six of the twelve brothers and says that the others have no names.

9. The two *Helgakviða Hundingsbana* and the *Helgakviða Hjörvarðssonar*; they are referred to in the remainder of the chapter as *HHn I*, *HHn II*, and *HHj*.

10. The *Hromundarsaga Greipssonar*; it is referred to in the rest of the chapter as *HrS*.

11. The episode of Regnerus and Svanhvita (2. ii, 1–10), referred to in the rest of the chapter as *RS*.

12. The mention of Helgo as *Hundingi interemptor* (2. v, 3) acknowledges the translation of *Helgi Hundingsbani*; and an allusion to this same cognomen occurs also a little later (2. v, 6).

I say "diversely interpreted" because for some, for the majority of authors until recent times, what we are dealing with here is two or even three heroes who have the same name but independent existences: *Helgi Hundingsbani* ("H. murderer of Hundingr"), *Helgi Hjörvarðsson* ("H. son of Hjörvarðr"), and a *Helgi Haddingjaskati* ("H. the champion of the Haddingjar") whom a prose fragment at the end of the *Helgakviða Hundingsbana II* (after str. 50, the last) says is the reincarnation of Helgi Hundingsbani.

Hermann Schneider, on the other hand, in the treatise *Germanische Heldensage* in the re-edition of the *Grundriss der germanischen Philologie*,[13] made it his task to stress all that these three characters and their various legends have in common. One does, in fact, sense a kinship between the plots of all three stories that is as undeniable as it is difficult to express in precise formulas. I think that Schneider is correct. What we are faced with here is not one great *subject* precisely defined, preserved to a large extent in its variants, as with the *Iliad* or the Sigurdr legends, but rather a small number of *themes* that recur in these narratives linked together in varying ways. "Our material presents us here," Schneider observes, "with a state of affairs that has no analogy in heroic poetry. Usually, each character has a constant legend linked to it. The legend may be lengthened, reworked, given a different course, the hero may enter into relations with new figures, the poets may multiply the doublets; but certain essential lines, certain scenes, certain features linked to the hero of the story remain unmodifiable. Thus the phenomenon with which we now find ourselves faced is one not to be found anywhere else: all that recurs is a very generalized legendary framework, and in every case it is filled out anew as though the previous poet had made no contribution whatever; more: in every case characters appear in the same rôle with different names . . ." But even that does not seem to me to go far enough: even the principal names, such as Helgi itself, for example, are found employed for a variety of rôles, and on occasion conflicting ones.

Schneider has singled out the most important of these themes that have apparently survived the disintegration of an older plot and formed pockets of resistance around which different legendary structures have been rebuilt two, three, or even four times.

13. II Band, 1. Abteilung, II. Buch: *Nordgermanische Heldensage* (1933), pp. 250–98.

1. The hero must avenge his father (*HHn II*) or his grandfather (*HHJ*) or his brother (*HrS*); in one story (*HHn II*), the orphaned hero who must avenge his father is brought up by a foster father; in the same story, at the outset, it seems to be presupposed that it was the Hundingjar who killed the hero's father (hence his appellation after he has exacted vengeance of "Hundingr's murderer"); *RS* seems to presuppose something of the sort also.

2. In his search for vengeance the hero enjoys the protection of a supernatural female being (Valkyrie . . .) who provides him with weapons, protects him in battle, or attacks his enemies: *HHn I* (*HHn II* implies it), *HHj*, *HrS*, *RS*.

3. The hero finally succumbs himself to a counter-vendetta: all versions except *RS*, which clearly has had its end cut.

And it is certainly worthy of note that the first of these themes is fundamental in the Hadingus saga while both the others also appear in it, in slightly different forms.

1. Hadingus is obsessed with the idea of avenging his father by killing the murderer-usurper, and does eventually exact his revenge; he is an orphan, and he is brought up by a foster father with a view to preparing him for vengeance.

2. Hadingus does indeed enjoy the love and to a certain degree the protection of a superhuman female being. But here the change is considerable. Harthgrepa has nothing of the Valkyrie, the Odinic warrior-maid, about her; on the contrary, far from helping the hero attain his revenge, she tries to deter him from it, and from the pursuit of arms in general, in order to convert him to a life of sensual pleasure alone; moreover, she is his wet nurse before becoming his "official mistress."

3. There is certainly opposition of race and lineage between Hadingus and Hundingus (whose grandfather was the murderer of Hadingus's father; whose grandfather, father, and brother Hadingus has killed in the course of his vendetta). With the arrival of Hundingus this hereditary hostility has abruptly, and inexplicably, been transformed into a close and faithful friendship. Except that this friendship is the very thing that proves fatal to both men: though one cannot say that Hadingus is "Hundingsbani," the murderer of Hundingus, he is nonetheless the occasion of his death, since it is during a premature funeral feast given in his friend's honor that

Hundingus is drowned; and, moreover, it is upon hearing of the death of Hundingus that Hadingus, trying to go one better as it were, commits suicide. Reduced to its purely material consequences and leaving aside all psychological explanations, the death of each of the two "friendly" heirs of hostile lines is brought about by the other.

These three coincidences between the Hadingus saga and the three constant themes of the Helgi legends confirm that it is not independent of that group of legends, in which the hero is in fact called on one occasion, let us not forget, Helgi, "champion of the Haddingjar." But I must immediately stress the fact that these coincidences bear upon points that have been left unexplained by the confrontation with Njörðr: the vocation to kill the father's murderer; the hereditary hostility with a family including a Hundingus; the upbringing with a foster father; and at the end, the compensatory pair of deaths. And even Hadingus's liaison with Harthgrepa allows us to perceive a dividing line between the qualities that are extensions of a Vane goddess from the Njörðr mythology and all that derives from the supernatural woman of the Valkyrie type, from the Helgi legends: the incest, the open advocacy of sensual pleasure, the condemnation of weapons and war, the low magic, these belong to the Vane side of Harthgrepa; the protection[14]—in the "huge hand" episode—is the Sigrún, Kara, Sváva, Svanhvita side of her.

To this set of coincidences we may also add a feature that concerns Helgi as well as the Haddingjar. Helgi has a brother who plays an important part in HHn I (Sinfjötli), HHj (Heðinn), and HS (Hröngviðr), and "the Haddingjar" are by definition two brothers: this is made clear, as we have seen, in the borrowing made for the battle of Sámsey from these legends, duo Haddingi, tveir Haddingjar; similarly in the saga of Hromundr it is "two Haddingjar, kings of Sweden," whom Helgi champions against Hromundr. Now let us return to the very beginning of the Hadingus saga (v, 1): Hadingus and Guthormus his brother are two babies whom their tutor carries off together and entrusts, still together, to two giants after Suipdagerus has killed their

14. When Hadingus wishes to return to Denmark, (vi, 4) we read that Harthgrepa's love was such that *virili more culta prosequi non dubitaret laboribusque ejus ac periculis interesse voluptatis loco duceret*. In the episode of the "great hand" (vi, 6), we read: *quo monstro territus Hadingus nutricis opem implorat*; whereupon Harthgrepa makes use of her gift for dilating or contracting herself at will (*tunc Harthgrepa artus explicans ac magno se turgore distendens . . .*), and seizes the threatening hand, which Hadingus has then only to cut off.

father. All we hear of the other brother, Guthormus, after this is that he later returned to Denmark and submitted himself to the usurper, after which there is no further mention of him. One has the impression that the author was unsure what to do with the "brother couple" idea, decided not to eliminate it altogether, but then swept it under the carpet as soon as he could.

It therefore seems that in some of its episodes—those that our previous studies could not explain—the career of Hadingus is an extension of the career of a "Haddingjaskati" hero or even, directly, of a Haddingr; so that his name is thus fundamental. We are now in a position to formulate our problem more precisely as follows: how are we to envisage the process by which our author, given these "Haddingian" data and the name Hadingus, went on to undertake the operation we have been investigating up till now—to wit, the fictional reworking of the mythical career of the god Njörðr? What affinity was there between the name and personality of the Haddingjar and the god Njörðr?

We are now on the fringe of a mythological problem that over a long period has been approached from other directions. Karl Müllenhoff[15] has indeed constructed a considerable thesis on this subject, although one can find all its principal elements already expressed, less ambitiously, in the *Deutsche Mythologie* of Jacob Grimm revised by Elard Hugo Meyer.[16] Early in this century, Andreas Heusler[17] and the more moderate Karl Helm[18] declared their undoubtedly excessive skepticism. Lastly, in his *Deutsche Heldensage*, Hermann Schneider had cause to interest himself in the subject, and though he described Müllenhoff's construction as dated he nevertheless retained important elements from it. It is not our concern here to follow these authors in their arguments[19] but rather to achieve a clear formulation of this problem, which is in fact that of the "third function god-couples,"

---

15. In several articles in the *Zeitschift für deutsches Alterthum*, in particular 30, pp. 217–60; in his *Deutsche Altertumskunde* 2 (1887): 11–34, and 4 (1900): 486–87.

16. 1 (1875): 286–89.

17. *Reallexikon der germanischen Altertumskunde*, by Johannes Hoops, 2 (1913–15): s.v. (the three) "Helgi" (pp. 497–500; on H. Haddingjarskati, pp. 497–98); 3 (1915–16) s.v. "Ortnid" (p. 382–83).

18. *Altgermanische Religiongeschichte* 1 (1913): 323–24.

19. In particular I shall leave aside all that concerns the German heroes: Hartung, Hertnid, Ortnid.

whether brothers or not and whether twins or not, in the early Germanic religions. Here are the elements we have to deal with:

1. Toward the end of his *Germania*, in chapter 43, dealing with the Suevi inhabiting the northeast region between the Oder and the Vistula, Tacitus makes some interesting comments on two peoples (or what he believes to be peoples); the second of these are the Harii, whose curious war customs he describes, and who have sometimes been thought to be in fact a Männerbund rather than a people or tribe (cf. Óðinn's *Einherjar*); the first, whose name is left rather in doubt (Naharnali, Naharvali . . .[20]) honor a divine couple whom Tacitus assimilates to Castor and Pollux, even though the remainder of his description speaks only of brothers, not of twins.

> Among the Narharvali a wood consecrated to an ancient cult is to be seen. It is presided over by a priest dressed as a woman. The gods he tends, it is said, are according to a Roman interpretation Castor and Pollux: such is the value of these divine persons, and their name is Alcis. They have no statue and offer no sign of foreign influence; it is as brothers, as young men that they are worshipped.

We know what these two-brother cults such as those of the Dioscuri or the Nāsatya represent in the Indo-European world: they occur on the level of the third function, and indeed the detail referring to the priest's clothing (*sacerdos muliebri ornatu*) tends to confirm this; it recalls that disturbing *ergi* or "effemination" that according to Snorri (*Ynglingasaga*, 7) accompanies and renders shameful the practice of *seiðr*, the low magic specific to the Vanes.[21] And Saxo (6. v, 10) takes pains to underline the repugnance of his virile hero Starkatherus at living in Sweden, in the country ruled by the great Vane god Freyr:

> . . . he went into the land of the Swedes, where he lived at leisure for seven years' space with the sons of Frey. At last he left them and betook himself to Hakon, the tyrant of Denmark, because when stationed at Upsala, at the time of the sacrifices, he was disgusted by effeminate gestures [*effeminatos corporum motus*] and the clapping of the mimes on the stage, and by the unmanly clatter of the bells, not even enduring to look upon it.

20. The manuscripts give: *Naharnalos, Naharualos, Nahanarualos, Nahanaruolos, Nahanarulos.*
21. See above, p. 68, and n. 14.

Ergi, effeminatos corporum motus: both terms that link up with and situate the *sacerdos muliebri ornatu* tending the temple of the Nahavarli Heavenly Twins.[22] And this Frö or Freyr, it must be added, forms a couple with Nöjrðr, a father-son couple, perhaps earlier still a brother-couple, but at all events a couple bound together by a very close tie, as Elias Wéssen among others has shown.[23]

2. Another Germanic people, the Vandals, who once lived in these northeastern regions before achieving their later notoriety in various parts of Europe, also had traditions among their national and dynastic legends that were concerned with two brothers whom we likewise have reason to interpret as Dioscuri.

In Paulus Diaconus's *History of the Lombards* (1, 7–8), the Winnili, while being led on an expedition outside Scandinavia by Ybor and Agio, meet the Vandali led by the brothers Ambri and Assi. The Vandals invoke Godan, the Winnili address themselves to Godan's wife, Frea, who tricks her husband into giving the victory to the Winnili. Whereupon the latter change their name and become the Lombardi.[24]

Cassius Dio (*Epitome*, 12) tells how under Marcus Aurelius in A.D. 167 a people he refers to in Greek as "Ἀστιγγοι, led by two characters named *Raos* and *Raptos*, began to migrate south and settled in what is now northern Hungary. In the *Historia Augusta*, J. Capitolinus (*M. Antonius* 14, 22) names this same people in two different passages *Victuali* and *Victovali* (allies of the Marcomanni and kin to the Quades), but later, when describing the triumph of Mark Antony (ibid., 17), it seems clear that it is the same people to which he gives the name *Vandali*. And he is right: it is indeed the Vandals he is dealing with. The information given by Dion Cassius is only slightly erroneous, in the sense that his "Ἀστιγγοι is the name not of the people but of its royal dynasty: we are assured of this fact by Jordanes' *History of the*

22. Axel Olrik, *Danske Studier* (1905), p. 53, has suggested a link with the fact that among the Lapps the sacrificer wears a woman's linen bonnet over which is placed a crown of leaves and flowers, plus a white kerchief over the shoulders. But Edgar Reuterskiöld, *De nordiska Lapparnas Religion* (1912), pp. 124–25, adds that according to other documents this only happened when the sacrifices were to female divinities.

23. "Studier till Sveriges hedna mytologi och fornhistoria," in the *Uppsala Universitets Årsskrift* (1924), pp. 126–29; in one bardic strophe, and perhaps in two, of the *Egilssaga Skallagrímssonar*, it appears that the group *Freyr ok Njörðr* governs a singular verb.

24. *Mythes et dieux des Germains* (1939), pp. 73–77.

Gots (22, 113),[25] by Johannes Lydos (*De magistratibus*, 3, 55), and above all by Cassiodorus, upon whom Jordanes has based his arguments and who in the first letter of book 9 of his *Variae* (*Athalricus rex, Hilderico regi Vandalorum*) says: *Nam et hoc nobilitati vestrae fuisset adjectum, si inter Hastingorum stirpem retinuissetis Amali sanguinis purpuream dignitatem.* It was common at this time, as it was later, for the name of a Germanic dynasty to be confused with that of the people it ruled. Thus in *Beowulf* the *Scyldingas* are not merely the Danish kings of the Skjöldungar dynasty but the Danes as a whole.

Thus Ἀστιγγοι (H)astingi is the name of the ruling Vandal kings. Müllenhoff thought that the Naharvales, who are never mentioned again after Tacitus's references to them, had become the Vandals, or had at least become amalgamated with them, the Vandal kings then becoming the hereditary priests of the two Alcis brothers, whose individual names are provided by the Vandal names of the two eponyms, Raos and Raptos. More recently, John Loewenthal has interpreted[26] these two names—which appear to be a Greek transcription of the Germanic *Rauʒaʒ*[27] and *Raftaʒ*[28] meaning "Reed" and "Beam"—in the light of the earliest representation of the Spartan Dioscuri, who like the Alcis of the Naharvali had no statues but were represented, or doubtless rather symbolized, by two δόκανα, two parallel beams linked together by crosspieces.[29] All of which is certainly attractive.

But the name of the (H)astingi in itself tells us enough: it is the

25. [The Goth king Geberich] *primitias regni sui mox in Wandalica gente extendere cupiens, contra Visumar eorum regem* [qui] *Astingorum e stirpe, quae inter eos eminet, genusque indicat bellicosissimum, Deuxippo historico referente* ...

26. *Beiträge zur Geschichte der deutschen Sprache und Literatur* 45 (1920–21): 248–49. Norwegian scholars, linking these "planks" to descriptions of Lapp altars, have made certain bold hypotheses: Magnus Olsen, *Hedenske kultminder* ... (1914, p. 254; see above, p. 25, n. 18). At all events the existence of a province of Norway containing the name of the Haddingjar—*Hallingdal,* formerly *Haddingjadalr*—poses particular problems (I have found nothing throwing light on any point of the Haddingjar legend in the regional folklore books by: J. E. Nielsen, *Søgnir fraa Hallingdal* [1868]; Andras Mehlum, *Hallingdal og Hallingen* [1891]; Hallvard A. Bergh, *Folkeminnex fraa Valdres og Hallingdal* [1924]; cf. also Nils Lid, "Jolesveinar og grœderikdomsguder," in *Skrifter utgitt ev det Norske videnskaps-academi i Oslo, Historisk-filosofik Klasse* 5 (1932): 103.

27. Old Icelandic *reyr* (Swedish *rör*, etc.) O. H. German *rór* (German *Rohr*).

28. Old Icelandic *raptr* (Swedish *raft*, etc.), Anglo-Saxon and Middle Low German *rafter*, meaning beam, roof beam.

29. Plutarch *De fraterno amore* (beginning = *Moralia*, 478 AB); moreover, the two-brother couple has a priestess.

expected continental form corresponding to the Scandinavian *Haddingjar* and confirms its meaning. The Common Germanic word *haʒdar*, which by regular derivation[30] gives the Scandinavian *haddr* and the Anglo-Saxon *heord*, signified "a woman's hair or mode of dressing the hair." In the case of *haddr* this meaning is established in particular by two Eddic poems, the *Guðrúnarkviða* (*I*, 15) and the *Guðrúnarhvöt* (16). In the first, faced with Sigurðr's corpse,

> Gudrún collapsed onto the cushion,
> her hair fell unloosed [*haddr losnaði*], her cheek blushed red . . .

In the second, during a summary of her misfortunes Gudrún refers to the shining hair of her daughter (*hadd Svanhildar*) being trampled by horses' hooves. And Snorri, listing the poetic periphrases for gold, includes "the hair of Sif," *Sifjar haddr*, with the added information on this occasion that *haddr* is reserved solely for women's hair.

The circle is visibly closing: the priest of the two Alcis is *muliebri ornatu*; the Vandal Hastingi, who appear to have Dioscuri as eponyms, as well as their Scandinavian homonyms the "two Haddingjar" have a name, *Haʒdingōʒ*, derived from *haʒdaʒ*, "a woman's hair or mode of dressing it." The two cases, at least as far as type is concerned, overlap: in both we have traces and evidence of a similar third-function cult, and all the accounts of the Haddingjar must be epic remodelings of early Dioscuric myths.

There is one awkward objection to this series of deductions by Müllenhoff, put forward by Andreas Heusler, that has not yet been answered.[31] After expressing doubts about certain extensions of the argument that I prefer not to discuss here (the German hero Hertnid, for example), Heusler says: "What arouses one's doubts is above all the fact that the epic narratives do not provide the necessary bridge: the female hair upon which the whole thesis hangs has left no traces anywhere in them."

This statement is inaccurate. It is amazing that no use has been made in these discussions of an episode in the "Haddingjar stories"

---

30. The phonetic equation is the same, for example, in: Old Icelandic, *oddr*, "point" (Swedish, *udd*, "point" or "cape," etc.), Anglo-Saxon, *ord*, "point; beginning," Old High German, *ort* "point, end; beginning; corner" (German *Ort*, "place"), based on a common Germanic substantive *uʒdaʒ*.

31. *Reallexikon der germanischen Altertumskunde* 3, Johannes Hoops, p. 383: cf. above, p. 114, n. 17.

that does in fact involve these heroes with a character who not only has a female hairdo but is also, like the priest of the Naharvali Alcis, dressed *muliebri ornatu*. We have two versions of the episode.

1. In the Hromundr saga,[32] Hromundr himself, the champion of the Norwegian king Óláfr who has killed Helgi, the champion of the two Swedish kings the Haddingjar, has been wounded; his protectress leaves him in the care of a peasant named Hagal to be nursed back to health. One of "King Haddingr's" advisers, the wily Blindr, reveals to his master that Hromundr is alive and staying with Hagal. The king sends Blindr with a small band of men to find him, but Hagal's wife hides Hromundr. A little later Blindr and his men return. This time Hromundr is dressed as a woman and is turning the mill. He gives the visitors a baleful glare, but they leave once more without suspecting anything. It is not till they are on their way home that Blindr realizes the truth: too late; Óláfr later attacks Haddingr, whom Hromundr kills, and Blindr is hanged.

2. In the prose section that begins *HHn II*—the poem that ends, as we have seen, by the indication that Helgi, "Hundingr's murderer," has been reincarnated as Helgi, "the Haddingjar's champion"— the episode is reversed in that it is Helgi himself who benefits from such a disguise. The young Helgi, son of King Sigmundr, is brought up by a foster father named Hagal. Under the name of Hamal, son of Hagal, he goes to the court of King Hundingr, his family's foe, but his behavior awakens the suspicions of a councillor, Blindr the Bad. When Helgi leaves the court with a band of men, Blindr follows him. Helgi's only recourse is to disguise himself as a serving maid and go inside a mill (*tók klæði ambóttar ok gekk at mala*); Helgi's eyes and strong hands worry Blindr (two strophes), but Hagal succeeds in convincing him that this serving girl is a captured Valkyrie (two strophes). Shortly afterward Helgi sallies forth again to kill Hundingr, thereby earning the cognomen by which he is known until such time as he enters his other existence as "Champion of the Haddingjar."

Clearly this is the same episode in both cases, only as so often happens in the Helgi complex it is attributed in the first example to an adversary of the hero and in the second to the hero himself. And it fills in the lacuna in Müllenhoff's deductions exploited by Heusler.

---

32. Summary of the episode in Hermann Schneider, *Germanische Heldensage* 2 : 274.

And it is worth noting in passing how very much at home this character is—not merely dressed as a serving girl but also busy in a mill—in our "third function."

Thus it seems on the one hand:

1. That *Haȝdingōȝ was on the mythical level, among certain Germanic peoples on both sides of the Baltic, a name equivalent to the *Alcis* of the *Germania*, one of the names of the Dioscuric couple, or in other words of the two associated gods corresponding to the Indo-Iranian Nāsatya, the patrons of fertility, wealth, health, and even, in the ṚgVeda, the tutelary deities of the seafarer;

2. That the *Haȝdingōȝ, not only among the Vandals (Hastingi) but also among certain Scandinavian peoples (the "Haddingjar kings"), bore a certain relationship to the kings, to the ruling house, probably as eponymous ancestors.

And on the other:

1. Njörðr and Freyr are also typical third-function gods, and though conceived of in our texts as a "father-son" couple, nevertheless they still constitute a closely linked couple of neighboring if not equivalent masculine gods;

2. In the Ynglingar ruling house of Uppsala (cf. the Inguaeones of Tacitus), Njörðr and Freyr (the Freyr of "Fróði's peace," the Swedish equivalent of the Danish Fróði, Friðfróði) are the two earliest ancestors.

It is therefore hardly surprising that in places homologous to those occupied by Njörðr and Freyr in the genealogy of the Swedish Ynglingar, Saxo or his sources should have inserted a Hadingus and a Frotho (Frotho I)—a Frotho corresponding partially to Fróði, Friðfróði, and wholly to Freyr, and a Hadingus whose career is a reworking of Njörðr's: from the very earliest times, since pagan days, there had undoubtedly been an affinity, if not an equivalence, between what in Scandinavia became on the one hand the "two Haddingjar" and on the other Njörðr and Freyr.[33]

33. Magnus Olsen thought (see above, p. 117, n. 26) that the two Haddingjar were Freyr and Ullr, because the only two place names with a divine first element in Hallingdal are *Freysakr* and *Ullinsaker*. But I believe that the god Ullr belongs to a quite different province of mythology: cf. my *Mythes et dieux des Germains* (1939), pp. 37–41, and *Mitra-Varuna*, (2d ed.; 1948), pp. 144–47 (with the correction made above, p. 103, n. 16, on the interpretation of Mithothyn).

It would be futile to delve into the question more deeply:[34] in whatever way it may prove necessary to envisage the literary construction involved, it is this fundamental affinity between the two mythical concepts "Haddingjar" and "Njörðr-Freyr" that made it possible.

34. It would involve the complex problem of the various systematizations of the Skjöldungar dynasty both in Saxo and elsewhere: good accounts of it will be found in Paul Herrmann, *Kommentar*, p. 71 et seq., and in Raymond Wilson Chambers, *Beowulf* (3d ed.; 1921 [Wrenn, 1959]). Despite the ironic comments of Carl Wilhelm Von Sydow, *Namn och Bygd* 12 (1924): 63–95, account should be taken of the *vegetable myth* and *agrarian myth* elements involved in the names and legends of the dynasty's eponym—in Anglo-Saxon *Scyld Scefing* (*sceaf* = modern "sheaf") and which after the present study will seem even better grounded.

CONCLUSION

In the preceding chapters I have simply been making an anatomical comparison, as it were, between the myth handed down by Snorri and the saga used by Saxo.[1] The homologous portions have been superimposed, demonstrating in certain places an identical sequence, an identical line, so that the saga can be interpreted as a literary structure derived from the religious structure of the myth. At the same time, the oddities of Saxo's plan, the two mythological digressions, have been accounted for and shown to be analogous to certain useless organs in an adult or senile body that are to be explained by the structure of the young or embryo animal. The object of the present study was limited to such a demonstration, though someone else may perhaps wish to extend it with a second project that philosophers and literary historians alike will consider of greater importance.

The problem is fundamentally the same as the one I encountered in 1942, when I put forward the opinion that we should view the Roman legend of young Horatius as a fictional transposition of a martial initiation or promotion myth that, in the light of practices observed in various parts of the world by field ethnographers, it is now possible for us to reconstruct thanks to a study of Irish and Indian legends. I attempted at that time to bring out not only the homology

1. I retain the 1953 text with one or two amendments of style. Since then the first part of *Mythe et épopée* 1 (1968), on the transposition of an extremely archaic mythology into the epic plot of the Mahābhārata, has provided a much richer and more varied example of the type of operation indicated here. In the case of Rome itself, the career of Horatius, and in general the events constituting the "saga" of the warrior king Tullus Hostilius, has been studied in greater detail in the first part of *Aspects de la fonction guerrière chez les Indo-Européens* (1966), reprinted with little change as the first part of *Heur et malheur du guerrier* (1969; *The Destiny of the Warrior*, University of Chicago Press, 1971). The story of Horatius and the Curiatii is the etiological myth of the ceremony on 1 October at the *Tigillum Sororium*, the original purpose of which was no doubt the purification of the Roman army returning from its summer campaigning.

of the original organism and the terminal organism of the Indo-European myth and Livy's narrative, but also what in a physiological sense made the transposition feasible, in other words the substitution of a story centered on an individual, governed by human passions, for a scenario originally wholly composed of gestures and governed by the immemorial customs of society.

The *furor* of the Roman hero, together with its resultant excess and reparation, is no longer a functional, blind gift, as much to be feared as it is desired, resulting automatically from victory over the triple enemy. True, it has not become independent of that victory, but it issues from it only through the intermediary of an internal, emotional drama: it is personal, tribal, national pride, added to scorn for female weaknesses, that inflames the warrior's soul with such terrible but human anger. Similarly, Horatius's victory over the "triple adversary" is now simply the result of the chances of war and of the sole surviving Roman's wily stratagem. Horatius's sister appearing before the terrible conqueror at the city gates is no longer fulfilling a social office, carrying out a social mission: she is there solely at the dictate of her heart. Lastly, the threat of death hanging over the victorious but now criminal hero, and the purification that is substituted for his punishment, has been clothed in an at once rational yet emotive form that as early as Livy is already lending itself to finely phrased analyses of complex emotions and outpourings of noble rhetoric. In all this the episodes of the original initiation scenario certainly subsist, and even follow one another in the same order as before, but they are now governed by a dramatic plot that has retained almost nothing of the mystical sequence that linked them originally, and that we can follow so clearly in the Irish story of Cúchulainn's initiation into war: battle waged by young man against a triple foe (or three brothers) having as its consequence the first manifestation of the *gift of fury* that is to make him an extraordinary warrior; *social necessity* for the domestication of this ambivalent fury, to which end a woman, a close relation, is *sent* to meet him at the city gate, where he pours virile scorn on her pleading; finally, *"normalizing" medication* applied by the city to the warrior-madman whom the woman's hapless intervention has at least enabled them to capture.

The Hadingus saga clearly offers the possibility for a study of the same kind, and in better conditions, since the point of departure, the Njörðr myth, does not have to be reconstructed: it has been summarized, briefly but clearly, in Snorri's *Edda* and *Ynglingasaga*. We are thus in a better position to follow, beneath the preserved episodes and the preserved order of the episodes, the substitution of a *psychological* and completely *personal* narrative for a story of purely *social* value in which the personal events and changes that affected Njörðr were merely the repercussions of *collective* events and changes.

The object of the myth was in fact to show how the complete divine society was formed. To this end it first pictured the Vanes and the Ases in opposite camps, then reconciled and allied them, presenting each group as possessing its own characteristic functions and a morality corresponding to those functions. In consequence, the all-important pivot of the story was the war, followed by the pact between the two types of gods, and although Njörðr lived *before* that war and that pact in an incestuous union that he went on to renounce, *after* having accepted subordination to Óðinn, in both cases he was simply and inevitably conforming—without personal passion or will—to the two different sets of "regulations" corresponding to the two differing "environments."

The saga, on the contrary, as we have seen, finds these groups of gods and their collective regulations an encumbrance: it preserves them only in the encysted form of the two mythological digressions, of which the second at least is wholly unconnected with Hadingus himself. The entire action is now motivated by the will or passions of the three main characters: the hero and his two successive protectors, the sensual foster mother who draws him into an equivalent of incest and the omnipotent old one-eyed man who makes him over into an "Odinic hero." The first part in particular, that dominated by Harthgrepa, does still express if you like the conflict between the voluptuous Vane *type* and the energetic and warlike Ase *type*, but it expresses it as a conflict of *desires* in the *souls* of Harthgrepa and Hadingus, not as a conflict of *customs* between two *classes* of beings. Harthgrepa's poem is of particular interest in this respect. The reader returning to this passage at his leisure will have no difficulty in formulating the developments implied by this fact.

I shall conclude by stressing the importance of the results obtained from the point of view of Scandinavian mythography.

First, when recognized as a transposition of the mythical career of

Njörðr, the Hadingus saga offers confirmation of the statements of Snorri, of whose work it is manifestly independent: it proves, if proof is still required in certain quarters, that the war of the Ases and the Vanes as well as the complex configuration represented by Njörðr are neither fantasies nor falsifications cooked up by "the Reykjaholt school," but authentic and traditional data.

Second, Saxo's fictionalized version is much fuller than the few lines devoted to the same subject in Snorri's two books. In the saga, it is true, it is immediately obvious that many features certainly do not derive from the myth: everything in the second half centered on the notion of the "Odinic hero," for example. But there is one feature for which the probability of derivation from the myth is very high and whose mythical original has not in fact come down to us. This is the scene in which Hadingus so catastrophically acquires the familiarity with the *winds* and the *sea* that is later to be one of his privileges, and that, in the myth, is also a characteristic of the god Njörðr. The evidence preserved in Scandinavian fable tells us how, through what initial misfortune (loss of an eye and hanging; sacrifice of his right hand) gods such as Óðinn or Týr earned the right to their special power (foretelling the future, legal acumen); in the case of Njörðr, who is, moreover, little mentioned, nothing of the sort is recorded. It seems to me, therefore, that there is a sound argument for filling in this lacuna with the help of the evidence drawn from this fictional transposition based on a more complete form of the myth. We ought, without doubt, to "re-mythicize" the episode that Saxo develops at length in his I, viii, 11–12, together with the functional poem it contains: it is hardly possible that Njörðr should have been the one odd man out in the divine world, and it must have been through painful struggle that he, too, weathering an initial misfortune, acquired the stormy and shifting province recognized as his by Snorri and confirmed by Scandinavian place names. This legitimate reconstruction is a valuable addition to our studies.[2]

2. As I have said in the Preface, the center of my interest in Saxo's work has shifted in the years since this was written. Since we are fortunate enough, in the first nine books of the *Gesta Danorum*, to have at our disposal a number of mythical narratives transposed into fictional narratives, it is the procedures common to these operations as a whole that I have studied above all. Appendixes 2, 3, and 4 are presented in this spirit.

HANGING AND DROWNING

To Michel Lejeune

In the lectures of 1949–50 we examined the Hadingus saga from the birth to the death of the hero, and I pointed out, as many have done before me, that the form of voluntary death chosen by Hadingus is sufficient in itself to characterize him—despite the god Njörðr hidden within him—as an "Odinic hero." Óðinn is not merely the god of hanged men, the god who consults corpses hanging from gibbets: he actually gave the example for this form of death by hanging himself as well, as he tells us in a famous poem in the Edda (Hávamál, str. 138), and since Hugo Pipping some scholars are inclined to link this strange ordeal with certain magical ceremonies performed by Siberian shamans;[1] moreover, we know from the Víkarr episode in the Starkadr saga that when Óðinn orders a human victim to be "dispatched" to him, those performing the sacrifice have no doubts about the procedure to adopt: they hang the victim. Finally, by this suicide Hadingus is simply conforming to a prophecy made by the one-eyed old man that ought without doubt to be construed, as we have said, as a pact in attenuated form: Othinus has faithfully protected him in many a battle, has engineered his escape on several occasions from vis hostilis, from personal perils that in normal circumstances he ought not to have survived: one has only to think of the trap set by Uffo, who invites Hadingus and his men to a banquet, then massacres his guests, Hadingus alone being successful in escaping (viii, 17); of Tosto pursuing Hadingus (viii, cf. above, pp. 47–48) and Hadingus's single combat with the same Tosto (viii, 22); of the plot hatched by Hadingus's daughter and her husband, from which he emerges unscathed only because he has been alerted by a dream (viii, 23–26). We must assume that as repayment for this exemplary behavior on the one-eyed old man's part, for the

1. Mircea Eliade, Le chamanisme (2d ed.; 1968), p. 299. For Óðinn as god of the hanged, see above, p. 44 and n. 19.

fulfilling of the promise on his side implied by the prophecy, Hadingus recognized himself as bound to carry out his side of the bargain also implied in it, which is to say that he has always kept on the alert not to miss an eventual sign from his divine partner; and in consequence, when he thinks he has in fact received that sign, he gives himself up to voluntarium mortis genus, *as the old man had predicted, and in the form that will permit him to go and join his benefactor in that mysterious abode already twice revealed to him* (vi, 7; viii, 14).

There is therefore nothing surprising here insofar as the saga's hero is concerned. But the form of the sign he receives and understands is less expected. First, it brings into the picture in the rôle of Hadingus's dearest friend a character—Hundingus—who ought by rights to be his mortal enemy, since Hadingus and his family are responsible for the deaths of his father Uffo, his grandfather Asmundus, and his great grandfather Suibdagerus. Second, it succeeds in establishing an interdependence between the deaths of Hundingus and Hadingus that amounts to a literary structure. This structure, which is Hadingus's final distinguishing characteristic, was examined the next year, in December 1950 and January 1951, in two lectures at the Collège de France, the material of which was published in an appendix (pp. 135–59) to The Saga of Hadingus.

Hadingus's death is the consequence of another death (Saxo, I. viii, 27):

> 27. Meanwhile Hundingus, king of the Swedes, heard false tidings that Hadingus was dead, and resolved to greet these tidings with obsequies. So he gathered his nobles together, and filled a jar of extraordinary size with ale, and had this set in the midst of the feasters for their delight, and, to omit no mark of solemnity, himself assumed a servant's part, not hesitating to play the cupbearer. And while he was passing through the palace in fulfillment of his office, he stumbled and fell into the jar, and, being choked by the liquor, gave up the ghost; thus atoning either to Orcus, whom he was appeasing by a baseless performance of the rites, or to Hadingus, about whose death he had spoken falsely. Hadingus, when he heard this, wished to pay like thanks to his worshipper, and, not enduring to survive his death, hanged himself in sight of the whole people.

The death of Hundingus is very different from that of his friend. We know that it is a doublet of that attributed by the *Ynglingatal*[2] (str. 1) and the *Ynglingasaga* (chap. 11) in their still mythical portion to Fjölnir, son and successor to the king-god Freyr, himself the son and successor of the king-god Njörðr. Here is the text, in which it is again a Danish friendship that lies at the root of the accident:[3]

> 11. Fjölnir, son of Yngvifreyr, reigned at that time over Sweden and the wealth of Upsala. He was a powerful man, enriched by fair harvests and fair peace. At that time, at Hleiðra (in Danish Zealand), there lived Fródi-of-the-Peace, *Friðfróði*. They were close friends and visited one another's houses.
>
> When Fjölnir went to Zealand to visit Fróði, a great feast was prepared to which many of the people of that country were invited. Fróði had a great dwelling. There a great vat was made, many ells high and constructed of great staves joined together. It stood in a lower room. On the story above there was a wooden floor with an opening through which to pour in liquid, so that the vat was full of mead. It was a very strong drink.
>
> When evening came Fjölnir was led to the upper story, onto the wooden floor (near the hole). In the night, the king came out onto the balcony to satisfy a need. He was full of sleep and dead drunk. When he returned later to go back to bed he went past (his door) and went into the door of the other room, the one containing the hole. He stumbled, fell into the vat of mead, and drowned himself in it. Here is what þjóðolfr of Hvin says of it:[4]

2. The *Ynglingatal* is very probably a poem by the bard þjóðólfr, the Sage of Hvin, written in the late ninth century; we possess his work in only fragmentary form as quotations from it given by Snorri early in the thirteenth century, here (a strophe of the *Ynglingatal* as a conclusion to each chapter or autonomous fragment of a chapter from the eleventh onward in the *Ynglingasaga*) and in the *Edda*. The *Ynglingatal* has been republished ("reconstructed") and translated into Swedish by Ivar Lindquist, *Norröna Lovkväden fran 800- och 900-talen* 1 (1928): 58–73, and also republished in the posthumous collection by Albin Kock, *Den norsk-isländska skaldediktningen* 1 (1946): 4–9. On the relationship of the *Ynglingatal* to the *Ynglingasaga* see below, p. 139.

3. Summarized in these terms, together with the next chapter (on Sveigðir: see below, pp. 137–38) in the *Historia Norwegiae*: "*Froyr* vero genuit *Fiolni*, qui in dolio medonis dimersus est, cujus filius *Swegthir* nanum in petram persequitur nec redisse dicitur, quo pro certo fabulosum creditur." Ari's genealogical table simply gives: "... III Freyr, IV Fjölnir who died in the house of Friðfróði, V Svegðir ..."

4. This strophe—the first of the poem, or at least the first of those preserved—is apparently incomplete; judging by the position of *auk* in this strophe and the majority of others (though not in all), it is the first third that must be missing, but we cannot say for sure. There is a small grammatical and etymological argument centering on the verb *viða*, but it changes neither the construction nor the meaning. The notion of "fate" in this strophe as in many others is implied by the last word, the verb *skyldi*.

1. *It was fulfilled in Fróði's dwelling,*
The word heralding death that had gone to Fjölnir;
to the king, the windless-sea-of-the-bull's-horn
   [i.e., the liquid drunk from a horn, mead]
caused ruin, as fate would have it.

This passage, or rather these two linked passages, have given rise to a great many studies, the most famous of them[5] being that of the Uppsala professor, at that time *rector magnificus*, Henrik Schück, a literary historian given to losing himself, with a joyous abandon as fatal as Fjölnir's, in the exegesis of mythologies (1904). Over those pages, however, indeed over that whole book, despite the harm it has done to a number of minds, it befits an adoptive Uppsalian to lower the pious veil of Noah.[6]

Another study, more serious at the outset but soon exceeding its rights, was the contribution—so deeply impregnated with the spirit of Mannhardt—made by Wolf von Unwerth, professor at the University of Marburg (1917).[7] At that time Magnus Olsen had just finished (1914)[8] developing his brilliant and as yet unchallenged hypothesis linking *Byggvir*, the spirit of Barley (*bygg*), who appears in the *Lokasenna*, with a minor guardian spirit of barley and rural economy observed among the Finns and southeastern Estonians, *Pellon Pekko*: the Oslo scholar saw *Pekko* as a very early Finnish borrowing from the proto-Scandinavian *beggwu-*, which also gave *bygg*; which meant that *Pellon Pekko*, made up of two words of Germanic origin (*pelto*, genetive *pellon*, "field"), signified precisely "Field Barley"; and in the same research work Magnus Olsen had also dug up a forgotten "field god" from Norwegian toponymy named *Fillinn*, which is to say *Feldinaʒ*, who could be linked to his cousin over the Baltic, the Germanic *Pellon Pekko*, who had become a naturalized Finn. And at that time, too, Frazer's influence was predominant throughout the history of religions, so that everyone lived under the fond illusion that all "Spirits of the Corn" are more or less equivalent, more or

5. *Studier i nordisk litteratur- och religionshistoria* I (1904): 29–47.
6. In *Fornvännen* 36 (1941): 24–26; Schück also returned to and enlarged his theories in an article entitled "Odin, Vili och Vé."
7. Fiolnir, in the *Arkiv för Nordisk Filologi* 29 (1917): 320–35.
8. *Hedenske kultminder* (see above, p. 25, n. 18), pp. 103–6, 114–15. *Fillinn* said to date "from the early iron age." See my summary of the matter in "Deux petits dieux scandinaves, Byggvir et Beyla," in *La Nouvelle Clio* (1952), pp. 1–30.

less interchangeable. As a consequence, Wolf von Unwerth saw the word for field in *Fjölnir* too, explaining it as *Fjöldnir*, which is to say *FelduníR*, which in turn was to be explained as either (1) a hypocorism comparable to *Vingnir*, the name for Þórr, contracted from the composite Ving-Þórr, and formed from a composite whose first element was *feldu-*, probably *Feldu-Beggwuʒ, and thus an exact equivalent of *Pellon Pekko*; or (2) a word formed with the suffix -*nir*[9] with *feldu-* alone in the sense of "spirit of the field"; or (3) (for those who refuse to believe in the admittedly suspect[10] existence of a Scandinavian stem in -*u* for a noun meaning field), a word formed with the suffix -*uniR* added to the usual *felda-*, again in the sense of "field spirit." As for the matter of the argument, using the least unreasonable part of Schück's study, he interpreted the legend of the drowned Fjölnir as follows: "Fjölnir, the equivalent of "[Byggvir] spirit of the field" and of Pellon [Pekko], perished in the horn liquid; which means that the god of barley or of the field [of barley] lost his life in the beer." Beer, as in Saxo, not the mead that Snorri must have derived from an arbitrary interpretation of the very generalized periphrasis with which Þjóðolfr, his source, had obscured the original beer.

This construction, based upon Magnus Olsen's *Byggvir* and *Pekko* hypothesis, did not survive it: criticism, at first won over, later reversed its decision, and it was shown that the Finnish *Pellon Pekko* or *Pekka* in fact means "Peter of the field" (*Pekka* being a diminutive of *Pietari*, "Peter" and this Peter was found to tie in with a fairly abundant series of Christian saints put to use as protectors of this or that agricultural activity. *Pellon Pekko* is therefore not modeled on a Germanic expression and does not prove the existence of a composite *Feldu-Beggwuʒ (Field Barley) of which *Felduníʒ, Fjölnir could be a contraction. Fjölnir cannot therefore be what the second and third explanations of his name claim he is either—i.e., a "field spirit"—for the simple reason that *nothing* in his legend connects him in any way with fields: whether filled with mead or with beer, the vat in which Fjölnir drowns is located in the royal palace, like the one in which

9. Cf. *Fjósnir*, a symbolic proper noun in the *Rígsþula* (from *fjós*, "dunghill"); *Mélnir*, the name of a horse (from *mel*, "bit"); Thor's hammer *Mjöllnir* (from *mjöllr*, *mjallr*, "glittering"); cf. below, p. 152, n. 56.
10. The extremely fragile basis for this supposition is derived from a few Old Swedish forms that can be explained otherwise.

Hundingus drowns, and not in a rustic or peasant setting bearing any relation to agriculture.[11]

This attempted explanation suffered, I think, as have all those made up till now, from the fact that the problem was badly posited, and incomplete. The analogy with the Saxo story ought to have warned the exegetes that Fjölnir's death by drowning is perhaps only one half of a whole,[12] since the parallel death of the Swedish Hundingus, *drowned* accidentally, is inseparable from that of the Dane Hadingus who *hangs* himself of his own free will in order to go to Óðinn.[13] And this suspicion would have been confirmed if they had taken into account a fourth version we have of the story, the one provided by a Faeroes ballad collected in 1840, of which the following is a literal translation:[14]

> 178. *Óðin goes from Asgardur*
> *—the sagas say—*
> *then from there sailed on*
> *as far as Siggjumtá*[15]
> 179. [16] . . .
> 180. *He sailed as far as Siggjumtá*

11. As for the etymology of the matter it is best to say here and now (cf. below, pp. 151–53) that though *Fjölnir* is not the "field" spirit so absent from his story he is even less the "hider" (verb *fela*, "to hide"); nor the "hider of the dead," the god of the dead (Schück, 1904); nor the "hider of the mead," Óðinn (Noreen, 1892; Kjærr, 1914). The etymological derivation from "field" also has against it, from the strictly philological point of view, the fact that it is one more in a series of similar efforts in which philologists have abused their faculty for presupposing the dropping of an internal syllable with a consonant essential to their explanations (here -*d*-).

12. Cf. Atsuhiko Yoshida, "Piasos noyé, Cléité pendue et le moulin de Cyzique, essai de mythologie comparée, "*Revue de l'histore des religions* 168 (1965): 155–64.

13. Reality can sometimes make fools of the cleverest interpreters of myths. Here is a quotation from *Le Figaro* of 8 March 1950, p. 2, col. 6: "Marseilles, 7 March. Suffering from persecution mania and also very upset by the recent death of one of his friends, C. C., whose body was found in a well, an Italian woodcutter of Sanary, aged 48, attempted suicide. He climbed into a tree, put a noose around his neck, tied it to a branch, and threw himself into the void. The rope broke, and the desperate man fell eighty feet . . . into the icy sea. Witnesses of the scene succeeded in hauling him out." Hadingus was luckier: his noose dispatched him to life eternal with Óðinn.

14. In the *Corpus Carminum Faeroensium* (= *Færoya Kvæði*) in course of publication (cf. below. p. 139, n. 28), it forms the end of variant C of the ballad "*Óðin í Ásgœrðum, ella Frúgvin Málniða*": t III, fasc 2 (Copenhagen, 1945), pp. 243a–44b. The name Óðin (with only one *n*) is pronounced in the Faeroes more or less "*ouin.*"

15. I.e., Sigtúna, in Uppland, as in the *Ynglingasaga*, chap. 5.

16. Strophe 179 is more or less a repetition of 178; these ballads were accompaniments to dances, and the poet-reciter tended to use repetition as a method of keeping in step with the dancers.

—as the saga says again—,
he subjected all Sweden,
the Russians and the Norwegians.

181. He had Siggjumtá built,
folk remember it still:
in Sweden he bears the name of king,
in Norway no less.

182. He taught them a faith
that did them little service:
"If you are in need in any way,
call on the name of Óðin."

183. Veraldur,[17] son of Óðin,
went to present himself to his father:
"I wish to go to the south lands
to find myself a wife."

184. "Listen, Veraldur, my son,
such a thing will not end happily.
If you go into the south lands,
you won't come back."

185. Veraldur had himself built a boat
of great solidity;
he sailed toward the south lands
that very fall.

186. He dropped his anchor
on the white sand;
Veraldur, son of Óðin, was first
to set foot on land.

187. In the middle of the garden,
he put his furs over his shoulders;
and thus fitted he advances
into the great hall.

188. And thus fitted he advances
into the great hall
where the king of Zealand was seated at table
with five hundred men.

17. I.e., Freyr. The name *Veraldur* is a curious formation from the cognomen of Freyr recorded by Snorri at the end of chap. 10 of the *Ynglingasaga*, and which is not found anywhere else except in a passage from the *Flateyjarbók* paraphrasing the Snorri text: *veraldar goð*, "god of the world" (or, "of mankind": Old Icelandic, *veröld*—cf. Eng., *world*, Germ., *Welt*, etc.—contains *verr*, "man," and *öld*, "age, period; people"). This cognomen, scarcely supported by other evidence from early Scandinavian literature, is confirmed by the copying (and semitranscription) in Norwegian Lapp in which Freyr is named *Veralden Olmay* (*olmay* = "man").

189. *Veraldur walked into the hall*
     —it was the custom in those days—
     he does all in a single word,
     he salutes them and makes his request.

190. *Veraldur stands on the floor of the hall,*
     he presents his request:
     "Happiness be with you, brave king of Zealand,
     give me your daughter!"

191. *"Be welcome, Veraldur, Óðin's son,*
     you are a noble champion.
     Enter our stone hall,
     drink mead and wine!"

192. *Veraldur entered the hall of stone*
     that was full of deceit:
     it was open beneath his feet,
     he fell into the brewing vat.

193. *Veraldur, Óðin's son, said*
     as he fell through the hole:
     "This is what my father wished to tell me
     when I left our home."

194. *He learnt of this, the king Óðin,*
     he was in his bed:
     his son, in Zealand, was fallen
     into a brewing vat.

195. *"I was old and gray,*
     yet I had a presentiment of it . . ."
     When Óðin heard this news,
     he fell on the ground.

196. *It was a feast day,*
     it all happened quickly:
     Óðin was struck with a mortal sickness
     that very night.

197. *Óðin utters these words,*
     he holds his golden ring:
     "Call together the men and women
     living all around!"

198. *Óðin utters these words,*
     he was a very good king:
     "Now it pleases me to go up to heaven,
     to live like a king up there.

199. *"When you see that I am giving up my ghost,*

> then I shall be going to Ásgarður
> to live in my own country.
> 200. "Listen, men and women,
> to what I shall say to you:
> if you find yourselves in any need,
> then you must pray to me:
> 201. "I shall be faithful to you,
> remember me:
> you shall come to Ásgarður,
> and there shall you find me."[18]

As with Saxo's paragraph, it is noteworthy that these lines provide a sequel to the death of the hero drowned in the vat. In fact the accidental drowning, in the internal economy of what is in fact a ballad wholly devoted to Óðinn, is merely an introduction to what follows: from grief, and of his own free will, another character dies in another manner, dies in the most Odinic manner possible, since it is Óðinn himself who "goes to heaven," who returns to his kingdom, where he promises to receive the dead of his earthly people later.

The observation of this structure naturally leads us to read on and see what in the *Ynglingatal* (str. 2) and in the *Ynglingasaga* (end of 11 and 12) follows the death of Fjölnir, which is to say the account of Fjölnir's son Sveigðir:[19]

> 11. ... Sveigðir took the kingship after his father. He made a solemn vow to go in search of the Home of the Gods (*Goðheimr*) and of Óðinn the old. He traveled through the vast world with twelve men.[20] He went into Turkey and into Great-Sweden [i.e., Russia], met many of his kin there, and stayed five years.[21] Then he returned to Sweden. He stayed a while at home. He had taken a wife named Vana in the Land of the Vanes (*Vanaheimr*).[22] Their son was Vanlandi.
>
> 12. Sveigðir left again in search of the Home of the Gods. To the east of Sweden there is a great tract of land named "At the Rock." A rock as high as a great house stands there. In the evening, after sunset, as Sveigðir was coming back from a drinking bout to the men's sleeping

18. Strophes 198–201 recall the beginning of chap. 9 of the *Ynglingasaga*, matter exterior and anterior to the Fjölnir story.

19. Summary in *Historia Norwegiae*; see above, p. 131, n. 3.

20. Thus imitating Óðinn himself with his twelve assistants in the *Gylfaginning*.

21. From Snorri's point of view these countries had in the past been stages in Óðinn's migration from Black Sea to Scandinavia: *Ynglingasaga*, 1–2 and 5.

22. Marching on the Home of the Ases: *Ynglingasaga*, 1–2.

room he looked at the stone and saw a dwarf seated at its foot. Sveigðir and his men were very drunk and ran toward the stone. The dwarf stood up in front of the door, called to Sveigðir, and invited him to enter in if he wished to come to Óðinn. Sveigðir hurled himself into the rock which immediately closed behind him, and Sveigðir never came back. Here is what Þjóðolfr of Hvin says:

2. *Terrified by daylight, one of the descendants of the Durnir* [= of the dwarfs],[23]

> *the guardian of the hall, tricked Sveigðir,*
> *when into the rock, the great-hearted*
> *son of Dusli,*[24] *behind the dwarf, hurled himself in.*
> *And the glittering hall of the Mímir-of-the-Gems*[25] *and his kin,*
> *peopled with giants, opened like a maw to [swallow] the king.*[26]

There is one feature here—and an essential one, since it gives the entire story its meaning and unity—that gives assurance of our not being mistaken in linking this chapter to our investigation: in another way, but as clearly as in Saxo and the ballad, a wholly Odinic death, the voluntary death of a character who is seeking for and succeeds in joining Óðinn in the Home of the Gods, follows the accidental death by drowning in the vat. Moreover, like Njörðr and Freyr, both of whom are gods, Fjölnir and Sveigðir are also, and alone, mythical characters: it is with Sveigðir's son and successor, Vanlandi, that the vaguely historic elements begin to appear in this genealogy.[27]

23. Taking *Durnis niðja* as a *partitive* genitive dependent upon *salvörðöðr*. Others translate it as a *possessive* genitive (which is perhaps more in keeping with these strophes stylistically) "the guardian of the hall *of the* descendants of Durnir," "the hall of the dwarfs" being a poetic periphrasis for the rock.

24. Unknown and of uncertain meaning. But it obviously refers to Sveigðir himself. Ivar Lindquist suggests (taking *Dusla*, in *Dusla konr*, as a genitive plural), with a question mark, "son of the goblins."

25. Unknown: no doubt a periphrasis for Óðinn; "peopled with giants" is odd: the gods represented as giants?

26. His appetite whetted by his treatment of Fjölnir, Henrik Schück has applied the same exegetic method, if so it can be called, to this chapter and strophe (1: 47–51).

27. Birger Nerman, "Den svenska Ynglingaättens gravar," in *Ríg* 2 (1919): 48. Cf. the summary of this author's work by Olof Janse, notes on the first pagan Swedish kings in the *Revue des études anciennes* (1924), pp. 243–49. Nerman's views have naturally been contested. Other opinions will be found, for example, in Sune Lindqvist, "Ynglingaättens gravskick," *Fornvännen* 16 (1921): 83–194, and by the same author, *Uppsala högar och Ottarshögen* (1936); in vol. 46 (1938–43), of *Upplands Forminnens-Förenings Tidskrift*, entirely devoted to the excavations at Vendel; in Göte Klingberg, "Uppsala högar och traditionen," ibid. 47 (1944–52): 231–35 (bibliography of the arguments and replies of Nerman up to 1943); in Sune Lindqvist, "Uppsala högars datering," *Förnvännen* 44 (1949): 33–48; and in Nils Åberg, "Vendelgravarna och Uppsala högar i deras historiska miljö," ibid., pp. 193–204; etc.

We do not, of course, know the source of the Faeroes ballad. It was a literary source certainly, and Icelandic, as is almost always the case, and very closely akin to the *Ynglingasaga*. But the coincidences that are immediately noticeable between these strophes and the Saxo story in passages where the latter differs from the *Ynglingasaga* make it impossible to think that the ballad source was, or was exclusively, the *Ynglingasaga*.[28] As for the relationship between the *Ynglingatal* and the *Ynglingasaga*, it is no longer possible today to maintain the radical thesis—that of Henrik Schück and many others—according to which Snorri had no other sources at his disposal, nor even any traditional commentary on the *Ynglingatal*, so that all his material is derived from the latter poem, its obscurity liberally interpreted, with the result that we need take no account of any of the data provided by the *Ynglingasaga*: such a thēsis is a kind of hypercriticism enabling mock-rigorous minds to indulge themselves without let or hindrance in their own imaginative fantasies and errors of logic.[29] Discarding any preconceived ideas as to the relationships of the

28. There was no early Faeroes literature corresponding to the Icelandic and we have no Faeroes manuscripts: Icelandic then Danish were the languages of the educated, and the dialect (scarcely less archaic today than Icelandic, but with a very distorted pronunciation) was not used in writing. But using Icelandic sources that we cannot always be sure of, and later on Norwegian ballads as well, local poets began—fairly early, it seems—composing ballads for use in folk festivities. It was remarked on long ago that the Faeroes *Sjúrður* (*Sigurðr*) cycle contains fragments independent of all known Nordic texts and sometimes more satisfying. A few of the ballads were noted down as early as the seventeenth century, but the "revelation" took place in the early twentieth century with the first systematic investigation, that of the naturalist H. C. Ljungberg, who had gone to the islands to study the seaweed there and then became interested in the poems. Since then, all the cantons have been well explored and emptied of their treasure. The happy result of this collecting work (notably by J. Ch. Svabo as early as the late eighteenth century and by P. C. Müller, Hentze, J. H. Schröter, H. Hansen, N. Nolsó, and V. Hammershaimb in the nineteenth) is the great work of Svend Grundtvig and Jörgen Bloch, *Færoya Kvæði* or *Corpus Carminum Faeroensium*, in sixteen manuscripts in quarto volumes kept in the Royal Library in Copenhagen, containing 234 ballads in nearly 900 versions, or about 70,000 lines. A presentation of this collection was made by Axel Olrik, then a humble "cand. mag." in the *Arkiv för Nordisk Filologi* 6 (1890): 246–61. Since just before the second World War the great Faeroes specialist Christian Matras has been publishing the collection in large quarto volumes. When the publication is finished a German commentary is promised. The interest of the ballad whose last strophes we are dealing with here was pointed out by Helmut De Boer, "Mythologisches aus den färoischen Folkevisen," in *Göteborgs Högskolas Årsskrift* 21 (1920): 54.

29. The present study will provide one reason for rehabilitating Snorri: how, if he was inventing everything arbitrarily on the basis of Þjóðólfr's strophes, could he have followed his Fjölnir story with an "Odinic" hero and an "Odinic" death not imposed by the Sveigðir strophe, thus recreating, with differences excluding the possibility of any borrowing from it, the Hundingus-Hadingus schema?

various texts, we must, therefore, undertake a complete comparison and set out precisely what the analogies and differences between them are (*Yt* = *Ynglingatal*, str. 1 and 2; *Ys* = *Ynglingasaga*, chaps. 11 and 12; *S* = Saxo, 1. viii, 27; *F* = Faeroes ballad, str. 178–201).

1. The four texts all present a death by drowning in a vat with an ensuing Odinic death. But in *S* and *F* the first is morally the cause of the second (by delicacy of scruple and gratitude in *S*, by grief in *F*), whereas in *Yt* and *Ys* there is simply a temporal succession, after a considerable lapse of time, with no causal link: these two dramatic deaths are merely the first of the many enumerated in both poem and saga, and whose succession actually forms the essential kernel of the material dealt with in both works.[30] It may be suspected, however, that it is *Yt* and *Ys*, in order to make the mythical diptych fit into their merely enumerative mold of "ends of reigns," that have deliberately broken the closer bond of interdependence between the first two deaths on their list.

2. a) In all four texts the drowning is involuntary. It is purely accidental in *Ys* and *S*; *Yt* makes certainty on this point impossible; in *F* it is the result of treachery (a common theme in the ballads, as is that of the request for a daughter's hand). It has been prophesied in *Yt* ("it was fulfilled the word heralding death . . .") and in *F* (str. 184); in *S* it is the death of the Odinic hero that has been foretold (viii, 16).

b) In all four texts the drowning takes place during a feast or drinking bout. The drowned man, in every case Swedish, dies on a visit to Denmark in *Yt*, *Ys*, and *F*; *S* has him die in his own Swedish palace, but during a ceremony in honor of a Danish friend.

c) The vat contains mead (*Ys*) or beer (*S*), or is a brewing vat (*F*); *Yt* is not specific on this point.

3. In *S* and *F* the Odinic death is clearly voluntary and takes place in the presence of subjects specifically assembled for the purpose of watching it; in *F* it is Óðin himself who goes up to heaven, vanishing

---

30. In the *Ynglingasaga* prologue Snorri says that Þjóðólfr's poem names thirty of Rögn-valdr's ancestors and "tells of the death and burial place of each." The literary genre thus created or made famous at the end of the ninth century went on to prosper: in the late tenth century the bard Eyvindr Skáldaspillir was imitating, and even reworking, the *Yngingatal* in his *Háleygjatal* (Ernst Albin Kock, *Den Norskisländska skaldediktningen* 1 [1946]: 37–39); again in the late twelfth century a poet was composing a *Nóregs konungatal* in this form relating the deaths of the Norwegian kings (ibid., pp. 278–88). There is a Danish ballad treating the deaths of the Danish kings in the same way: *Dansk kongetal*, in the *Danmarks gamle Folkeviser* by Svend Grundtvig (3 [1862]: no. 115). It is a sort of Scandinavian counter-part of the genre that flourished in Rome under the Empire relating the *exitus illustrium virorum* (cf. Friedrich A. Marx, *Philologus* 42 [1937–38]: 83–103).

rather than dying; in S the Odinic hero hangs himself, a death that guarantees him access to Óðinn's abode. In Ys and probably in Yt the Odinic hero has spent his life searching for Óðinn, and disappears into a rock, to a certain extent voluntarily, at the invitation of a dwarf who promises him that he will find Óðinn in that way.

4. a) In Yt and Ys the drowned man and the Odinic hero are father and son, both Swedish; in F, son and father, both Swedish; in S, close friends, one Swedish the other Danish, and moreover the drowned man is quite young, the Odinic hero very old.

b) In Yt and Ys the two characters are both kings, successive kings, and of equal importance in Þjóðólfr's and Snorri's reviews of the Ynglingar rulers (a consequence of 1). In S they are kings again, but of two different peoples and on the throne at the same time. In F they are a king and his son. In the wholes (saga and ballad) of which the S and F accounts are the conclusions the drowned hero is merely episodic, secondary in relation to the Odinic hero, and all that happens to him is intended only as an explanation of how the Odinic hero either kills himself or disappears.

c) In Yt, Ys, and S the two characters are mortal kings. In F they are two gods, but conceived of as men (which is also the case, in the previous chapters of the Ynglingasaga, with the god-kings Óðinn, Njörðr, and Freyr, as well as with Saxo's one-eyed "old man" and later, when he mentions him, with the "King Frö").

This first inextricable network of correspondences and differences makes it clear that of the four texts only Yt and Ys are fully in agreement[31] and form a unit, but that none of the three versions to which the four texts can thus be reduced is wholly reducible to one of the others; and that none of them can therefore be ignored.

As to interpretation, two points of view are clearly of particular importance: the natures of the characters and the circumstances of the deaths. It is easy to see that both characters and deaths are antithetical:

5. a) If the second character who dies is of the Odinic type, linked to the Ase leader, the first, the one who drowns, is of the "Freyr," the Vane type. It is F that makes this contrast clearest, since the characters in it are Veraldur, i.e., Freyr, and Óðin themselves, and this fact is all the more remarkable in that this is the sole mention of Freyr in the

---

31. Though Yt and F alone of the four (and with the notable exclusion of Ys) contain the prophecy relating to the death of the drowned hero (2, a).

entire Faroes ballad literature. But in the other versions, though less clearly stated, this antithesis is nonetheless fundamental: in S, since the moment he is taken under the wing of the one-eyed old man, Hadingus is a typical "Óðinn hero"; as for the drowned man, Hundingus, he is a member of the Swedish ruling house that in Saxo's eyes is the family of Frö or Freyr itself. In Ys (and doubtless in Yt as well), Fjölnir is Freyr's own son; he has been characterized like the latter by the fertility and prosperity of his reign, which continues Freyr's own reign without any change or fresh difficulty; Sveigðir, from beginning to end, from the moment when he binds himself by his vow to search for the god and find him, thinks of nothing but Óðinn and shows no concern at all for his kingdom. We are therefore justified *in referring to the two heroes from now on, for simplicity's sake, as being in the one case "Vanic" and in the other "Odinic."*

b) However, within these antithetical couples the two characters are intimately linked: either closely akin (Yt, Ys, F) or faithful friends (S). Moreover, in S and Ys (and doubtless in Yt), the Odinic character, despite this dominant characteristic, is not radically separated from the "Vanes": in S Hadingus has *become* an Odinic hero, but he was *initially*, and still remains, a fictional remodeling of Njörðr, the typical Vane god, thus uniting the two qualities; in Ys, Óðinn's devoted follower Sveigðir is not only a Vane by blood, being the son of Fjölnir and the grandson of Freyr, but during the course of his first search for Óðinn he encounters mainly his Vane kin, marries a wife named Vana in Vanaheimr, the Home of the Vanes, and names his son Vanlandi. (There is no ground or means for examining F from this point of view, since the poet does not differentiate between his characters in such terms and is no more aware than any other of the Faroes ballad authors of a division of the gods into Ases and Vanes.) *Thus in Ys, probably in Yt, in S, and doubtless therefore in the purest form of the double myth, the two characters, including the Odinic hero, are of Vane origin:* it is a solemn promise (Ys) or "election" on the god's part (S) that binds them to Óðinn.

6. a) The death of the Vanic character comes about by drowning, in a large vat of beer or mead, *as the result of a fall, of a movement from high to low*: though the scene in S is not clear on this point, Ys on the other hand describes the fall as taking place through a hole in a wooden floor, from the first story into the vat below on the ground floor; according to F there is a hole in the ground and the vat is apparently in a cellar. On the other hand, in both S and F the death of the Odinic character takes place by *elevation*: ascent and disappearance into heaven in F, macabre ascent

onto the gallows in *S*; in *Yt* and *Ys* there is no ascent, but nor is there any descent, and *Ys* says that the "Odinic" rock into which Sveigðir plunges and vanishes is of uncustomary height: "high as a big house," *mikill sem stór hús.*

b) The contrast in the direction of the deaths is followed by a similar contrast in the "afterlives" involved. The Odinic hero is assured of his life after death, and that is why he chooses to "disappear": he is going to the place where his master Óðinn lives (*Yt, Ys, S*) or returning, in the case of Óðin himself, to his own realm above where he will later welcome mankind (*F*). The Vanic hero dies without any such hope, without any life after death, and apparently never escapes the fermented substance in which he chokes to death; in particular, the Óðin of *F*, when returning to heaven and inviting "his" men to join him there, seems to have no hope of being reunited there with the Veraldur whose death he is mourning. In other terms, the *Odinic hero* survives *in* the *supra-* or *paraterrestrial* mythical world that is his true homeland (*F*) or of which he has had the revelation (*S*) or of whose existence he has been assured by an infallible tradition (*Ys* and doubtless *Yt*); the *Vanic hero* goes into dissolution, *is assimilated into* the substance of the earth, *in its most material form: food, drink.* The *Ys* version makes it possible to push this formulation to its extreme: the vat into which Fjölnir disappears forever is a vat of mead, of the mead that Óðinn's chosen in the other world will continue to quaff for all eternity.

The antithetical structure that thus appears is akin to that set out by Snorri himself, in his prologue to the *Ynglingasaga*, with regard to the treatment of corpses, and later in fact illustrated by Óðinn's funeral on the one hand and those of Njörðr the "Odinized Vane" and Freyr on the other. The prologue even puts forward a chronological theory, though it is an invented one, since the Ases did not precede the Vanes in time, or vice versa, and neither are "tribes," or gods of two distinct peoples, but two contemporaneous and interdependent levels of one and the same mythology. However, this theory has the advantage of expressing the contrast between them clearly enough:

In a first age called the age of cremation (*brunaöld*), the dead had to be burned and memorial stones erected. Then, when Freyr had been placed beneath a barrow (*heygðr*) at Uppsala, many chiefs preferred such barrows to upright stones when paying funeral honors to their kin. And when the king of the Danes, Danr the Proud, had raised a barrow for himself into which he ordered that he should be borne after his death together with his treasure, his armor, his horse in full panoply, and many other possessions, most of his descendants afterward did likewise and the age of the barrow (*haugsöld*) was established in Denmark, whereas among the Swedes and Norwegians the age of cremation continued longer.

The first ritual is illustrated and commented on in the following terms when Óðinn dies (chap. 9):

> Once dead, Óðinn was burned, and this cremation was a magnificent event. It was believed in those times that the higher the smoke rose in the air the more surely the dead man being burned would himself be raised (*háleitr*, "he who observes from on high") into heaven, and that the more of his possessions that were burned with him the richer he would be there.

At the end of the same chapter, referring to Njörðr, he writes: [32]

> Njörðr fell ill of a mortal sickness. Before dying he had himself marked with the mark of Óðinn. The Swedes burned him . . .

In chapter 10, however, the death of Freyr gives rise to a macabre scene that ends quite differently.[33] His reign had been prodigiously prosperous, rich, and peaceful, so that the taxes had always flowed in freely.

> When he fell ill his followers held council among themselves. They hid him away and had a big barrow built with a door and three windows. When he was dead they bore him within with hurried secrecy, telling the Swedes that he was still alive inside. They kept him there in this way for three years, and the people continued to pay their taxes, throwing the coins of gold and silver and copper into the barrow by the three windows. And during this time abundance and peace continued in the land . . . . In the end all the Swedes knew that Freyr was dead; but since abundance and peace were continuing in their land they believed that it would always be so as long as Freyr remained in Sweden, and so they did not wish to burn him.

These passages make the methods and intentions of the two funerary procedures clear enough. In the case of the cremation funeral the main concern was with *the dead man himself*, who must be guaranteed a fine ascent and a prosperous existence in the other world. With the

32. See above, p. 44.
33. See below, Appendix 5.

barrow it is the *country* that is the main object of concern: the dead man is a pledge of abundance kept in the earth so that it shall produce good harvests. In other words, there is a class of privileged dead men who go to heaven, to the Home of the Gods, to live with Óðinn as his friends, as Snorri also says at the beginning of chapter 9; the others remain bound to the soil, hidden in the earth itself, transmitting to it the fertile powers of which they have given proof during their lifetimes, and which the earth transforms into nourishment for those who are left. These two concepts must be at the root of the contrasting representations of Óðinn's Valhöll[34] and the underworld realm of Hel ("Hölle," from the same root as Latin *celare*, "to hide"), representations that we must take care to avoid "chronologizing"[35] since they are in fact complementary: in order that society may develop harmoniously throughout the generations to come it is essential that not only in this world but also in the other, its counterpart, certain distinct functions shall be distinctly fulfilled; even when dead, Óðinn's men—the leaders, wizards, and warriors—continue to live a privileged life separate from that of the masses; while Freyr's men—the rich peasants and the mass of the people, whose values and merits have all been circumscribed by the harvests of their fields and the cattle in their meadows—continue also to fulfill their duties by secret means that imply contact and fusion with the element that concerns them.

Albeit in another form, it is my view that Fjölnir, Hundingus, and Veraldur drowning in their nurturing vat on the one hand, and Sveigðir, Hadingus, and Óðinn emigrating into immortality on the other, all belong to the same functional mystique.

I have pointed out that the two characters forming the couple in *Yt*, *Ys*, and *S*, despite their antithetical natures, were of Vane origin, and in his account of the major gods Snorri's account points in the same direction, contrasting the Odinic funeral by burning accorded to

---

34. I cannot follow Magnus Olsen in the brilliant article in which he derives Valhöll from the Roman *Colosseum*: "Valhall med de mange dörer," in *Acta Philologica Scandinavica* 6 (1931–32): 151–70 (reworked in *Norrøne Studier*, 1938); cf. Jan de Vries, *Altgermanische Religionsgeschichte* 2 (2d ed.; 1957): 377–79.

35. The reconstruction by Knut Stjerna, "Mossfynden och Valhallstron," in *Från filologiska föreningen i Lund, språkliga uppsatser* 2 (till, Axel Kock, 1906): 137–61, is completely contrived.

Njörðr with the burial of Freyr, even though both these gods should by rights be classed as Vanes. In these three versions, all no doubt nearer to earlier beliefs than the Faeroes ballad, it is as though the myth wished to place equal emphasis on: (1) the difference between the two dead men and their two fates, *post mortem*; (2) the close kinship, at the level of the third function, between the two characters being used in the theorem.

It is a situation that recalls, among other Indo-European peoples, the divergent ends of the two members, otherwise closely united, of the dioscuric couple, in other words of the twins who, in India for example, and as early as the Indo-Iranians in the form of the Nāsatya, were the conventional third-function gods, bringers of health, vitality, wealth, and progeny.[36]

Of the Greek twins, one is the son of a mortal and the other a son of Zeus. During their lifetime this difference of origin has had scarcely any effect; but when it comes to their deaths it is quite different. The first succumbs humanly, wretchedly, unwillingly, in the hollow tree trunk in which he has taken refuge; his despairing brother, longing for death, is then offered the opportunity by Zeus of being transported to the home of the gods, since he is in fact a god, and the condition upon which the young and magnanimous hero accepts this brilliant future is of course well-known: henceforward, combining and sharing their one mortal and one immortal nature, Castor and Polydeuce each alternately knows the joys of Olympus and the sleep of the grave. Let us turn to the magnificent passage in Pindar's tenth *Nemean*:[37]

> *They change abode each day, and live alternately with Zeus, their beloved father, then, under the deep earth, in the valleys of Therapnes; thus they both live out the same fate, for Pollux chose it rather than be always a god and dwell in heaven after Castor was killed in combat. Angered at the theft of his oxen, Idas had wounded him with his brazen lance. It was Lyncaeus, keeping watch from high Taygetus, who had spied him out below, hidden in the hollow trunk of an oak . . .*[38]

36. See now *Mythe et épopée* 1 (1968): 76–81 (differentiating characteristics of each of the twins [Pāṇḍava] following Stig Wikander); 87–89 (the god-twins among the other Indo-Europeans).

37. This text offers one of the rare Greek examples (all the more important in that it involves the Dioscuri) superimposable upon the Indo-Iranian trifunctional structure: (1) The ruler Zeus; (2) the warriors Ares and Athene; (3) the Dioscuri.

38. δρυὸς ἐν στελέχει. The στέλεχος, properly speaking, is the base of the trunk, "the crown of the root, whence the stem or trunk springs" (Liddell and Scott).

(But Pollux avenges his brother and kills Lynceus, while Zeus in person blasts Idas with his bolt; then:)

> With haste the Tyndarid returned to the side of the hero, his brother; he found him still living, but with failing breath. Mingling his sobs with warm tears he cried in a loud voice: "Oh son of Kronos, oh father, what cure can there now be for my suffering? Decree death for me too, decree that I may die with him, oh Ruler . . ."
>
> Thus he cried, and Zeus came to him, and stood before him face to face, and made this reply: "You are my son; Castor was engendered in your mother's womb after you by the hero her husband, by a drop of human semen. This absolute choice I therefore give you: if you yourself wish to escape from death and hateful old age by coming to live on Olympus with me, in the company of Athene and Ares of the dark lance, that is your birthright. But if you stand by your brother and if you wish him to share equally with you in all things, then you shall spend one half of your life beneath the earth and the other in the golden palace of the sky." He spoke, and Pollux did not hesitate in his mind for a moment. He opened the eyes, then rekindled the voice of Castor of the brazen belt.

In Rome, the canonic god of the third function is Quirinus. But the Romans knew (we have been in rather too much of a hurry to accept, and I myself accepted this point of view too quickly, that the "apotheosis of Romulus" was a late, Hellenistic notion) that Quirinus was none other than Romulus, one of the twin founders deified after death. Again, let us compare the deaths of these two twins: the wretched, irreversible end, without tomorrow or compensation, that Remus meets out on the boundary furrow, and the ascent into a divine world, the celestial and active immortality of Romulus-Quirinus.[39]

The material also exists for broadening this comparison and relating it to findings in other parts of the Indo-European world. First in India, where Stig Wikander has now succeeded in "splitting the Aśvin-Nāsatya": apart from the fact that these twins appear like the Greek Dioscuri to be unequal in status from birth, one being the son of a god and the other of a man,[40] we have familiar texts interpreting their

---

39. E.g., Ovid, *Metamorphoses* 14. 808–15, depicts Mars asking Jupiter, in accordance with an earlier promise, to deify the survivor of his two sons:

> Unus erit quem tu tolles in caerula caeli,
> dixisti: rata sit verborum summa tuorum.

On this whole topic see *La religion romaine archaïque* (1966), pp. 247–48 and 252–53.

40. In *Rg̊Veda*, 1, 181, 4: one is the son of "Sumakha" (unknown) the other of the Sky. See Stig Wikander, "Nakúla et Sahadeva," *Orientalia Suecana* 6 (1957): 66–95, and my *Mythe et épopée* 1, (1968): 76–89.

association with reference to other couples such as the Sky and the Earth, or the Day and the Night,[41] and texts as early as the Vedic hymns tell us that their common chariot had one wheel on the earth and one wheel in the sky.[42] In Iran, the twin Entities substituted by Zoroastrianism for the Indo-Iranian Nāsatya[43] are differentiated under the names of *Haurvatāt* ("Health"), the patron of water, *liquids*, and liquors, and *Amərətāt* (the "Non-Death," "Immortality"), patron of plants and *trees*.

Though the Scandinavian couples under consideration are not Dioscuric in the full sense of the word, they are nevertheless couples closely linked in the extreme.[44] It therefore seems as though the northern mythologies have simply transferred to them a representation that the Indo-Europeans applied to their Twins, and that was part of the complex theology of life and death involving not only the third function but the two others as well.

Once replaced in the complex whole of which it is one part, Fjölnir's death then appears in a quite different light from any it has been seen in up till now. In the Fjölnir-Sveigðir and Hundingus-Hadingus diptych the Vanic hero, having remained purely Vanic, dies a death characteristic of his type, being assimilated into a particularly substantial and precious form of matter; the Vanic hero who has become Odinic, on the other hand, attains to personal immortality in order to go and join his master in the supra- or paraterrestrial world. This twofold tale is a simple illustration, without any further intention or pretension, of the coexistence of different worlds and different destinies, and of their relationship with the major functions that structure not only religion but also the entire life of society and the ideology behind it.

It was therefore an error, a widespread one during the past fifty years, to apply to Fjölnir *in isolation*, to Fjölnir's death, a series of commonplaces drawn from the compilations of Mannhardt and

41. *Śatapatha brāhmaṇa*, 4, 1, 5, 16; *Nirukta*, 12, 1 . . .
42. *R̥gVeda*, 1, 30, 19, where the expression "on the bull's head" as opposed to "around the sky" can hardly denote anything but the earth; cf. 5, 73, 3; 8, 22, 4.
43. The proof of this appears in my book *Naissance d'Archanges* (1945). Cf. James Darmester, *Haurvatât et Ameretât* (1875), pp. 4–14. For the other areas see *Mythe et épopée* I (1968): 87–86.
44. See above, pp. 114–21, in particular pp. 115 (n. 20) and 120.

Frazer that were on a lesser scale altogether: misunderstood human sacrifice transposed into fictional anecdote; misunderstood ritual of a *Gerstengott*, of a *Korndämon*.

Yet it ought to have occurred to someone that the pagan Scandinavians, and Snorri too, always displayed a perfect understanding of any human sacrifice they had to deal with, and always presented it as such: the practice was not so far removed from the thirteenth century. In the *Ynglingasaga* we find kings sacrificed to Óðinn, and the author states quite clearly both that they are sacrificial victims and also what request accompanied the ritual.[45] Side by side with these we also find kings who perish by violent death, by accident, or by murder; yet, however picturesque their death scenes may be, we have no right to consider them as being sacrifices:[46] the fact that King Agni in chapter 19 is hanged by his wife in circumstances recalling the terrible vengeance of Poe's "Hop-Frog" is insufficient grounds, for example, for referring to his death as "a misunderstood sacrifice to Óðinn." And this observation, be it said in passing, should be extended also to the legendary Celtic incidents that are often linked with the death of Fjölnir, and that Stefan Czarnowski in a scholarly but amazingly naïve and self-confident book interprets as fictionalized human sacrifices:[47] the hero whose house is besieged and set afire,

45. E.g., *Ynglingasaga*, 15: because there had been a bad harvest three years running, "the chiefs held council [at Uppsala] and agreed that it was their king Dómaldi who must be the cause of this calamity, and also that they must offer him up as a sacrifice for the harvest and direct an attack against him and kill him and sprinkle the altar with his blood; and this they did."

46. The same reservation applies to the article in which the ingenious Danish scholar Gudmund Schütte attempted to interpret as fictionalized sacrifices or "god murders" not only the deaths of many of the Ynglingar but also those of several Danish kings in the *Dansk kongetal* ballad (see above, p. 140, n. 30): "Gudebraebning i nordisk Ritus," in *Samlaren* 35 (1915): 21–36.

47. *Le culte des héros et ses conditions sociales; saint Patrick, héros national de l'Irlande* (1919), p. 116. The Irish Muircertach (a historical character of the sixth century, subject of tenth-century poems and epic tales), victim of a "Melusinian" wife, is besieged in his burning palace, takes refuge in a barrel of wine, *isin dabaigh fina*, and is drowned; the roof falls in on his head and burns him (*Revue celtique* 23 [1902]: 424). Flann, attacked and trapped likewise in his burning house by Diarmaid, goes into a "bathtub," *i ndabaig fotraiccthi*, and perishes there (Standish O'Grady, *Silva Gadelica* [1892] text: 1: 73; translation: 2: 77). Diarmaid, similarly besieged and trapped in his turn by the Ulates, drowns in his beer barrel, *issin dabaigh chormma*; a burning beam falls on him and all his body is consumed except his head (ibid., 1: 82; 2: 88). The fact that the deaths of Muicertack and Diarmaid fall on the same day as the great feast of *Samhain*, and that of Flann on the feast day of *Beltaine*, does not justify us in viewing them as deriving originally from "feast myths," as transpositions of religious rites: in Irish epic literature there is a general fondness for linking important events with one of the big annual feast days.

and who takes refuge in the cellar only to drown in a vat of wine or beer, is an epic theme that could well have been inspired by real and by no means rare events (since the Irish like the Scandinavians were fond of burning their foes inside their houses),[48] without it being necessary to bring either religion or the gods into the matter every time.[49]

As for the "spirits of the corn," the example of Byggvir, the personification of barley, likewise proves that the early Scandinavians could recognize them perfectly well for what they were and accorded them their rightful place, which is not a large one. Attempts have also been made to establish a link between the Fjölnir legend[50] and that of Kvásir; but again the results do not bear scrutiny. The Kvásir legend is presented quite straightforwardly as what it is, in other words an explanation of the *origin* and the remarkable *properties* of hydromel or mead: it is not at all astonishing that mead should induce poetic inspiration and wisdom since it is simply a transformation of the blood drained from the extraordinarily wise Kvásir into the three vessels. But there is nothing of the sort in Fjölnir's case. The story at no point mentions either the origin or the properties of either mead or beer; both beer and mead are already in existence, together with the essential property, which is to intoxicate, the techniques for

48. The Nordic sagas are as well endowed with examples of foes burned to death in their own houses as are the Irish epic tales. Moreover, when there is a sacrificial intention behind the act the author says so clearly; e.g., in *Ynglingasaga* 43, which tells how the Swedes, on account of a number of bad harvests, sacrificed their king Óláfr Trételgja, whom they blamed for being miserly in his dealings with the gods: "Then the Swedes gathered together an army, made a raid against King Óláfr, surrounded his house, and burned him inside it; then they consecrated him to Óðinn, offering him up as a victim in exchange for a prosperous year."

49. Anyone determined to see the deaths of Hundingus and Hadingus as "sacrifices" would do better to look for systematic parallels not among the Germanic peoples but among the Celts, where they occur in circumstances that underline the antithetical functional values of vat-drowning and hanging (which for us is the essential, since this double representation comes into play, with or without interdependence, in both rituals and myths). Speaking of the Esus, Taranis, Teutates triad (gods who may represent the first, second, and third functions: *Tarpeia* [1947], p. 113), the Berne scholia on Lucan (*Pharsalia* 1: 445–46) give (with *interpretationes latinae* that are unreliable and erroneous) the modes of sacrifice appropriate to each: for Esus, *homo in arbore supenditur* (first function; cf. Óðinn); for Teutates, *in plenum semicupium homo in caput demittitur ut ibi suffocetur* (third function; cf. Fryr, Fjölnir); as for Taranis (cf. Þórr), like the Germanic Hercules, i.e., *þunaraʒ*, mentioned by Tacitus (*Germania*, chap. 9, 1), he does not receive human sacrifices at all (in the better of the two series of scholia; the other assigns him victims burned in the wicker figures also referred to by Caesar).

50. Since Schück, "Odin, Vili och Vé" (see above, p. 132, n. 5).

producing them, and the etiquette of the banquets at which they are consumed: all this has already been acquired by society when the accident occurs, and the hero's immersion in the liquid neither transforms nor adds to it in any way. When explaining a myth it is imprudent, and almost always misleading, to accept as a starting point that the form in which we know it has somehow lost all the features that we are presupposing as essential to it, as constituting a "first" and "forgotten" meaning.

The names are of no great importance: as a general rule, making exception of such cases as the Haddingjar, Byggvir, Óðinn, or Þórr in which the explanation is self-evident, etymology is not a great deal of help in clarifying Scandinavian mythology. The light thrown on Loki or Heimdallr is provided by their adventures, not by their names. And a number of hypotheses that have proved quite useless have been based on Sveigðir's name. In the case of Fjölnir, however, the following considerations may be offered as of some use:

We know that outside this one text, in which the hero Fjölnir has *no relation whatever* with Óðinn and in which his nature, his behavior, and even his death all indicate that he belongs to the "Freyr type," the name Fjölnir is never anything but one of Óðinn's numerous *cognomina*. Attempts have been made to construe this fact as the sign of an "evolution": the critical mind is ever ready to manufacture "history" out of very sparse raw material. According to this theory, Óðinn was a latecomer who took over this cognomen and a few others from the god Freyr, supposedly a predecessor whose position he more or less usurped.[51] I myself have very little faith in this *ersatz* kind of history, any more than I have in the recent arrival or usurpations of Óðinn, who was in reality an early god, early enough to exist in Common Germanic, and distinct from Freyr in being a first-function deity. The explanation seems to me rather simpler: the word *Fjölnir* must have a wide enough meaning to fit characters as different as a

---

51. Hjalmar Falk, "De nordiske huvedguders utviklingshistorie," in the *Arkiv för Nordisk Filologi* 39 (1927): 43, with reference to the *Odehsheite* by the same author. In another form, but related to his inadmissible thesis, Wolf von Unwerth, *art. cit.* (see above, p. 132, n. 7), pp. 333–34. For Jan de Vries, *Altgermanische Religionsgeschichte* 2 (1937): 271, n. 1, it is by virtue of the hydromel, Óðinn's drink, in which he is drowned, that Fjölnir, or rather his name, later became Óðinn's too (but see the second edition (1957) 2: 196 and n. 2). I hope to show, however, that this problem is a false one.

wizard and ruler like Óðinn and a god or hero of plenty such as Freyr's son and successor in the *Ynglingasaga*. The obvious etymology, though it has only rarely been put forward,[52] sees *Fjölnir* as a secondary derivation in -*nir* from the adverb *fjöl* "much," the Scandinavian counterpart of the Sanskrit *purú*, the Greek πολύ, the Gothic and Old High German *filu*, and Modern German *viel*.

In Vedic Sanskrit there are numerous epithets for gods beginning with *puru-*, and according to the nature of the second element they are applicable to various gods, principally Indra and the Aśvin-Nāsatya: Indra and Soma are *purukŕt*, "who acts much"; Indra, Soma, and Agni are *purukṣú*, "who have much wealth"; Indra is *purugūrtá*, *puruhūtá*, "much praised or called upon," and also *purutmán*, "having much vital energy"; Agni is *purucétana*, "much visible" (or in many forms); the Aśvin are *purudáṁsa(s)*, "having many technical talents," *purumántu*, "having much advice," *purubhū́*, "who are present, who appear much," *purumandrá*, "dear to many," *purubhúj*, "having or giving many pleasures"; Agni and the Aśvin are *purupriyá*, "loved of many"; and so on. Moreover, as a result no doubt of these formations, the Vedic language sometimes qualifies Indra,[53] the Aśvin,[54] and Agni[55] with the simple superlative *purú* without any second term as a further qualification: *purutáma*, *purūtáma*, which of course one cannot translate literally.

In the same way, the Scandinavians, and all the Germanic-speaking peoples, formed many composite words with the first term *fjöl-*, *filu-*, and so forth, which were used as proper nouns,[56] epithets, or even cognomens: *fjölkyngi*, "much learning," is "magic," and the

52. Sveinbjörn Egilsson, *Lexicon poeticum antiquae linguae septentrionalis*, 2d ed. by Finnur Jónsson (1931), p. 137b, s.v. "Fjölnir"; Hans Naumann, "Altnordische Namenstudien," in *Acta Germanica*, N.R. 1 (1912): 33, 53.

53. *Ṛg Veda*, 1, 5, 2, in which the superlative of *purú* is immediately followed by an analytic expression containing *puru-*: *purútmam purūṇā́m íśanaṃ vā́ryāṇām*, "the very *purú* master (*íś*) of many desirable things (*purūṇā́m*) or treasures (*vā́r*)."

54. *Ṛg Veda*, 1, 73, 1, in which the superlative of *purú* is preceded by an adjective formed with the first term *puru-*: *purudáṁsā purutámā purājā́* "[the two Aśvin], the very [*puru-*] clever, the very-*purú*, the firstborn." But see Louis Renou, *Etudes védiques et pāṇinéennes* 3 (1957): 64 (*ṚV*, 1, 124, 6a), cf. pp. 72, 92: *purutáma* said to be semiordinal and meaning "eminent among many."

55. *Ṛg Veda*, 8, 91, 7.

56. Naumann, "Altnordische Namenstudien" (see above, p. 151, n. 51), no. 42, pp. 33–34: outside Scandinavia, Ostrogothic *Felithank*, *Filimer*; Hercul Φιλιμουθ, Gepid Φιλήγαγος; Visigothic *Filimir*; Lombard *Filicausus*; Frankish *Filibert*; Bavarian *Filomuot* (cf. Old Icelandic *Fjölmóði*); Anglo-Saxon *Feolugeld* . . .

being who is *fjölkunnigr* is "well versed in magic"; both Óðinn (*Grimnismál*, 47, 4) and, elsewhere, the dwarfs are said to be *fjölsviðr*, "full of wisdom"; the all-powerful god is *fjölhress*, "very much on form"; a hero or a giant may be *fjölvarr*, "very prudent, or *fjölverkr*, "very active"; gold is *fjölvinjaðr*, "having many friends"; a rich king, or fortune, is *fjölgóðr*, "having much wealth"; and so on.

It is easy to see how a hypocoristic, summarizing all the gifts and powers that Óðinn possesses in particular forms of "abundance," in the manner of the Vedic *purutáma*, could have been applied to him as a sort of blanket term: he is the being above all others to whom one can apply a whole host of epithets beginning with *fjöl-*; and such— formed from *fjöl* with the suffix *-nir* in accordance with a type of formation well represented in Old Icelandic[57]—is doubtless the meaning of the name *Fjölnir*.[58] But on the other hand it is also conceivable that this same epithet could have been taken, once at least, as an autonomous proper name, to designate a mythical third-function king, an extension of his father Freyr, a personification of abundance like that father, and of whom Snorri says: *hann var ríkr ok ársæll ok friðsæll*, "he was powerful and had harvest and peace in abundance."

57. Elof Hellquist, "Bidrag till läru om den nordiska nominalbildningen," 1, *Arkiv för Nordisk Filologi* 7 (1891): 22–23; cf. above, p. 152, n. 52.
58. Egilsson, *Lexicon poeticum* . . . (see above, p. 152, n. 52) suggests completing to "he who [knows] much" or "he who [has] many [forms]." In reality, the epithet summarizes a vast number of possible composite epithets of this type without being a substitute for any particular one of them: it is a symbol of summation, almost of integration.

GRAM

To Michel Foucault

As early as his 1843 article in which the first analogies between Njörðr and Hadingus were pointed out, Wilhelm Müller had noted that Hadingus's son was named Frotho, Frotho the first, which is to say Fróði, a known variant of Freyr, who is in fact the son of Njörðr. Müller further remarked that Frotho succeeded Hadingus on his throne just as in the "history" of the Uppsala dynasty, according to Snorri, Freyr also succeeded his father Njörðr. It would have therefore seemed natural in the circumstances if Müller and those who came after him, confirming and developing the parallels between Njörðr and Hadingus, men such as Ferdinand Detter and Rudolf Much, had extended their comparisons to the predecessors of the "father-son couple" in both dynasties, that of the Swedish Ynglingar and that of the Danish Skjöldungar. Nevertheless, they did not do so, and I myself have waited ten years since the publication of my Saga de Hadingus before succeeding in finding my way around a difficulty that must certainly have deterred them.

This difficulty is obvious enough: in the historicization of the myths that provided the Ynglingasaga with its divine beginnings Njörðr and Freyr are the second and third kings; and their solitary predecessor is Óðinn. This order of succession is to be explained by the similarly historicized myth of the war between the Ases and the Vanes, with which it is expressly linked: during Òðinn's reign, at the conclusion of this war, the major Vane gods, i.e., Njörðr plus his son Freyr and his daughter Freyja, were transferred to the home of the Ases, first as hostages, but very soon as associate gods with full rights, thus constituting together with the Ases a complete and balanced divine society in which the fertility functions proper to the Vanes, as well as the magical and martial functions proper to the Ases, were all adequately fulfilled. In consequence, when Óðinn dies—for in this account of the matter,

157

claiming as it does to be history, the gods are men and die like men—it is Njörðr who replaces him, without any interposing ruler, at the head of the entire society, thus preparing the way for his son Freyr, Yngvifreyr, who becomes the eponym of the ruling family. Hadingus, on the other hand, has been preceded on the throne by a great many rulers, including the eponym Scioldus (Skjöldr). Saxo's list includes four "pre-Skjöldungar," or in other words four rulers prior to Scioldus, then Scioldus, then Gram, then Hadingus. Other versions exist, but they differ solely as to the very early members of the dynasty: when Hadingus figures in it he does so always some way from the beginning and after Scioldus. And we do not need to look either very long or very hard to see that neither Gram, Hadingus's father, Scioldus, Gram's father, nor Scioldus's father or uncle or grandfather present any Odinic traits.

Thus limited, however, the problem is badly posited. It is clear that it is not specifically the Ynglingasaga that Saxo or his source has made use of. But perhaps independently of the Ynglingasaga, and in a different way, he has employed the same procedure: the transposition into a series of "kings," not of just one or two gods at random, but of an entire divine structure. For that is precisely what the Ynglingasaga did in fact, but taking as its basis a binary theological structure that ignores all other male gods in the Ases-Vanes war besides Óðinn on the Ase side and Njörðr and Freyr on the Vane side; and these are presented as three successive kings, Óðinn succeeded by Njörðr, Njörðr by Freyr. But comparative studies, in particular a comparison of the Ases-Vanes war and the homologous war of the proto-Romans and the Sabines in early Roman history, show that this binary structure in reality conceals a ternary structure, that of the "three functions": because we are dealing with a war, and because the two sides destined to form a single society by their reconciliation must fight "well," the second function, the martial function, becomes (as it were) attenuated, and the differentiation of the two opposing sides is expressed solely in terms of the first (the Ases and the companions of the last god Romulus) and the third (the prosperous Vanes and the rich Sabines); hence the disappearance from among the protagonists of the character who would be representative of the second function: the commoner of the two Roman versions opposes Romulus and the Sabine king alone, dropping Romulus's Etruscan ally Lucumon, whose province is the waging of war; while the Scandinavian story contains no mention at all of þórr.

Yet it is quite conceivable that sequences of kings, whether arranged in dynasties or not, could have been formed by a direct transposition of the complete, trifunctional theology, without any reference to the mythological episode of "the first war" that altered its constitution. And in fact we do find the four pre-Etruscan Roman kings, the two founders Romulus and Numa, then Tullius, then Ancus, successively presenting the characteristics of the first function (in its two complementary aspects), then the second, then the third—a sequence that would be covered in Scandinavia, mutatis mutandis, *by the wizard Óðinn and Týr in his guise as god of the þing, then by the fighter Þórr, then by the couple Njörðr-Freyr, the bringers of wealth. We know that the Scandinavian "canonic list" is in fact simpler than this: in the "idols" of the temple in Old Uppsala it was visibly reduced to Óðinn, Þórr, and Freyr; and elsewhere, in set phrases, to Óðinn, Þórr, Njörðr, and Freyr; Týr is in any case eliminated, for reasons that seem to be becoming apparent. Might it not be this list, partially at least, that Saxo or his source made use of, from the eponym onward, to constitute the first sections of the* Skjöldungasaga: *Scioldus, Gram, Hadingus, Frotho? This working hypothesis was investigated in two lectures given at the Collège de France on 16 and 23 February 1961. This appendix will deal solely with the material concerning Gram considered as a transposition of Þórr. A few words will suffice for Frotho I and Scioldus.*

The problem of Frotho I—who occupies Saxo's second book—is in reality the problem of the Frothones. The history of the Skjöldungar in fact includes several characters transposed from Fróði-Freyr, dividing the constitutive elements of his particular divine type among them. Some have been given rather more than their fair share, but even among the others enough of the elements remain for the type to be recognizable. Frotho I is one of these latter: his reign begins with the conquest of a prodigious treasure, and an allusion is made to his connection with the famous "mill of Fróði" that continued to grind out gold indefinitely and that we also meet in the Edda. *But as Axel Olrik had pointed out as early as 1910, in an appendix to his* Danmarks Heltedigtning, *thanks to the homonymy existing between them, the first heir of the mythical Fróði also drew some of his substance from a Viking named Frode, who died in Ireland in about 830 after having terrorized Scotland and England in the company of his brother.*

As for Scioldus—on whose account tradition did not apparently have much to offer to "history"—he occupies with a great deal of majesty the position where we would expect to find Óðinn; but Óðinn has yielded that position to a model, to models, who in the eyes of Saxo the pious monk, the ardent patriot, and also the good courtier, possessed more prestige than the devilish imposter of the mythologists, and in any case gave better expression to his ideal of royalty: the Valdemar kings, to whom Denmark owed a power and a brilliance that it had not known since Knut the Great; the rulers who conquered several German provinces, codified the laws of Skania, Sealand, and Jutland, and showed themselves truly humane in the administration of their empire. Scioldus was in consequence made into a conqueror of the "Saxons," promulgated salutary laws after having rescinded the former "impious" laws, and distinguished himself by his benevolence and generosity (I, iii, 1–2). Paul Herrmann has said everything essential on this topic, noting in addition that in the Angers fragment the margin corresponding to the reign of Scioldus is covered in notes and corrections all of which suggest the desire to provide a glorious prototype for the deeds of Valdemar II, known as "the Legislator" or "the Victorious." It was to Valdemar, after all, that the Gesta Danorum *were dedicated:* Te ergo, salutaris princeps et parens noster, cuius illustrissimam a priscis temporibus prosapiam dicturus sum, clarisssima lux patriae, Waldemare, dubium laboris progressum favore prosequi rogo . . . . *And in two almost Ciceronian sentences it seems that Saxo is concentrating upon the name of that prince all the merits that he attributes elsewhere to Scioldus.*

Unlike the story of Hadingus, that of Gram, though well provided with poems, is not developed at length (I, iv, eighteen paragraphs, mostly short ones, in the edition of Jørgen Olrik and Hans Raeder). Here is Elton's translation of it:

> 1. Soon after, he had by her a son, Gram, whose wondrous parts savoured so strongly of his father's virtues, that he was deemed to tread in their very footsteps. The days of Gram's youth were enriched with surpassing gifts of mind and body, and he raised them to the crest of renown. Posterity did such homage to his greatness that in the most ancient poems of the Danes royal dignity is implied in his very name.[1] He practiced with the most zealous training whatsoever serves to sharpen and strengthen the bodily powers. Taught by the fencers, he trained himself by sedulous practice to parry and deal blows. He took to wife the daughter of his upbringer, Roar, she being his foster-sister and of his own years, in order the better to show his gratefulness for his nursing. A little while after he gave her in marriage to a certain Bessus,

---

1. *Gramr* is one of the designations of the king.

since he had ofttimes used his strenuous service. In this partner of his warlike deeds he put his trust; and he has left it a question whether he has won more renown by Bessus's valour or his own.

Gram, chancing to hear that Gro, daughter of Sigtrugus, king of the Swedes, was plighted to a certain giant, and holding accursed an union so unworthy of the blood royal, entered on a Swedish war; being destined to emulate the prowess of Hercules in resisting the attempts of monsters. He went into Gotland, and, in order to frighten people out of his path, strode on clad in goats' skins, swathed in the motley hides of beasts, and grasping in his right hand a dreadful club, thus feigning the attire of a giant: when he met Gro herself riding with a very small escort of women on foot, and making her way, as it chanced, to the forest-pools to bathe.[2] She thought it was her betrothed who had hastened to meet her, and was scared with feminine alarm at so strange a garb: so, flinging up the reins, and shaking terribly all over, she began in the song of her country, thus:

3. "I see that a hateful giant is coming to the king and darkens the highways with his stride. Or my eyes play me false; for it has oft befallen bold warriors to skulk behind the skin of a beast."

Then began Bessus:

"Maiden, seated on the shoulders of the steed, tell me, pouring forth in thy turn words of answer, what is thy name, and of what line art thou born?"

Gro replied:

"Gro is my name; my sire is a king, glorious in blood, gleaming in armour. Disclose to us, thou also, who thou art, or whence sprung!"

4. To whom Bessus:

"I am Bessus, brave in battle, ruthless to foes, a terror to nations, and oft drenching my right hand in the blood of foes."

Then said Gro:

"Who, prithee, commands your lines? Under what captain raise ye the war-standards? What prince controls the battle? Under whose guidance is the war made ready?"

5. Bessus in answer:

"Gram, the blest in battle, rules the array: force nor fear can swerve him; flaming pyre and cruel sword and ocean billow have never made

2. *Bellum Sueticum auspicatur Heraculeae virtutis exemplo monstrorum nisibus obstaturus. Inita Gothia cum deturbandorum obviorum gratia caprinis tergoribus amictus ac variis ferarum pellibus circumdatus horrificumque dextra gestamen complexus giganteas simularet exuvias, ipsam Gro silvestres forte latices cum paucis admodum pedissequis lavandi gratia petentem equo obviam habuit.*

him afraid. Led by him, maiden, we raise the golden standards of war."

Gro once more:

"Turn your feet and go back hence, lest Sigtrugus vanquish you all with his own array, and fasten you to a cruel stake, your throats haltered with the cord, and doom your carcases to the stiff noose, and, glaring evilly, thrust out your corpses to the hungry raven."

6. Bessus again:

"Gram, ere he shall shut his own eyes in death, shall first make him a ghost, and, smiting him on the crest, shall send him to Tartarus. We fear no camp of the Swedes. Why threaten us with ghastly dooms, maiden?"

7. Gro answered him:

"Behold, I will ride thence to see again the roof of my father which I know, that I may not rashly set eyes on the array of the brother[3] who is coming. And I pray that your death-doom may tarry for you who abide."

Bessus replied:

"Daughter to thy father, go back with good cheer; nor imprecate swift death upon us, nor let choler shake they bosom. For often has a woman, harsh at first and hard to a wooer, yielded the second time."

8. Whereupon Gram could brook no longer to be silent, and pitching his tones gruffly, to mimic a gruesome and superhuman voice, accosted the maiden thus:

"*Let not the maiden fear the brother of the fleet giant, nor turn pale because I am nigh her. For I am sent by Grip[?], and never seek the couch and embrace of damsels save when their wish matches mine.*"

9. Gro answered:

"Who so mad as to wish to be the leman of giants? Or what woman could love the bed that genders monsters? Who could be the wife of demons, and know the seed whose fruit is monstrous? Or who would fain share her couch with a barbarous giant? Who caresses thorns with her fingers? Who would mingle honest kisses with mire? Who would unite shaggy limbs to smooth ones which correspond not? Full ease of love cannot be taken when nature cries out against it: nor doth the love customary in the use of women sort with monsters."

Gram rejoined:

"Oft with conquering hand I have tamed the necks of mighty kings, defeating with stronger arm their insolent pride. Thence take red-glowing hold, that the troth may be made firm by the gift, and that the faith to be brought to our wedlock may stand fast."

---

3. We do not know whose brother this refers to. Perhaps that of the giant-fiancé?

Thus speaking, he cast off his disguises, and revealed his natural comeliness; and by a single sight of him he filled the damsel with well-nigh as much joy as he had struck her with fear before at his counterfeit. She was even incited to his embraces by the splendour of his beauty; nor did he fail to offer her the gifts of love.[4]

11. Going further, he learnt from those he met, that the road was beset by two robbers. These he slew simply by charging them as they rushed covetously forth to despoil him. This done, loth to seem to have done any service to the soil of an enemy, he put timbers under the carcases of the slain, fastened them thereto, and stretched them so as to counterfeit an upright standing position; so that in their death they might menace in seeming those whom their life had harmed in truth; and that, terrible even after their decease, they might block the road in effigy as much as they had once in deed. Whence it appears that in slaying the robbers he took thought for himself and not for Sweden; for he betokened by so singular an act how great a hatred of Sweden filled him.

12. Having heard from the diviners that Sigtrugus could only be conquered by gold, he straightway fixed a knob of gold to a wooden mace, equipped himself therewith in the war wherein he attacked the king, and obtained his desire. This exploit was besung by Bessus in a most zealous strain of eulogy:

"Gram, the fierce wielder of the prosperous club, knowing not the steel, rained blows on the outstretched sword, and with his wooden weapon beat off the lances of the mighty.

"Following the decrees and will of the gods, he brought low the glory of the powerless Swedes, doing their king to death and crushing him with the stiff gold.

"For he pondered on the arts of war: he wielded in his clasp the ruddy-flashing wood, and victoriously with noble stroke made their fallen captain writhe.

"Shrewdly he conquered with the hardness of gold him whom fate forbade should be slain by steel; unsworded, waging war with the worthier metal.

"This treasure, for which its deviser claims glory and the height of honour, shall abide yet more illustrious hereafter, known far and wide in ampler fame."

13. Having now slain Sigtrugus, the king of Sweden, Gram desired to

---

4. *Quo dicto discussis larvis nativum oris decorem confessus tantum praene voluptatis vero sui aspectu puellae attulit quantum adulterino terroris incussit; quam etiam formae suae luculentia ad concubitum provocatam amatoriis donis prosequi non omisit.*

confirm his possession of the empire which he had won in war; and therefore, suspecting Guarinus, the governor of Gotland, of aspiring to the crown, he challenged him to combat and slew him. This man's brethren, of whom he had seven lawfully born and nine the sons of a concubine, sought to avenge their brother's death, but Gram, in an unequal contest, cut them off.

14. Gram, for his marvellous prowess, was granted a share in the sovereignty by his father, who was now in extreme age, and thought it better and likewise more convenient to give his own blood a portion of the supremacy of the realm, than now in the setting of his life to administer it without a partner. Therefore Ringus, a nobly born Zea-lander, stirred the greater part of the Danes with desire for insurrec-tion; fancying that one of these men was unripe for his rank, and that the other had run the course of his powers, alleging the weakness in years of both, and declaring that the wandering wits of an old man made the one, and that of a boy the other, unfit for royal power. But they fought and crushed him, making him an example to all men, that no season of life is to be deemed incompatible with valour.

15. Many other deeds also King Gram did. He declared war against Sumblus, king of the Finns; but when he set eyes upon the king's daughter, Signe, he laid down his arms, the foeman turned into the suitor, and, promising to put away his own wife [= Gro], he plighted troth with her. But, while much busied with a war against Norway, which he had taken up against King Suibdagerus for debauching his sister and his daughter, he heard from a messenger that Signe had, by Sum-blus's treachery, been promised in marriage to Henricus, king of Saxony. Then, inclining to love the maiden more than his soldiers, he left his army, privily made his way to Finland, and came in upon the wedding, which was already begun. Putting on a garb of the utmost meanness, he lay down at table in a seat of no honour. When asked what he brought, he professed skill in leechcraft. At last, when all were drenched in drunkenness, he gazed at the maiden, and amid the revels of the riotous banquet, cursing deep the fickleness of women, and vaunting loud his own deeds of valour, he poured out the greatness of his wrath in a song like this:

16. "Singly against eight at once I drove the darts of death, and smote nine with back-swung sword, when I slew Suarinus, who wrongfully assumed his honours and tried to win fame unmerited; wherefore I have oft dyed in foreign blood my blade red with death and reeking with slaughter, and have never blenched at the clash of dagger or the sheen of helmet. Now Signe, the daughter of Sumblus, vilely spurns me

and endures vows not mine, cursing her ancient troth; and, conceiving an ill-ordered love, commits a notable act of female lightness; for she entangles, lures, and bestains princes, rebuffing beyond all others the lordly of birth; yet remaining firm to none, but ever wavering, and bringing to birth impulses doubtful and divided,"

17. And as he spoke he leapt up from where he lay, and there he cut Henricus down while at the sacred board and the embraces of his friends, carried off his bride from amongst the bridesmaids, felled most of the guests, and bore her off with him in his ship. Thus the bridal was turned into a funeral; and the Finns might learn the lesson, that hands should not be laid upon the loves of other men.

18. After this Suibdagerus, king of Norway, destroyed Gram, who was attempting to avenge the outrage on his sister and the attempt on his daughter's chastity. This battle was notable for the presence of the Saxon forces, who were incited to help Suibdagerus, not so much by love of him as by desire to avenge Henricus.

I, v, 1. Guthormus and Hadingus the sons of Gram (Gro being the mother of the first and Signe of the second), were sent over to Sweden in a ship by their foster-father, Brage (Suibdagerus being now master of Denmark), and put in charge of the giants Wagnophthus and Haphlius for guard as well as rearing . . ."[5]

Everything in this first great Viking portrait painted by Saxo is not of course taken from Þórr, but the reader must surely have recognized him in several passages as the transposed model: the God who often reminds us of the giants he fights, who has his "Ase-fury," his *ásamóðr*, just as they have their *jötunmóðr*, both exploding into the same symptoms. It will be sufficient for our purpose here to point out the principal characteristics he shares with Gram.

1. Gram decides to "resist the attempts of monsters," and sets out to wage war against a giant who has been bold enough to claim the hand of a princess, thus fulfilling one of the usual offices of Þórr, who similarly punishes the giant Þrýmr for having demanded the hand of Freyja, and the giant Hrungir for having, among other insolences, demanded the goddesses. Gram also enters upon his campaign in an outfit that Saxo terms Herculean—*Herculeae virtutis exemplo*—but which in his mind's eye is exactly that of Þórr, since it is in the guise of Hercules that Saxo, like Tacitus's continental sources of information

5. This is the beginning of the Hadingus saga; see above, p. 10, and below, p. 233.

earlier, presents this god: the famous hammer is transformed by his pen into the club of the Greco-Roman hero, as for example when Thor intervenes with a formidable club in the theomachy of the Balderus story (III, ii, 10).[6]

2. The name of the heroine Gro, in this first episode, the one narrated at greatest length, alone betrays the origin of the material: her meeting with Gram-Hercules is inspired by that between Gróa and þórr, which we know from Snorri's *Edda* (*Skáldskaparmál*, 17, p. 104), and which follows þórr's duel with Hrungnir: the god has succeeded in killing the giant, but the giant's weapon, a sharpening stone, has remained embedded in the god's head:[7]

> þórr was returning home, the stone in his head, when he met the future-seeing *völva* named Gróa, wife to Aurvandill the Valiant. She sang her incantations over þórr until the stone began to loosen in the wound. þórr, feeling much relief, conceived the hope of being rid of the stone altogether and wished to reward Gróa for her pains by bringing her joy. He therefore told her the news that he had come back from the North by crossing the (mythical) river Elivágar, and that he had brought back from the North, from the Home of the Giants, her husband Aurvandill in a basket on his back, offering as proof the fact that one of the latter's toes, protruding from the basket, had frozen, so that he, þórr, had broken it off and hurled it high in the sky, and had turned it into the star named "Aurvandill's Toe." He said, moreover, that before long Aurvandill would return home. The joy of Gróa was such that it made her forget her incantations and the sharpening stone ceased to loosen in the wound: it is embedded in þórr's head to this day.

The plot material of the Gram-Hercules and "Princess" Gro episode is different: Saxo has assimilated this strange and mythical episode into the commonplace theme of the good hero delivering the beautiful maiden from the monster to whom she has been betrothed against her will. But even with this new content important fragments of the original framework subsist. When Gram encounters his Gro she

---

6. *Sed et Thoro inusitato clavae libratu cuncta clipeorum obstacula lacerabat, tantum ad se incessendum hostes invitans quantum socios ad tuendum. Nullum erat armaturae genus quod impellenti non cederet. Nemo ferientem tuto excipere poterat. Quicquid ictu urgebat obruit. Non clipei, non cassides impactum pertulere robur. Nulli corporis aut virium magnitudo subsidio fuit.* Cf. below, p. 176, c.

7. *Heur et malheur du guerrier* (1969), pp. 141–45.

is troubled by a different affliction˙from that affecting the Gróa
þórr meets—but both are afflicted, and the causes of their affliction
are similar: Gro knows that she must marry a giant, Gróa believes
that she has lost her husband, who is apparently a captive among the
giants. In both cases the scene consists of two contrasting sections:
Gróa and Gro both remain afflicted until the moment when þórr and
Gram decide to turn this affliction into joy with a piece of good news
concerning their husbands that they could perfectly well have impart-
ed at the outset. At the impact of this sudden revelation both women
abandon themselves to a joy so ungovernable that the one forgets her
incantations and the other all restraint: Gro's terror turns to *voluptas*,
and the young princess falls into Gram's arms.[8]

3. Gram has an inseparable companion, Bessus, whose "strenuous
service" he had ofttimes used, and who takes such a large part in his
exploits and expeditions that "he has left it a question whether he has
won more renown by Bessus's valour or his own" (1. iv, 1). This too
fits in perfectly with our knowledge of þórr, who is always accompanied by a servant—Loki in his dealings with þrýmr and Gerröðr,
þjazi against Hrungnir—a less considerable figure than Bessus, it is
true, but one who often renders his master signal services and whom
the Lapp drum painters, who were unable to record any but the most
important features of divine figures, always found room for in their
depictions of þórr, standing beside the god, unarmed and rather
smaller in size.[9] It is also noteworthy that in the Gro episode, although
we hear about the "array" Gram is leading, Gram and Bessus are
the only active participants.

4. Thanks to the presence of Bessus, it has been made possible for
Saxo to achieve a remarkable collation of the Gro episode theme—
distress turned to joy—with a characteristic motif of the Eddic
þrymskvida, that of disguise. When þórr and Loki arrive at þrymr's
home disguised as a fiancée and her lady-in-waiting, the giant does not
suspect their true identities, even though þórr's behavior does occasion some doubts; the god remains silent, however, and it is between
þrymr and Loki that dialogue is exchanged, with Loki continuing to
allay the giant's suspicions until the moment when the hammer is
produced for the visiting ladies and þórr suddenly throws off his

---

8. *Enn Gróa var sva fegin at . . .; tantum paene voluptatis vero sui aspectu puellae attulit . . .*
9. "Tordenguden og hans dreng," *Danske Studier* 2 (1905): 129–46.

disguise to reveal his true identity. When Bessus and Gram meet Gro, Gram is disguised as a giant, and the princess believes that she is in the presence of the giant to whom she is betrothed, though reserving the possibility that there is disguise involved; Gram remains silent, and it is between Gro and Bessus that the dialogue is exchanged, Bessus actually naming himself and Gram by their true names but Gro continuing to believe that she is dealing with her "fiancé," a state of affairs that continues until Gram can "brook no longer to be silent," intervenes, and very quickly reveals his true identity.

5. The final episode (1. iv, 16), Gram's poem of self-praise and vituperation against the woman who, out of lightness, has preferred a rival to him, Gram, whose exploits have been so many, links up with the attitude and the lament of þórr in a version of the Starkaðr saga—which is, moreover, different from the version that Saxo has retained in his sixth book. The *Gautrekssaga* has the god explain his animosity against Starkaðr—the grandson of a homonymous giant killed by þórr and a girl whom þórr eventually won back and took home to her father—as follows: he cannot wish anything but ill, he says, to a stripling whose grandfather was a giant he, þórr, was obliged to slay, and whose grandmother as a girl had preferred that same giant to himself, "þórr of the Ases."[10]

6. The method by which Gram kills Sigtrugus (1. iv, 12) has a strange consequence: since the king cannot be conquered except by a weapon of gold, Gram fixes a "knob of gold" to the end of his wooden club; then the fate of this knob of gold after the exploit is described in these enigmatic terms: "This treasure, for which its deviser claims glory and the height of honour, shall abide yet more illustrious hereafter, known far and wide in ampler fame."[11]

The future *manebit* here seems to refer to a material preservation of the "knob of gold" after the exploit, or rather of the entire club with its golden knob in all probability, and, moreover, to a form of preservation intended to attract the lasting and universal homage of

---

10. *Heur et malheur du guerrier* (1969), p. 86, and from another point of view, *Mythe et épopée* 2 (1971): first part.

11.   Clarius post hoc agathum manebit
          agnitum late meliore fama
          cui suus laudem decorisque culmen
          arrogat auctor.

"fame." The allusion becomes easier to understand perhaps if we think of the figurative or symbolic representations of þórr about which we have evidence from two sources: three centuries ago, in his *Laponia*, Scheffer described as follows the wooden idol of the Lapp god *Hora Galles*, borrowed from the "*þórr karl*" or "Old Father Thor" of the Norwegian peasants: *in capite infigunt clavum ferreum, cum silicis particula, ut si videatur ignem Thor excutiat*; and Jan de Vries links this with the more abstract "divine nails" (*reginnaglar*) in the "posts of the seat of honor" (*öndvegissúlur*) set up in the great hall of Icelandic houses and placed under the protection of þórr. This fragment of flint fixed with a nail into the idol's head is explained by a detail of the Hrungnir myth, the story that immediately precedes the Gróa episode: a piece of the defeated giant's sharpening stone has remained embedded in the god's head and Gróa begins to extract it by means of her incantations; but then her joy at þórr's good news makes her forget the end of the spell so that the stone fragment, loose but inextirpable, remains in the god's head. The meaning of the incident is probably a naturalistic one: the god makes the thunder with his hammer, but it is the flint in his head that contains his store of lightning flashes and bolts.[12]

This chapter of Saxo's thus seems to have been put together with the life of þórr as a basis, though much more freely than in the case of the subsequent Hadingus saga modeled on the life of Njörðr. In Hadingus's case the author has followed and used the god's whole career, broadly speaking, including its Vane phase and its Odinic phase, while inserting between the two, in the form of his second mythological digression, the fragment of the myth (Ases and Vanes war) that occurred exactly in that place and justified the transition from one phase to the other, but which from the point of view of the *Gesta Danorum* was unsuited for transposition onto the human hero Hadingus. In Gram's case, either Saxo or his source—though it becomes increasingly probable that it was Saxo himself and not some *sagamaðr* who was responsible—composed a series of incidents by dipping into the varied myths surrounding the god þórr, a body of material in fact less coherent and less continuous than Njörðr's mythical biography;

12. *Heur et malheur du guerrier*, p. 145.

in particular he used the interdependent myths involving Hrungnir and Gróa the *völva* (meeting with lamenting woman; good news transforming alarm into excessive joy; the golden knob on the end of his club, modeled on the flint in the god's brow and the wooden representations of him;[13] but he introduced into these incidents other elements (disguised approach, talkative companion, disguise thrown off) taken from the story of þórr and Loki's expedition to the home of þrymr; lastly, he deliberately eliminated from this amalgam one part of the Gróa episode—mythologically the most important—that he had already made use of in a different way in a section of his work written before the first book: the mutilation of Aurvandill.[14]

This analysis of the sources used in the Gram episodes has enabled us to gain some insight into further methods of transposition that Saxo did not employ in the case of Hadingus.

13. The scene in which the two slain brigands are propped upright again so that they shall continue to appear alive and inspire terror (I. iv, II) is perhaps a corruption of the scene in which Hrungnir and his double, "the man of clay," are killed together—a scene on which light is thrown in its turn by that in which Höttr kills, then props up again on its paws, the monster that has been terrorizing the lands of King Hrólfr (*Heur et malheur du guerrier*, pp. 140–41, 142–43).

14. See below, Appendix 4.

BALDERUS AND HØTHERUS

To Otto Höfler

The vast mythical structure that rests upon the frail shoulders of "Balder the Beautiful" is certainly one of the earliest elements in ancient Scandinavian mythology.[1] In each generation, it is true, a few scholars always use it as a prime target for their criticisms: this is a game that could go on a long while, it is now invulnerable to attack, even by mistletoe.[2] But the fact remains that the game does still go on. Some stubbornly continue to discern either Christian or Iranian influences in the myth; others pull it apart, arguing either that the rôle of Loki is "early" or that the connection between Balder's murder and the Twilight of the Gods is a fundamental one. And for all these assaults the pages in Saxo's third book devoted to Balderus are looked upon as an inexhaustible arsenal of weapons. Why?

Apart from the one and scarcely significant fact—since it applies to almost all the mythical characters heroicized in the Gesta Danorum—that Saxo's Balderus is depicted as a Viking avid for exploits and combat, the divergences between his adventures, his fate, his very character and those of the god Baldr as depicted in the Eddic poems and in Snorri are so great that one is at first glance inclined to accept the existence of two independent traditions formed in two entirely different countries or environments, in short of two

1. The bibliographies of Baldr and the Ragnarök are vast. The essential may be found in recent text-books: Jan de Vries, *Altgermanische Religiongeschichte* 2 (2d. ed.; 1957): 214–38 (Baldr), 392–405 (the Ragnarök); Werner Betz, "Die altgermanische Religion," *Deutsche Philologie im Aufriss* (2d ed.; 1957), col. 2502–8 and 2521–23. My own opinion on these very controversial matters has been progressively developed in the third part of *Loki* (1948; German edition modified on this point, 1960), in the third part of *Les Dieux des Germains* (1959, "Le drame du monde, Baldr, Höðr, Loki"), and in the first part of *Mythe et épopée* 1 (1968): chap. 8 ("Anéantissement et renaissance"), in particular pp. 222–30. Also E. M. Meletinskiji, *Edda i rannye formy eposa* (1968), pp. 191–248, has offered some interesting remarks on Loki and Baldr.

2. I am thinking of the attempt by Aage Kabell to explain the mistletoe in the Baldr story as a translating error, *Baldr und die Mistel, Folklore Fellows Communications* 196 (1965).

theologies in which the god presented faces and played rôles that are wholly incompatible. But in doing so we would be depriving ourselves of a very rare advantage: an external means of checking the tradition of the two Eddas, or at the least an assurance that the "Eddic version" was not the only one, that it was no more than one "interpretation," one "construction" among others —and doubtless a late one—of mythical data that we would then be justified in thinking had previously existed in a rougher and more fluid state. In particular, because Loki's name does not appear in the Gesta story, and because Balderus's death does not bring about anything that can be considered—either in the short or the long run—as a heroicized cosmic catastrophe, scholars are very fond of setting Snorri and Saxo up against one another on these two scores, not simply in order to appraise the differences between them but in order to put Snorri, and Snorri alone, into the dunce's corner.

They are certainly wrong to do so, and not only with reference to these two particular points. For if we view Saxo's originalities as a totality, as we must, then we shall find that they are the result of a very personal labor of literary transposition whose guiding lines we are now in a position to discern, thanks to the enlightening precedent set by his Hadingus saga.

Here is how Snorri describes Baldr (*Gylfaginning*, 11 and 15, pp. 29–30, 33):

> 11. Another of Óðinn's sons is Baldr, and of him there is nothing to be said but good. He is the best and everyone praises him. He is so beautiful in his appearance and so bright of face that light shines out of him; and there is a white flower that men compare to Baldr's brows; it is the whitest of all flowers—and by that you may comprehend what the beauty of Baldr is, at once of hair and face. He is the wisest of the Ases, and the most skilled in speech, and the most inclined to mercy. But he has this trait in his nature that none of his decrees can be applied. He dwells in the place named Breiðablik, which is in the sky. In this place there can be nothing that is impure.
>
> 15. Höðr is the name of one of the Ases. He is blind. He is strong also. But the gods would have preferred that there had never been need to name him, for the work of his hands will long be remembered among gods and men.

As for the event narrated in chapters 33–35 (pp. 65–68), here is a summary of it:

As a result of ominous dreams that Baldr has dreamed (cf. in the *Edda*, the *Baldrs draumar*), Frigg, Óðinn's wife and Baldr's mother, consults with other gods, then makes everything in the universe—animals, plants, metals, stones—swear not to do him any harm. Reassured by this, the Ases then organize an extraordinary game to which Baldr amiably agrees: they all surround the young god in their þing and strike him with, or hurl at him, all kinds of projectiles. And nothing wounds him.

But Loki, taking the shape of a woman, goes to Frigg and cunningly leads her to reveal the fatal secret to him: she has received sworn assurance from everything in the world not to harm Baldr, but she has omitted to extract such a promise from the mistletoe, because it was so obviously incapable of doing harm. Loki hurries away to pick a branch of mistletoe and places it in the hand of the blind Höðr, who has been standing gloomily aloof from the game; then he guides the blind god toward the target, Höðr strikes the young god with the mistletoe, and Baldr falls dead.

The world then goes into mourning. Óðinn, who knows the future, is more downcast even than the others. A messenger sent to the goddess who keeps watch over the imprisoned dead returns with a message that brings hope: she will release Baldr if everything in the world, without exception, weeps. Everything that exists therefore begins to weep, Snorri says—men, animals, earth, stones, trees, and all kinds of metal, "as you must have seen things weeping when they emerge from the frost and come into a great heat." But Loki, taking the form of a witch, refuses to weep, and Baldr remains among the dead until the Twilight of the Gods.

Such is the tradition recounted by Snorri for the use of the Icelandic bards and their prosaic heirs the philologists: it doubtless represents the Scandinavian vulgate. The fiction written by Saxo for the use of his prince is very different. And first in the matter of the characters involved. Since Loki does not appear as such, the two protagonists both fully responsible for their actions, are Baldr and Höðr, under the names of Balderus and Høtherus. Moreover, the "good" and "bad" rôles have been reversed. Snorri's Baldr is entirely sympathetic, and though his *handbani* Höðr is not by our standards guilty of a murder, since he was only its blind and directed instrument, he is nevertheless a "fateful" character of whom Snorri says that the Ases would have rather he had never existed. Balderus, on the other hand, is entirely antipathetic. Jealous, an aggressor, unscrupulous, he has all the wrongs on his side (3. ii, 4: *infectissimo odio dignum*) and, moreover, in defeat he is ridiculous (3. ii, 11: *Balderus ridiculus fuga*). Later, when Høtherus whom he persecutes and whose beloved he attempts to ravish, triumphs over him in battle and then, finally, kills him, we are satisfied and relieved just as we are when the good man punishes the bad man in a novel.

How much of the plot recounted by Snorri can we recognize in Saxo? The list has been drawn up long since:

1. Where Balderus is concerned:

a) Balderus is killed by Høtherus (3. iii, 7) as Baldr is by Höðr, and killed, moreover, despite the invulnerability that safeguards him against all weapons except one—the sword that Høtherus takes from Mimingus on the advice of Gevarus (3. ii, 5 and 6) and that is the counterpart of the mistletoe wand placed in Höðr's hand by Loki. It must be pointed out, however, that in the scene of the killing itself neither this sword nor the invulnerability are even mentioned, and that Høtherus owes his superiority in the actual event solely to the fact that he has managed to obtain, and eat, certain magic food intended for Balderus.

b) Immediately before his death, but after he has received the fatal wound, Balderus has a premonitory dream that Saxo describes in two lines and that recalls the *Baldrs draumar* placed elsewhere in Snorri.

c) Balderus has retained Baldr's social rank: being a son of Othinus he is *semideus*; which in Saxo is in fact the sole reason for his invulnerability, whereas that of Baldr is the consequence of the oath exacted from all things by Frigg, his mother. This divine parentage assures him of the military support of the gods (3. ii, 10), whereas in Snorri, who has no battle in his account, he enjoys only their sympathy; then later, as in the Scandinavian traditional version, it assures him of a miraculous avenger (3. iv).

d) Though Balderus is no longer, as Baldr was, the beloved husband of Nanna, nevertheless he feels a lively passion for her.

e) The abundance of water, equivalent to tears, that wells out of the whole earth, out of all the things in it, after the death of Baldr and is intended as the means of his resurrection, seems to have been used by Saxo in a quite different context, reduced to the form of one of the more ordinary miracles: it is the living Balderus who draws the water from the earth for a very practical reason (3. ii, 12):

> Thus conquering Balderus, in order to slake his soldiers, who were parched with thirst, with the blessing of a timely draught, pierced the earth deep and disclosed a fresh spring (*novos humi latices terram altius rimatus aperuit*). The thirsty ranks made with gaping lips (*hianti ore*) for the water that gushed forth everywhere (*erumpentes scatebras*). The traces of these springs, eternized by the name (of the place), are thought not quite to have dried up, though they have ceased to well so freely as of old.[3]

2. In the case of Höðr:

As we have just seen, Høtherus kills Balderus in circumstances partially, but no more than partially, similar to those of Baldr's murder by Höðr. That is all. The essential characteristic of Höðr has vanished: Høtherus is not blind, and though he accepts advice he nevertheless remains fully master of his own actions. As for the linking of the *arcus* in which he has *peritia* in youth—among other things, swimming and wrestling in particular: 3. ii, 1—with the weapon used to murder Baldr (the mistletoe branch that Loki causes the blind Höðr to throw at him), we must certainly put that down as no more than a product of Paul Herrmann's ingeniousness (*Kommentar* [1922], p. 204).

These preserved elements, some of which give the impression of literary fossils, amount to very little—both in volume and even in importance—in the plot of Saxo's story. In addition, however, we also find what one may call reversed elements, all of them reversed in the same direction. By this I mean that there are certain features ascribed to Baldr in Snorri that Saxo has retained but taken away from his Balderus and assigned either to his enemy Høtherus or to an ally of Høtherus. Three of these transferences have been recognized for a long time:
a) Though Balderus is inflamed with love for Nanna, this love is

---

3. Cf. also the water welling out of Balderus's funeral barrow as a defense against tomb-robbers (3. iii, 8): Paul Herrmann, *Kommentar*, pp. 216–47. For an eastern parallel to "Tears for Baldr" see my note "Balderiana Minora," 3, *Indo-Iranica*, Mélanges présentés à *Georg Morgenstierne* (1964), pp. 70–72.

both insulting to her and ill-starred (3. ii, 3 and 9). The reciprocal love is between Høtherus and Nanna, and it is Høtherus, the fortunate victor over Balderus, who marries Nanna (3. ii, 11).

b) The magic ring of Draupnir plays a rôle in the Scandinavian legend of Baldr: Óðinn places it on his son's pyre, and Baldr takes it with him into the other world, then sends it back to his father charged with the new magic property of secreting gold every ninth night. In the Saxo version this ring recurs, transformed into an *armilla* that has the mysterious virtue of "increasing the riches of its possessor";[4] but it is not Balderus who receives it, it is Høtherus, and in very different circumstances: he wins it from Mimingus at the same time as the sword he needs, the only weapon that can kill Balderus; and the two talismans are linked (*ita armillam ensemque in expedito fore, quorum alterum opum, alterum belli fortuna comitaretur;* 3. ii, 5 and 6).

c) The magnificent funeral accorded to Baldr, the cremation on his ship described at such length by Snorri and so celebrated throughout Nordic poetry, is assigned[5] to an ally of Høtherus (3. ii, 11) killed in the great battle that the latter has fought against Balderus and his allies, Othinus, Thoro, and all the gods; it has, however, been corrupted, in the sense that the dead man's ashes are eventually deposited in a barrow.

These transferences are indicative of one of Saxo's methods of procedure: indifferent and no doubt impervious to the former theological value of the stories he was using and of the gods he was transposing to make his heroes, the Danish writer took them apart quite unscrupulously and reconstructed them to suit himself. I propose now to show that apart from the three recognized transferences there are several others we ought to take into account, all of them similar to the first three in that it is again Høtherus who benefits from them at the expense of Balderus.

1. Snorri defines Baldr's character in three terms: He is the wisest of the Ases (*vitrastr Ásanna*) and the most skilled speaker (*fegrst talaðr*) and the most inclined to mercy (*líknsamastr*). In Saxo, on the other hand, we find two consecutive and symmetrical paragraphs (3. ii, 7 and 8) intended to illustrate these last two qualities in Høtherus in

4. Paul Herrmann, *Kommentar*, p. 221.
5. Ibid., p. 211.

the most striking manner and to explain how they came to earn him his two principal allies against Balderus.

a) (para. 7) As soon as Høtherus has won the equally magical *ensem* and *armillam* from Mimingus, Gelderus the king of Saxony tries to seize them from him in his turn. He attacks Høtherus's fleet but is defeated and forced to surrender. How does Høtherus react to this unjustified aggression? He greets the aggressor with the most friendly physiognomy and the most kindly words and was completely victorious over him no less by his humanity than by the skill of his military tactics (*quem Høtherus amicissimo vultu benignissimoque sermone exceptum non minus humanitate quam arte perdomuit*). These expressions (*amicissimo vultu beningnissimoque sermone, humanitate*) are an expansion of the attitude of the man prepared to grant mercy, ready for reconciliation, expressed by the adjective *liknsamr*.

b) (para. 8) Immediately after this (*ea tempestate*), Høtherus renders service to the king of Halogia, Helgo, who is aspiring to the hand of Thora, daughter of Guso, king of the Finni and the Byarmi. Being afflicted with what, even to those close to him, is considered an extremely unpleasing speech defect, Helgo has sent several *legationes* to Guso, thereby breaking with the custom that requires young men to go and make their demand for themselves, and the Finnish king has haughtily refused his requests. Whereupon, knowing Høtherus's powers as an orator, Helgo begs his aid (*Høtherum, quem politioris facundiae noverat, suis favere studiis obsecrabat*). Høtherus agrees, goes to see Guso, and talks with such eloquence that the king totally reverses his attitude (*cumque pro Helgone per summam eloquii suavitatem egisset, refert Guso mentem filiae consulendam, ne quid contra nolentem paterna videretur severitate praesumptum. Accersitam, an proco allubesceret percontatus, annuentis Helgoni nuptias pollicetur. Igitur Høtherus obseratas Gusonis aures ad ea quae precabatur exaudienda rotundae volubilisque facundiae dulcedine patefecit.*) The insistence of the writer on this point is sufficient proof of his wish to stress the eloquence of Høtherus and the success it earns him; he does so both by direct affirmation, in hyperbolic expressions that are as it were glosses on Snorri's *fegrst talaðr* (*politioris facundiae; per summam eloquii suavitatem; totundae volubilisque facundiae dulcedine*), and also by contrast, creating the strange figure of the character *tanto oris vitio obsitus ut non solum exteras, sed etiam domesticas aures erubesceret.*

These twin paragraphs—from whatever source Saxo took their subject matter and the names involved[6]—therefore have a defining function and demonstrate, in the form of a little drama and an equally pleasing little comedy, how Høtherus had the gift of winning men's hearts by means of two well-defined qualities—two of the three qualities that Baldr in the Scandinavian tradition possessed to the highest degree. The third quality, wisdom or sagacity (*vitrastr*), is also demonstrated by Høtherus throughout his entire biography, but being less specific to him it has not given rise to a paragraph parallel to the two others.

Another transference from Baldr to Høtherus is detectable in another, secondary episode of his career. In this case, however, it is no longer a character trait that is involved but a particular scene, one of the essential components of the Baldr myth.

2. Before his tragic death, strong in his invulnerability, Baldr gladly took the leading rôle in a picturesque kind of game. This involved his standing in the middle of the open space normally used by the Ases for their most serious meetings and being literally bombarded by them with all kinds of projectiles that he did nothing to fend off: "Baldr and the Ases entertained themselves in this way," Snorri says; "he stood in the open þing and all the others either shot arrows at him, or struck him with sword blows, or threw stones at him; but whatever they did he received no harm, and that seemed to all a great privilege." (*þá var at skemtun Baldrs ok Ásanna, at hann skyldi standa upp á þingum, enn allir aðrir skyldu, sumir skjóta á hann, sumir höggva til, sumir berja grjóti. Enn hvat sem at var gjört, sakaði hann ekki, ok þótti þetta öllum mikill frami*).

What remains of all this in Saxo? As far as Balderus is concerned, nothing. True, as I have remarked, Balderus on account of his divinity (3. ii, 5; *ne ferro quidem sacram corporis eius firmitatem cedere*) is in a like manner invulnerable except to the blows of one particular *ensis*. But in the event, on the two occasions when Høtherus and Balderus actually confront one another, there is no mention of either invulnerability or *ensem*, either in the first battle, from which Balderus escapes without glory but unhurt whereas Høtherus has just succeeded in chipping Thoro's club (3. ii, 10), or in the second meeting (3. iii, 7),

---

6. Ibid., pp. 208–15, suggesting many disputable parallels.

when Høtherus inflicts a mortal wound on Balderus (*obvii sibi Balderi latus hausit eumque seminecem prostravit*); in this latter instance we must admittedly assume that it is in fact the sword taken from Mimingus that has succeeded in wounding Balderus, since no other is capable of doing so, but Saxo himself neglects to recall this essential detail and is manifestly no longer concerned with it. And let us remark in passing that even Baldr's invulnerability, in another form, has been transferred to Høtherus, since he confronts the army of the gods *tunica ferrum spernente succinctus* (3. ii, 10), a garment that appears to have been given to him by the *virgines* of the woods whom he had met at the very outset of his difficulties with Balderus (3. ii, 4; cf. 3. iii, 4: *insecabilis vestis*).

In any case, however, Balderus's invulnerability, ignored by the author once he has stated it, certainly gives rise to no scene of "inoffensive bombardment" comparable to that of Baldr standing up in the Ases' þing so that they can verify his invulnerability. Whereas among the accessory or lateral adventures—not of Balderus, who, moreover, scarcely has any, but of Høtherus—we find a scene that does in fact recall that bombardment, and in which Saxo's expressions read like echoes of Snorri's. It is to be found in the episode mentioned earlier in which Gelderus, king of the Saxons, learning that Høtherus has gained possession of the sword and bracelet of Mimingus, attacks him with his fleet in order to wrest these precious objects from him (3. ii, 7). While Gelderus is still preparing for his attack, however, Gevarus—who according to Saxo is a diviner and wizard, and who seems to have assumed part of Loki's rôle in this whole affair[7]—summons Høtherus and advises him when he is attacked *Gelderi iacula patienter excipiat, non ante sua remissurus quam hostem missilibus carere conspiciat.* Høtherus does in fact apply this tactic. Here is the scene:

> Høtherus followed his advice and found its result fortunate. For he bade his men, when Gelderus began to charge, to stand their ground and defend their bodies with their shields, affirming that the victory in that battle must be won by patience. But the enemy nowhere kept back their missiles, spending them all in their extreme eagerness to fight (*iisdemque per summam pugnandi cupiditatem effusis*); and the more patiently they found Høtherus bear himself in his reception of their spears and lances,

7 *Loki* (German edition, 1960), p. 101.

the more furiously they began to hurl them (*hoc avidius hastas ac spicula torquere coepit, quo Høtherum in his excipiendis patientius se gerere comperit*). Some of these stuck in the shields and some in the ships, and few were the wounds they inflicted; many of them were seen to be shaken off idly and to do no hurt (*quae partim scutis partim navigiis infixa rarum dedere vulnus, complura innoxia ac frustra videbantur excussa*). For the soldiers of Høther performed the bidding of their king, and kept off the attack of the spears by a penthouse of interlocked shields (*siquidem Hotheri milites regis imperium exsequentes receptam telorum vim conserta clipeorum testudine repellebant*); while not a few of the spears smote lightly on the bosses and fell into the waves (*nec rarus quidem eorum numerus erat, quae levi ictu umbonibus impacta fluctibus incidebant*).

The plan succeeds: their missiles once foolishly squandered, it is the turn of Gelderus and his men to undergo the rain of enemy weapons: powerless, Gelderus raises the sign of surrender—giving Høtherus, as we have seen, the opportunity to display his "Balderian" quality of *liknsamastr*.

The commentators have described these proceedings as a maneuver and a ruse familiar from other battles (though they have nothing in common, despite Sophus Bugge, Friedrich Kauffmann, and Paul Herrmann, with the defense offered by the Saxon army of Cheldricus in the *nemus Caledonis*: Geoffrey de Monmouth, *Historia regum Britanniae*, 9, 3): (1) *testudinem clipeorum conserere*, Herrman says,[8] may be linked with the expression *at skjóta á skjaldborg* of which he finds examples in the *Egilssaga* and the *Flateyjarbók*; (2) as for the ruse consisting in saving up one's own missiles until the enemy has exhausted his, that is to be found not only in the *Fornmanna Sögur* but also elsewhere in Saxo himself, in the story of the first Frotho (2. iii, 1). Here is the passage:

> He put out to Ocean, and his first contest was with Witho, a rover of the Frisians; and in this battle he bade his crews patiently bear the first brunt of the enemy's charge by merely opposing their shields, ordering that they should not use their missiles before they perceived that the shower of the enemy's spears was utterly spent. This the Frisians hurled as vehemently as the Danes received it impassively; for Witho supposed that the long-suffering of Frotho was due to a wish for peace. High rose the blast of the trumpet, and loud whizzed the

8. *Kommentar*, p. 209, n. 1.

javelins everywhere, till at last the heedless Frisians had not a single lance remaining, and they were conquered by the missiles of the Danes.

It is instructive to compare this description with that of the battle in the biography of Balderus in book 3. King Frotho's ruse is presented both as a purely physical mechanism without mention of the extent of the casualties inflicted upon the *patientes* by the enemy's ballistic extravagance—and as a psychological mechanism, the function of which is to encourage the enemy to squander his javelins in the belief that the Danes are demoralized (*patientiam a pacis cupiditate profectam*). And naturally enough, since the selfsame ruse is being used, the description of the Høtherus versus Gelderus battle gives the same physical and psychological facts, and to some extent in the same terms (3: *hoc avidius hastas ac spicula torquere coepit* [Gelderus] *quo Høtherum in his excipiendis patientius se gerere comperit*; cf. 2: *quae tanto a Frisis avidius emissa quanto a Danis tolerabilius excepta*); but the author also adds details of another kind, entirely absent from the description in the second book; he takes pleasure in describing not merely the squandering of the enemy's weapons but also their inefficacity: *rarum dedere vulnus, complura innoxia ac frustra videbantur excussa; . . . nec rarus quidem eorum numerus erat, quae levi ictu umbonibus impacta fluctibus incidebant*). Thus the army of Høtherus is, as it were, invulnerable, and the weapons that strike it fall to the ground, inoffensive and vain. Is this not something very close to the game the Ases play in their þing? I have the feeling that, when he was writing his biography of Balderus, Saxo wished to keep in the scene of the bombardment suffered without risk or harm. And he did so by translating this bombardment-game into military terms, by assimilating it to the nearest form of Viking exploit, to a ruse of war that he combined with the *testudo* maneuver. The result is the spectacular quasi-invulnerability of Høtherus and his army under enemy bombardment. I cannot think that it was simply by chance that this scene—it is the only time that Saxo mentions the *testudo* maneuver—was inserted into the biography of Balderus rather than into any of the others, to the advantage of the very Høtherus whom we now know to have acquired so many of the elements belonging to the Scandinavian Baldr.

3. One of the important moments in Snorri's story is the universal anguish of the Ases at the news of Baldr's death, the void that death

opened beneath their feet, the feeling of loss that provokes their touching efforts to bring Baldr back from the other world. And one of the no less important traits in the character, the *náturá* of Baldr in Snorri's account is that no decree of his can be made good, can be realized, *at engi má haldast dómr hans*. This scene and this character trait appear combined and reinterpreted in earthly terms, again to the advantage of Høtherus, in a singular episode in Saxo III, iii, 3.

One day when he has been defeated by Balderus, Høtherus disappears, as though he were leaving this world, leaving a bitterly felt void behind him.[9]

> Here [in Jutland] he passed the winter season, and then went back to Sweden alone and unattended. There he summoned the grandees [*magnates*] and told them that he was weary of the light of life, *se lucis et vitae pigere*, because of the misfortunes wherewith Balderus had twice victoriously stricken him. Then he took farewell of all, and went by a circuitous path to a place that was hard of access, traversing forests uncivilised, *expertes humani cultus* . . . . Now he had been wont to give out from the top of a high hill decrees to the people when they came to consult him; and hence when they came they upbraided the sloth of the king, *regis inertiam causabantur*, and his absence was railed at by all with the bitterest complaint.

And it is at this point, after having wandered to the ends of those remote regions, that he comes to an *insuetum mortalibus nemus* where he meets the three *virgines* who "had once given him the invulnerable coat" and who now revive his confidence by telling him how to overcome Balderus.

The disappearance is here quite as total as in Snorri's story; but it is temporary only, from the society of men, not from "this world," and, moreover, provokes not tears but reproaches. On the other hand, the unexpected mention of the "habit" Høtherus had of delivering his decrees, *scita depromere* (*scita: dómr*) at the precise moment when he becomes deficient in that office—here a deficiency not of nature but secondary, voluntary, and temporary, just as the disappearance is in fact—can best be explained as a "historicized" version of the unfortunate *náturá* that rendered all Baldr's decrees useless: associating the two key words (*inertia* and *absentia*) and sub-

9. Ibid., p. 229.

stituting reproaches for laments, Saxo has managed to combine the reasons for pain that Baldr gave the Ases, the inefficacity of his decrees during his life, and his disappearance.

4. There is one last characteristic of Baldr's that seems to reappear in Saxo reinterpreted and attributed to Høtherus (3. ii, 5–6).

Gevarus, the kindly and somewhat wizardlike counselor who has inherited the function of *ráðbani* fulfilled by Loki in Snorri's account, tells Høtherus that there is only one sword (*ensis*) in the world capable of killing Balderus, and that this sword is in the possession of the "satyr" Mimingus, as is the *armilla*, a talisman of wealth. To win the sword is no easy task. He must first find his way to the remote country where Mimingus lives, beyond infinite regions of extreme cold—which may be accomplished, Gevarus says, by using reindeer to pull him. Then he will have to seize hold of the satyr and force him to give up the sword and bracelet: a familiar theme not only in Nordic tales but also in the Greek and Roman worlds. But here the theme is differentiated by the addition of a detail, a particular maneuver that is rather unclear, and that later, when the plan is being carried out, is presented somewhat differently.[10] Here is the advice Gevarus gives Høtherus—in *oratio obliqua*:

> And when he had got to the place [near Mimingus's abode], he should set up his tent away from the sun in such wise that it should catch the shadow of the cave where Mimingus was wont to be; while he should not in return cast a shade upon Mimingus, so that no unaccustomed darkness should be thrown and prevent the Satyr from going out.

Høtherus duly arrives at the cave, pitches his tent as directed, and spends several days and nights without sleep, hunting by day and meditating by night. Then this is what happens:

> Once as he watched all night, his spirit was drooping and dazed with anxiety, when the satyr cast a shadow on his tent. Aiming a spear at him, he brought him down with the blow, stopped him, and bound him, while he could not make his escape.

The maneuver is thus based, either in order to avoid warning the satyr or in order to alert his assailant, on the play of light and shade.

---

10. Ibid., p. 221.

From Müller to Herrmann, commentators attempting to understand how exactly the maneuver was meant to work have remarked
on the contradictions involved (the tent must be pitched in relation
to the sun, yet it is *pernox* when the capture is effected) and eventually given up the attempt. As was often the case when he was
transposing, laïcizing a mythical feature or ritual, it seems that Saxo
himself has not clearly pictured to himself what he was describing.
What could this mythical feature—a ritual feature being excluded
—have been? It is again to Baldr that we must turn for the answer.

The seventh divine abode, that which Baldr built for himself, is
named in strophe 12 of the *Grímnismál* and again in the *Gylfaginning*
as *Breiðablik* or "Wide-shining." The name can signify only one thing:
the dwelling is shining by nature and spreads its light far abroad. This
magical property of the dwelling, which is essential to it since it
provides it with its name, could not be retained as such and applied
to the dwelling, whether permanent or temporary, of a Viking chief,
whether Balderus or by transposition Høtherus. It must therefore
have been brought down from the heavenly to the earthly sphere. It
no longer has anything magical about it but is the result of human
cunning. Substituted for the widely shining dwelling we therefore
find the tent that by virtue of its skillful positioning (more skillful
than the description of it) never throws a shadow on the side where it
is important that it should not do so.

But in Snorri, corresponding to the shining of Baldr's dwelling (the
neuter *blik* is "nitor"), we also have the shining whiteness of the
building's owner: Baldr is so bright (*bjartr*) that light shines out of
him, *svá at lýsir af honum*—and there is a wild flower, the whitest of
all, *hvítast*, so white, *svá hvítt*, that it is compared to Baldr's brows.
Again, this characteristic could not be attributed in its original form
to a man. So Saxo has transposed it: it is no longer to a body but to a
piece of magical accoutrement that this *nitor* is given. From a group of
supernatural women he meets, Høtherus—once again profiting at
Balderus's expense—receives a baldrick that shines with extraordinary brightness: *eaedem namque nymphae accurati nitoris cingulum
potentemque victoriae zonam clementi benignitate ei largitae sunt* (3. iii,
6, end). This *accurati nitoris cingulum* has no direct mythological
precedent, whereas the *potens victoriae zona* is a borrowing from
þórr's wardrobe and is also to be found in the folklore of the Faroes

ballads; moreover, *nitor* applied to weapons is rare in Saxo[11] and consequently is fairly likely to be of particular significance here.

With this supernatural brightness we have exhausted both the material provided by Snorri's account of Baldr and the principal episodes of the god's life: they have all been systematically transferred to the account of Balderus's foe and bane Høtherus. And thus enlightened as to one of Saxo's literary procedures, we can now turn back to Balderus and try to discover what material the Danish scholar used to replace in his character all that he had extracted to build up Høtherus. Though in fact he has replaced very little: Balderus has much fewer adventures than Høtherus, who has become the true hero of the story; but the small amount of supplementary material, of compensation, that Balderus has been allowed all has a single and unmistakable origin: Saxo took it all from the Freyr myths. This suggestion is not a new one, and Paul Herrmann himself, after many others, formulated it very clearly, though admittedly only in order to reject it immediately on the strength of arguments that now seem very dated, and of which our investigations into Høtherus have now disposed once and for all. Essentially there are two elements involved:

1. The way in which Balderus falls in love with Nanna and is wasted away by thwarted passion recalls very closely the beginning of the *Skírnismál*, just as the speech with which Nanna eludes his request for her hand echoes the principal reason given by Gerðr, also in the *Skírnismál*, for refusing to accede to Freyr's request. In *Sk.*, 6, Freyr himself, whose distress is disquieting his whole retinue, tells his servant of the circumstances in which he saw Gerðr:

> *In the enclosure of Gymir, I saw walking*
> *a young girl with whom I fell in love;*
> *Her arms sparkled, and their lustre*
> *was reflected in all the air and the waves . . .*

In Saxo, 3. ii, 3, here is how the passion of Balderus is kindled:

---

11. In three passages *nitor* is applied to *galeae, arma, acumen*; in 4. viii, 2, Frotho Vegetus makes an offer to Frogerus (son of Othinus and trifunctional!) that they should exchange weapons and places; Frogerus, seduced by the *hostilium nitor armorum* (which are made of gold), imprudently accepts.

Now it befell that Balderus the son of Othinus was troubled at the sight of Nanna bathing, and was seized with boundless love. He was kindled by her fair and lustrous body, and his heart was set on fire by her manifest beauty; . . .

Paul Herrmann rejects the notion of linking these two texts with indignation:[12] whereas the chaste emotion that Freyr feels at the sight of Gerðr makes him think of Faust catching his first glimpse of Marguerite, the unbridled passion of Balderus at the sight of the naked Nanna puts him more in mind of the biblical elders peering sensually at Susanna in her bath, or of David lusting after Bathsheba in hers. For my part, however, I can see no difference: the fact that Freyr's passion was kindled by the sight of no more than Gerðr's bare arms and Balderus's by that of Nanna's entire body in her bath is one entirely due to circumstances and the emotional effect was just the same.

Moreover, after she has been obliged to surrender, Gerðr explains her initial rejection of Freyr with a very precise reason: she is of a different race (str. 38):

> However, I never thought that I would
> love one of the Vanes!

The objection is not a groundless one, and Freyr himself had foreseen it from the very beginning when he said to his servant (str. 7):

> Among the Ases and the Elves, not one allows
> that we two [Gerðr and he] may be united.

Such is the situation also between Balderus, a demi-god, and Nanna —not a graceful daughter of giants like Gerðr but a woman; and when Balderus comes in person to ask for her hand, the reason she gives for rejecting him is that it is impossible to unite a god to a mortal woman and, in general, to unite two beings set so far apart by the world order (3. ii, 9: nuptiis deum mortali sociari non posse; . . . neque enim stabilem dissonis esse nexum; . . . supernis terrestria non iugari, quae tanto originis intervallo discors rerum natura secreverit; . . . quod a divinae luculentia maiestatis infinitum distet humana mortalitas . . .)

That Saxo is here modeling himself on the Skírnismál is made all the more probable by the fact that at the end of the Balderus story, when Othinus makes it his duty to engender an avenger for him,

12. Kommentar, p. 218.

another section of the same eddic poem has been used: just as Skírnir vainly attempts to win over Gerðr by offering her jewels, then by threatening her with his sword, and finally forces her to yield with the threat of a terrible magic incantation, so Othinus attempts vainly to seduce Rinda by warlike exploits, then with jewels, then once more (a slip of transposition no doubt) with warlike exploits, and succeeds in gaining his end only after he has driven her mad with incantations.[13]

2. It is of the ritual outings of the Vane gods drawn in a chariot, and in particular of that of the god Freyr escorted by his priestess—as described in the Gunnarr Helmingr episode of the *Flateyjarbók* 1, ed. of 1860, p. 337[14]—that one is reminded by the end of Saxo, 3. ii, 12:

> Balderus was continually harassed by night with phantoms feigning the likeness of Nanna, and fell into such ill health that he could not so much as walk, and began the habit of going his journeys in a two-horse car or a four-wheeled carriage (*quamobrem biga redave emetiendorum itinerum consuetudinem habere coepit*). So great was the love that had steeped his heart and now had brought him down almost to the extremity of decline. For he thought that his victory had brought him nothing if Nanna was not his prize.

The motivation here is romantic, of course, but the resulting facts are nonetheless materially identical with the ritual procession of the Swedish Freyr. Moreover, immediately following this passage, in paragraph 13, the text contains proof of this origin. Without offering any connection with his fictional plot, simply breaking it off, in fact, exactly as he does on several occasions elsewhere, notably in the case of the two mythological digressions in the Hadingus saga,[15] Saxo continues with these words:

> Also Frø, the regent of the gods [*Fro quoque, deorum satrapa*], took his abode not far from Uppsala, where he exchanged for a ghastly and infamous sin-offering [*piaculum*] the old custom of prayer by sacrifice, which had been used by so many ages and generations. For he paid to the gods abominable offerings, by beginning to slaughter human victims.

This description of another ritual of the Uppsala Freyr is obviously

13. *Mythe et épopée* 1 (1968): 622–23 (and n. 1).
14. See below, pp. 207–9.
15. See above, chaps. 6–7.

a consequence of the preceding description of the journeys in the chariot transferred from Freyr to Balderus.

So that everything in the genesis of the Balderus story, at least with regard to the two protagonists, can now be seen as the simple product of literary artifice: the alterations, varying in their skillfulness but coherent nevertheless, and whose very accumulation confirms that this text does not in fact overlay some authentic variant of the Baldr myth, all derive from the fact that for some unknown reason Saxo decided to give Höðr-Høtherus the sympathetic and heroic rôle and to that end transferred all the characteristics and qualities of Baldr to him.

It is possible, however, that in the case of Höðr there was a much fuller account available to Saxo than the very brief one preserved by Snorri. Recent comparative research makes it, in fact, seem probable that this unhappy, blind god, whose sole intervention in Nordic mythology causes the great catastrophe of divine and cosmic history, was also more generally the god or embodiment of fate, and less of a *fatum* making unfathomable but possibly providential decisions than of mere chance, of "the capriciousness of things"; moreover, his name, which properly signifies "warrior," leads one to think that what was principally involved in his case was the capricious chance of war.[16]

Høtherus, being a purely epic character, could not, of course, retain the full weight of such a mythic value, but it is remarkable that he retains more of it than Snorri has apparently attributed to Höðr. Høtherus is in effect the only one of Saxo's heroes to maintain a close relationship with the supernatural beings who decide the outcome of battles. Not just once but twice, first at the beginning, then again just before the end of his rivalry with Balderus, he meets a number of *virgines* or *nymphas*, a cross between the Norns and the Valkyries, as it were, on whom "the fortune of wars" depends[17]. In 3. 11, 4, they describe their functions themselves: *illae suis ductibus auspiciisque maxime bellorum fortunam gubernari testantur; saepe enim se nemini conspicuas praeliis interesse, clandestinisque subsidiis optatos amicis praebere successus.* In 3. iii, 4, when Høtherus tells the same *virgines* of his

16. *Mythe et épopée* 1: 227–28.
17. *Kommentar*, pp. 218–19.

reversals in war, laments *gestarum infeliciter rerum fortunam,* and accuses them quite frankly of breach of faith and forgetfulness, they reply that although he has rarely emerged victorious from his battles he has nevertheless inflicted losses on his enemy equal to his own, and that he has dealt as much carnage as he has shared in (*at nymphae eum, quanquam raro victor exstiterit, aequam tamen hostibus cladem ingessisse dicebant, nec minoris stragis auctorem fuisse quam complicem*); it is at this point too that they reveal to him the means of overcoming Balderus, just as at their first meeting with him they had given him the *insecabilem vestem.* This familiarity of Høtherus with these *virgines* seems to me to be an extension of Höðr's earlier theological rôle. And it is perhaps also permissible to append here the way in which (3. iii, 1), in order to become king of Denmark, he recognizes and exploits the *rerum benficium,* the *fortunae beneficium* (cf. *quod vix spe complecti posset casu sibi collatum dicebat*), as well as his reflections on the instability of fortune in 3. iii, 5, that decide him to attack Balderus; not to mention the sword extorted from Mimingus, which is always accompanied by *belli fortuna.*

Such are the ways in which Saxo appears to have dealt with his raw material. Far from diminishing the value of his work as evidence, this analysis makes it possible for us to reconcile it with the Snorri account, from which at first glance it diverges so considerably but whose outline and details, once the general formula of the transposition has been grasped, it in fact confirms. And we find that the two major divergences with which the critics have made such great play, once replaced in this context, provide information that is totally the reverse of what those critics claim to derive from them. Loki, it is quite true, does not occur under that name, but by diminishing his rôle and making it work on the side of the good, Saxo has in fact transposed him into the character of Gevarus, Høtherus's counselor. As for the eschatological implications, though Saxo has indeed eliminated those he has also inserted within the Balderus story, albeit in the form of a single episode, a theomachia in which the gods suffer a massive defeat, an exceptional situation that is precisely that of the Ragnarök These two liberties taken by the "historian" with his model are of the same order of magnitude as those we have just examined with regard to the two protagonists.

HORWENDILLUS

To Claude Lévi-Strauss

The story of Aurvandill (Örvandill), in Snorri's Edda, is particularly irritating for mythologists. This character bears a name as well attested in Vestic as in Nordic, since a real-life Lombard called himself Auriwandalo, a twelfth-century German wrote an Orendel romance (O. H. G. Orentil), and in Old English earendel signified the morning star.[1] Moreover, this meaning of the word in Old English, fitting in so well with the Icelandic story of Aurvandill's toe being transformed into a star, makes it certain that the myth, with its astral outcome, was not limited to Scandinavia. But these two "favorable conjunctions" are nullified by the fact that at no point in the densely packed Orendel romance is there anything to link it to the Aurvandill episode, and also, more serious still, the fact that in Saxo the episode of Horwendillus—father of Amlethus, a lad with a literary future—seems to be equally different from both.

Leaving aside all the suggested interpretations (and Lord knows they add up to a heavy bundle),[2] and limiting myself to an analysis of the texts, it is this last point I wish to reconsider here. Contrary to current opinion, taking into account the way in which Saxo altered Scandinavian myths on other certain and attested occasions, I think that when it came to depicting his Horwendillus the sources and the tradition at his disposal were no different from those employed by Snorri, and that the very considerable divergences between the two accounts can be adequately explained by the Danish writer's habitual literary methods.

The material of this study was presented and discussed in a seminar at the

1. For the attempted etymological approaches, none of which can be considered conclusive, see Jan de Vries, *Altnordisches etymologishes Wörterbuch* (1961), s.v., pp. 20–21.

2. Since those examined or noted by Paul Herrmann, *Kommentar*, pp. 345–48, and Jan de Vries, *Altgermanische Religiongeschichte* 2 (2d ed.; 1957): 137–38, there have been quantities of further attempts. Atsuhiko Yoshida intends to examine them all soon.

Ecole des Hautes Etudes 21 and 28 April 1966 and published in 1969 in the
Mélanges *presented to Claude Lévi-Strauss.*

The myth of Aurvandill is to be found, very briefly recounted, in
Snorri's *Skáldskaparmál*, 17, p. 104. It has been quoted in its entirety
earlier,[3] but here are the essential elements: his victory over the giant
Hrungnir has left þórr in a sorry state: a sliver of the sharpening stone
his adversary used as a weapon has remained embedded in his head.
Returning from the Home of the Giants he meets the witch Gróa,
wife of Aurvandill the Valiant. By means of incantations Gróa gradu-
ally loosens the stone, and þórr is so pleased that he wants to reward
her with a piece of good news before the treatment is finished: he
tells her that her husband—whose disappearance has apparently been
causing her distress—will soon be home, that he, þórr, himself
carried Aurvandill back from the Home of the Giants in a basket, but
that while they were crossing the mythical river Elivágar one of
Aurvandill's toes became frozen and so he, þórr, broke it off and
threw it up into the sky, where it became a star. In her joy, Gróa
forgets the end of her spell, and the piece of sharpening stone stays
embedded in the god's head. We have seen earlier that Saxo used
almost all the material relating to Gróa and þórr in his first book,
transposing it to fit the Princess Gro and Gram, but that he eliminated
all the material relating to Aurvandill, which is to say the loss of the
toe destined for such a glittering future.

Now here is a summary of Saxo's story together with the principal
passages in quotation (3. vi, 1–3):

1. Horwendillus, a great Viking, had been prefect of Jutland for
three years when Collerus, the king of Norway, another Viking,
jealous of Horwendillus's fame, decided to try his skill in battle with
him. He searched for him a long time by sea. One day the two fleets
happened to anchor, unwittingly, on opposite sides of an island. The
place and the season tempted both leaders to go for a walk through
the glades, and in one of them they suddenly found themselves face
to face.

2. Horwendillus courteously asked Collerus what form of combat
he would prefer, a confrontation of the two armies or a duel between
just the two of them, confessing his own preference for the second.

3. See above, p. 166.

Collerus replied:

"Since thou hast granted me the choice of battle, I think it is best to employ that kind which needs only the endeavours of two, and is free from all the tumult. Certainly it is more venturesome, and allows of a speedier award of the victory. This thought we share, in this opinion we agree of our own accord. But since the issue remains doubtful, we must pay some regard to gentle dealing, and must not give way so far to our inclinations as to leave the last offices undone. Hatred is in our hearts; yet let piety be there also, which in its due time may take the place of rigour. For the rights of nature reconcile us, though we are parted by differences of purpose; they link us together, howsoever rancour estrange our spirits. Let us, therefore, have this pious stipulation, that the conqueror shall give funeral rites to the conquered. For all allow that these are the last duties of human kind, from which no righteous man shrinks. Let each army lay aside its sternness and perform this function in harmony. Let jealousy depart at death, let the feud be buried in the tomb. Let us not show such an example of cruelty as to persecute one another's dust, though hatred has come between us in our lives. It will be a boast for the victor if he has borne his beaten foe in a lordly funeral. For the man who pays the rightful dues over his dead enemy wins the goodwill of the survivor; and whoso devotes gentle dealing to him who is no more, conquers the living by his kindness. Also there is another disaster, not less lamentable, which sometimes befalls the living—the loss of some part of their body; and I think that succour is due to this just as much as to the worst hap that may befall. For often those who fight keep their lives safe, but suffer maiming; and this lot is commonly thought more dismal than any death; for death cuts off memory of all things, while the living cannot forget the devastation of his own body. Therefore this mischief also must be helped somehow; so let it be agreed, that the injury of either of us by the other shall be made good with ten talents of gold. For if it be righteous to have compassion on the calamities of another, how much more is it to pity one's own? No man but obeys nature's prompting; and he who slights it is a self-murderer."

3. After mutually pledging their faiths to these terms, they began the battle. Nor were their strangeness in meeting one another, nor the sweetness of that spring-green spot, so heeded as to prevent them from the fray. Horwendillus, in his too great ardour, became keener to attack his enemy than to defend his own body; and, heedless of his shield, had grasped his sword with both hands; and his boldness did not fail. For by his rain of blows he destroyed Collerus's shield and deprived him of

it, and at last hewed off his foot and drove him lifeless to the ground. Then, not to fail of his compact, he buried him royally, gave him a howe of lordly make and pompous obsequies.

After which there is nothing left for the victor to do but wait for the deathblow from his brother and leave his orphaned son, over the centuries, to the care of Shakespeare.

Is there any relationship at all between these apparently so totally divergent texts? Certainly. In the first place, let us remember, we can be certain that Saxo was familiar with a version close to that found in Snorri of the whole story in which Þórr, Gróa, and Aurvandill are linked. It is therefore probable *a priori* that he was familiar with a form of the mutilation of Aurvandill more or less as Snorri presents it, that is to say, a form in accordance with the Anglo-Saxon tradition underlying the Old English *earendel*. How then can we suppose that when he came to create a character named Horwendillus he would have ignored such a source and gone on instead either to invent an episode entirely from his own head or to make use of another Aurvandill tradition that has been entirely lost in any other form? Neither notion is probable. But what we now know—from the Hadingus saga (1. i–viii),[4] from the Gram saga (1. iv),[5] from the Balderus saga (3. i–iii),[6] and we can now add also the Starcatherus saga (4. v– 8. iii)[7]—of the literary methods he used when transposing mythology into historical fiction enables us to account for his Horwendillus solely on the basis of the only other attested Aurvandill story we have. Let us recall a few of those methods.

1. All the characters he borrows from mythology and legend, gods transposed into heroes or heroes used as such, are dressed by his pen in the same uniform: even the most pacific by nature and function, such as Njörðr and Freyr, such as Baldr, are transformed into bellicose kings, more often than not into Vikings, into *piratae*—Hadingus, the Frothones, Balderus—in a way that puts them on much the same level as his most fundamentally warlike models.

---

4. See above, pp. 129–53.
5. See above, pp. 157–70.
6. See above, pp. 173–91.
7. *Heur et malheur du guerrier* (1969), pp. 77–88; *Mythe et épopée* 2 (in course of publication): part one.

2. When the myth furnishes him with two conflicting characters, such as Baldr and Höðr, or when he himself sets up a character of his own in opposition to the one he has been supplied with by the myth, he is very fond of transferring material to the "adversary" that originally applied to the "principal hero." This is the case, as we have seen, from beginning to end of the Balderus story, which occurs in the third book of the *Gesta Danorum* only a little before the Horwendillus episode.

3. It often happens that Saxo will reduce to the status of an episodic, or attenuated, or distorted notation what was in fact the most characteristic trait of the character he is borrowing, or the most important feature in the structure of that character's career. For example, having clearly announced the three *facinora* that Starcatherus will commit and that will punctuate his triple life (6. v, 6), he slips the second one in so discreetly at the end of a brilliant battle scene (VII, v) that even so perspicacious an observer as Jan de Vries did not at first recognize it for what it was. This happens with particular frequency when the characteristic feature is more than usually at variance with probability, with the laws of nature. For instance, in the Hadingus saga the sole reference to one of the most theologically important attributes of the god Njörðr, his control over the winds and sailing, is reduced to this (1. viii, 15):

> Then Hadingus turned back and began to make homewards with his wife; some rovers bore down on him, but by swift sailing he baffled their snares; for though it was almost the same wind that helped both, they were behind him as he clove the billows, and, as they had only just as much sail, could not overtake him.

The supernatural power still subsists, quite evidently, but it has been reduced from a matter of magic to a question of technique, or at least presented in terms that avoid stressing the magic element.[8]

We must keep these three literary procedures in mind when attempting to evaluate the Horwendillus episode.

Firstly, Aurvandill has suffered the common fate of all Saxo's heroes and been transmuted into a warrior, a Viking—a process facilitated by the epithet left unexplained by Snorri: Aurvandill the

8. See above, pp. 23–26.

Valiant, *frœkinn*; and being a Viking, he becomes involved in an adventure typical of such Scandinavian warriors, the *hólmgangr*, a single-handed combat on an island,[9] fought according to a precise code of conditions, one of which, it is generally thought, Saxo seems to have misunderstood.[10]

In the second place, Horwendillus has been given as his adversary a homologue of himself, another Viking: the well-worn theme of the Viking tracking down and catching up with another has overlaid the adventure of which we catch only a glimpse in Snorri—one in which, before being rescued by Þórr, Aurvandill had been involved in some sort of conflict with the giants. And whereas it is Aurvandill who is worsted by the giants, and who later suffers physically during the process of his rescue, it is the adversary of Horwendillus who is defeated, and who suffers physically during the actual combat.

In the third place, the mutilation thus transferred to the adversary has very materially retained both its type and its anatomical location: Aurvandill loses a toe "broken off" by Þórr, Collerus loses an entire foot lopped off by Horwendillus—and to my knowledge he is the only combatant in the whole *Gesta Danorum* to perish in this way. But the circumstances and the consequences are entirely different: all the features that make the story of Aurvandill original—the toe first made brittle by the frost; the snapped-off digit hurled into the sky to become a star while the mutilated owner survives on earth—improbable and fantastic as they are, have been replaced by a commonplace story of a duel, with a fatal outcome as a result of the crippling wound, and spectacular compensation in the form of a lavish but wholly human funeral, without any magical or cosmic extension or connotation.

---

9. *Heur et malheur du guerrier*, p. 142.

10. The practice of *leysask af hólm*, of "buying oneself out of a duel"; when one of the adversaries is badly wounded he can save his life by paying the victor a ransom. Elsewhere, Saxo describes this bargaining process correctly (Herrmann, *Kommentar*, pp. 246–47), but here he reverses it: it is the victor who is to indemnify the crippled loser—and this alteration has been generally viewed, since Axel Olrik, as a misreading due to the influence of the spirit of chivalry, of the *ridderlighed i sin œdleste form*, prevalent around the time of Waldermar's reign (*Kilderne til Sakse Oldhistorie* 2 [1894]: 157). We cannot be so sure: the model he was working from does entail a sort of indemnity paid to the victim, since Þórr promotes the toe he snaps off to the rank of star, just as Horwendillus provides Collerus with magnificent funeral rites after lopping off his foot. Perhaps it was this rather than a misreading that led Saxo to make an intentional reversal of a rule that he understood perfectly well.

These changes are of the same type and magnitude as those that Saxo saw fit to make in other myths, and like them are no more than a writer's literary whims. His Latin version ought not therefore to be treated as original, independent evidence to be set against that provided by Snorri's account.

THE GESTATIO OF FROTHO III
AND THE FOLKLORE
OF THE FRODEBJERG

To the memory of Fernand Mossé

Saxo's historical writings have always enjoyed a legitimate prestige both among the people and the intellectuals of Denmark. As a result they have turned out to be at the bottom of many a folktale collected much later. The parallel that follows, put forward in February 1951 in a lecture at the Collège de France and published the following year in Etudes Germaniques *7, pp. 156–60, offers what is possibly one example of such an affiliation, and one particularly remarkable for the fact that the assimilation into folklore has been carried further than is usually the case. But it is also possible that the Frodebjerg tradition, noted in the nineteenth century, is independent of Saxo, deriving directly from an actual pre-Christian ritual in which Fróði was taken on a journey through the country, and that it was Saxo who made use of an earlier version of this tradition. Each of these interpretations entails some difficulties, and I myself am less inclined today than twenty years ago to adopt the second. In whichever way we attempt to explain it, however, the analogy between the "historical" text and the folk tradition is indisputable.*

If I reproduce this note here, even though it is concerned not with the first Frotho, the son of Hadingus, but with the third, it is because ultimately there is only one "Frotho problem" that applies to them all; and also because it provides a further datum to add to the important question of the periodic "outings" of the Vane gods.

In the Festschrift für Otto Höfler (1968), *pp. 389–409, Kurt Scheer has published a study entitled* "Freys und Fródis Bestattung," *in which the parallels he draws with Scythian (Ossetian) data derived from archeology and folklore lead him to take a very much wider, perhaps excessively wide view of the subject.*

205

The death of Freyr in the *Ynglingasaga* and that of Frotho III—seemingly the most faithful of all the Frothones to the probable mythology of the Danish god Fróði[1]—are followed by analogous scenes: the Swedish chiefs conceal the death of Freyr for three years, fearing that the taxes will cease to be paid; and in a similar way, fearing that Frotho's immense empire will become unruly and stop paying tribute money, the Danish chiefs embalm the corpse and for three years maintain the fiction that he is still living.[2] There is one detail in this last scene that Axel Olrik took as the basis for very broad hypotheses that are doubtless correct in principle but somewhat generously developed.[3]

The macabre hoax that prolongs the lives of Freyr and Frotho III in the minds of men is accorded a somewhat different fictional "treatment" in the two cases.

According to Snorri, in the *Ynglingasaga*, chap. 10, the Swedish chiefs held a council and decided to build a big barrow with three windows in it, and as soon as Freyr was dead they carried him inside it in secret, telling the people that he was still alive, *en er Freyr var dauðr, báru þeir hann leyniliga í hauginn ok sögðu Svíum, at hann lifði*. This situation lasted for three years, during all of which time the good people of Sweden regularly threw their gold, silver, and copper coins in through the three windows:[4] in this way "good harvests and peace,"

1. Recent authors are inclined to see this name as indicating "vigor" or "fertility" rather than "wisdom": Ernst Albin Kock, *Notationes Norrœnae* (1923 et seq.), 1780; Gustav Neckel, *Kommentierendes Glossar zur Edda* (2d ed.; 1936), s.v.; Erik G. Rooth, *Vrastmund*, *Ein Beitrag zur mittelhochdeutschen Wortgeschichte* (1939), p. 54 et seq.; Franz-Rolf Schröder, *Skaði und die Götter Skandinaviens* (1941), p. 40, n. 2; Jan de Vries, *Altnordisches etymologisches Wörterbuch* (1961), s.v. Fródi. Unlike Swedish and Norwegian place names, Danish place names provide no example certainly containing Freyr. Inversely, outside Denmark Fróði occurs only in *Frodhevi*, today *Frövi* in Uppland (and even then Jöran Sahlgren prefers to translate that name "dense forest," and the few legends linked with *Frude* (Östergötland) and *Frue* (Halland) are suspected of being literary in origin).
2. There is no reason for thinking, with Axel Olrik, in *Danmarks Heltedigtning* 2 (1910): 147, that Snorri simply transferred a legend specific to the Danish Fróði to the Swedish Freyr: the two stories make use of an identical and very old theme (applied to Zalmoxis, to Tarquin the Elder . . .) but using very different additional details.
3. Ibid., pp. 239–303, in particular, pp. 239–49, 257–62.
4. Rudolf Much, *Anzeiger für deutsches Altertum und deutsche Literatur* 28 (1902): 320, has tried to find an archeological prototype of these *gluggar*, "Lücken oder Fenster," in the "aus dem Schluss der Steinzeit oder der Übergangszeit zur Bronzeperiode stammenden Steingräbern, die ein grosses rundes oder rundliches Lock in der einen Giebelwand zeigen." He adds: "Auch zwei solche Löcher neben einander sind in einem Hügel bei Plas Newydd in Wales im Verschlusstein angebracht, und gelegentlich mögen wohl auch drei vorgekommen sein . . . Beachtenswert aber ist hier noch, das soweit es sich um Skandinavien handelt, solche Grabbauten mit Giebelöffnungen gerade nur im mittleren Schweden vorkommen."

ár ok friðr, were maintained. At the end of three years the Swedish people found out what had happened, but in view of the fact that the fertility and quiet of the land had in fact been maintained they were persuaded that such would always be the case as long as Freyr remained in Sweden; consequently they gave up the idea of cremating him and have ever since offered up sacrifices to him "for good harvests and for peace."

In Saxo, (5. xvi, 3) the Danish *proceres* conceal the death[5] of the king differently and do not place him in the barrow until they absolutely have to, at the end of the three years. Until then, having removed his entrails and salted his body, in order to forestall any *provinciarum defectionem* and to ensure the continued payment of *consuetam a subjectis pensionem*, they drive him around in the royal car (or on a litter), as though he is still the sick old man people had got used to seeing during his last years: *deportabatur itaque ab iis exanimum corpus, ut iam non funebri lecto, sed regali vehiculo gestari videretur, tanquam invalido seni nec satis virium compoti id muneris a milite debebatur*. It is only when his body, despite the salt, falls into decay that they bury him *regio funere* in a barrow *secus Weram Sialandae pontem*, saying that the king himself had chosen to die and be buried in the place *ubi regni eius praestantissima haberetur provincia*.

Thus Saxo's *proceres* continue for three years to drive or carry around the human form that the people believe to be Frotho and thereby obtain, apart from both internal and external peace, the continuance of the rich tributes that Frotho, thanks to the prosperity of the empire, had established as a custom. And this *gestatio* of Frotho's, though it is not found in the homologous account of Freyr's death, is nevertheless paralleled by a characteristic feature of the rituals specific to that god and also, in northern Germania, to the earliest known form of Njörðr, Tacitus's Nerthus:[6] seven tribes of the Suevii forming a religious federation "worship Nerthus, which is to say the Earth Mother, in common and believe that she participates

5. Frotho III does not die of illness like Freyr but is killed by a horn blow from a "sea cow," in reality a witch who has taken that shape. Parallels have been drawn with the death of one of Freyr's descendants, Egill, gored by a bull in *Ynglingasaga*, 26, and also—of course —with the accidental deaths of Adonis, Attis (Atys) . . .

6. *Germania* 40 (2–4)—Olrik, *Danmarks Heltedigtning*, pp. 257–58, followed by Neckel and several others, has also cited in this context the "Frazerian" rituals of the Near East referred to in the immediately preceding note. There is no need to go so far afield; one needs only to think of the numerous analogous practices unearthed in the medieval and modern Germanic world.

in the lives of men, that she passes from tribe to tribe in a chariot, *eamque intervenire rebus hominum, invehi populis arbitrantur.* There is on the island of Ocean a sacred wood, and in that wood a chariot dedicated to her, covered with stuffs: the priest alone has permission to touch it. He knows when the goddess is present in the sanctuary, and while she journeys forth in her chariot harnessed with heifers he escorts her with great marks of respect. Those are days of joy and feasting for the places she honors by her passing or her sojourn. They do not undertake wars, they do not bear arms, and all their iron is locked away: it is the only moment when they know, when they love peace. And this lasts until the priest leads the goddess, sated with the commerce of mortals, back into the temple . . .''

For a long while now a parallel has rightly been drawn between this ritual outing on the part of Nerthus and that described as part of the worship of Freyr in the version of the Óláfr Tryggvason saga preserved by the *Flateyjarbók*.[7] The priestess of Freyr, seduced by Gunnarr Helmingr, invites him to spend the winter in the sanctuary and tells him that later on he can accompany the god and herself during the tour of visits they will make ''at the time when he (= Freyr) makes the season clement again for men,'' *ok þykki mér ráð, at þu sér hér í vetr ok farir á veizlur með okkr Frey, þá er hann gerir mönnum árbót.* The god, in this Christian text, is an idol who is brought to life by the devil (*fjándinn*), and used by him as a means of conversing with men *ok svá mjöti (var) magnat líkneski Freys at fjándinn talaði við menn ór skurðgoð-inu* (rather than the *skúrgoðinu* of the text). During the tour, with the aid of the true God, Gunnarr knocks down the devil-idol, takes his place, is taken for Freyr wherever he goes, and takes full advantage of the lavish receptions accorded him by all the villages.

These two parallels make it probable that the feature recorded by Saxo is not of purely fictional origin but is based on an ancient ritual in the worship of Fróði: periodically, in the region adjacent to his supposed place of burial, he too was no doubt wheeled around from village to village in order to bestow his benefits on the inhabitants and their soil.

This interpretation is considerably strengthened by a local tradition,

---

7. Edition of 1860 (1: 337); conveniently reproduced in Franz Rolf Schröder, *Quellenbuch zur germanischen Religionsgeshichte*, *Trübners Philologische Bibliothek* 14 (1933): 72–74.

apparently overlooked by the mythographers, relating to the "barrow of Fróði"—*Frodebjerg* or *Frodehøj*—that long natural hill situated, in fact, *secus Weram Sialandae pontem*, or in other words near the *Værebro*, manifestly between the two mills, *Nedre* and *Övre Værebro Mølle*, lying alongside the *Værebro Aa* just before it descends into the gulf of Roeskilde.

The folklore surrounding this hill is on the whole as disappointing as the various excavations undertaken there since the seventeenth century.[8] All the traditions collected have been either learned in origin, more or less faithfully reproducing Saxo,[9] or else the kind of "inhabited barrow" stories[10] such as one meets in the sagas.[11] At first one is tempted to regret that Worm should have contented himself, in his *Danish Monuments* (1643), with the words: *Prope* [værebro] *collis ostenditur ab accolis, quadam sui parte quasi collapsus, ubi tumulatum referunt Frothonem, Frodehoi dictus, de quo mira ac varia vulgo fabulantur.*[12] But one feels there is good reason to suspect that this tantalizing statement was based on very little in the way of facts when we find the solemn archeologist requesting—and being given!—information about the stone on which a four-line epitaph of the mythical king was supposed to have been carved.[13]

8. In *Annaler för nordisk Oldkyndighed* (1838–39), pp. 370–74 (with a detailed map of the district, pl. 3, at the end of the book), there is a substantial "historisk antiquarisk Beskrivelse" (anon.) of the "*Frodeberg* eller *Frodehöi*" and a summary of the rather unfruitful attempts made at its archeological exploitation. The writer has reproduced the detailed description of Christian Molbech made in 1810 before the damage that was done to the hill.

9. Just Mathias Thiele, *Danmarks Folkesagne* 1 (1843): 15–16, summarizes Saxo but omits the *gestatio*: the burial takes place as soon as the "sea cow" has killed the king. He does add two extra features: (1) inside the barrow, one of the richest in the country, the king wears around his neck a golden chain so long that the other end is fixed to one of his toes; (2) when the queen arrived on the scene and learned of the accident that had befallen her husband she was overcome with emotion and pressed heavily upon the ground; the mark left by her foot can still be seen on "the queen's stone."

10. *Annaler* (cited above in n. 8), p. 373, and n. 3: toward the middle of the eighteenth century, two men, whose names are on record, were said to have dug up the mound in the hope of finding and taking treasure; they are said to have found Frode's sword, at least; but as they were struggling to pull it out one of them was terrified by the sight of "someone" riding upside down on a tailless horse and was unable to refrain from telling his companion what he could see; the silence having been broken in this way, the sword buried itself again in the earth of its own accord.

11. Cf. Grettir at the barrow of Kárr the Old, *Grettissaga Ásmundarsonar* 18 and the parallels cited in the edition of Boer (1900), p. 64, n. 8.

12. Olaus Worm, *Danicorum monumentorum libri sex* (1643), p. 105.

13. Ibid.: "Senes de hoc negotio interrogati, referunt lapidem cui epitaphium insculptum erat, a caementariis fractum et ad pontis reparationem una cum aliis nonnullis translatum."

But the folktale collection made by Just Mathias Thiele (1843), which in its "Historic Legends" section records only the bookish, official tradition,[14] unexpectedly returns to the Værebro in the section devoted to "The Devil."[15] Here is a translation of the text:

> In the bailiwick of Rœskilde, in the parish of Jyllinge, you may find the Værebro. It is now no more than a wooden bridge of modest aspect, but at one time it was made of great stones that today lie at the bottom of the bog. This bridge had not been built by the hand of man, and a curious story is told about it.
>
> In the days of Catholicism, when the Devil was still in the thrall of the priests, it happened that a poor peasant was charged with the task of carrying him, in a round box, from Jyllinge over to the vicar of Øl-stykke. The peasant had no idea it was the devil he was holding under his arm. So he sat down near the bog over which the Værebro passes today, and while he was making all sorts of guesses as to the contents of the box he began little by little to loosen the rope, and finally lifted the lid. Immediately the devil jumped out and began cudgeling the unfortunate peasant, crying all the time in German: "Was soll ich machen? What must I do?"
>
> Disagreeably surprised, the peasant did not know at first what to reply. But then, since the devil continued to cudgel him and ask the same question, he said to him: "Build a bridge here so that the likes of me can get over the bog!" Scarcely were the words out of his mouth before the devil, with all his imps, had piled stone on stone and set the bridge over the bog. The task finished, the devil set to cudgeling the peasant once more and crying as he had the first time: "Was soll ich machen? What must I do?"
>
> The peasant did not take long to think it over. He thought to himself that what was needed was a task that would really keep him busy, so he replied: "Gather together all the horse droppings in all the realms of the States of Denmark!" Scarcely were the words out of his mouth when the devil was piling dunghill upon dunghill, so that in the end they made a hill, which is today called the *Frutebjerg* (i.e., *Frodeshøj*).
>
> The peasant then thought to himself that the best thing would be to make the devil get back into the box, since he began to fear that

---

The reference is to the stone carved with the four lines given by Saxo (6. i, 1–2, p. 43) in Latin and said to have earned their author, Hiarnus, the privilege of being chosen as king after Frotho!

14. See above, n. 9.

15. 2: 95–96.

otherwise the priest might get cross. Meanwhile, however, the devil had started cudgeling him again worse then ever, still crying: "Was soll ich machen? What must I do?"

At which the peasant was seized with such anxiety, such distress, that he farted. "Listen!" he said to the devil who was cudgeling his shoulders, "if you can catch that fart for me you shall be my master; but if you can't you will have to squeeze yourself back into the box!"

Time was obviously of the essence, and the devil sped away forthwith on his quest. He ran through seven cantons hunting the fart. But when he returned he had only managed to secure a seventh part of it. Whereupon the peasant said to him: "Since you have not brought it back to me whole you must go back into the box!" There was nothing for the devil to do but obey, so he squeezed himself up small and slipped back into the box.

The peasant was delighted, and continued on his way with the box to the vicar at Ølstykke, from which place it was sent out from time to time in this way to be carried around the country, *hvorfra den, Tid efter anden, sendtes videre omkring i Landet.*

This story abounds in familiar folk motifs: the box opened out of curiosity, the impossible tasks, the devil building a bridge, the devil tricked . . . The total result is nevertheless original. It is remarkable for one thing that the Frodebjerg should be presented as the result of the piled up middens of all the provinces of Denmark: it is a notion that accords very well with the agricultural, fertilizing character one would expect in a homologue of Freyr.[16] But above all this tale preserves, linked with this site and this hill, the memory of a supernatural being, already a "Devil" in the story of Gunnarr Helmingr, who is moreover kept by force among men and obliged to serve them, and whom *"the priests" sent out from time to time to be carried round the country, sending him from parish to parish.* It is probable that we have here, in a christianized folk form, an independent survival of the ancient ritual of Fróði, which in another context, in the history of the country's kings, produced the *gestatio* of Frotho mentioned by Saxo.

16. The other legends Thiele records (*Danmarks Folksagen* 2: 37–39) relating to the formation of hills, dunes, or rocky eyots are quite different and have no relationship with rural economy: a troll or a witch was carrying sand or moving a mountain, but there happened—for example—to be a hole in her apron . . .

NJÖRÐR, NERTHUS, AND THE SCANDINAVIAN FOLKLORE OF SEA SPIRITS

To the memory of Kaj Barr

Despite the revival of interest the god Njörðr is at present enjoying, there is a class of considerations that does not seem to have been applied in his case, even though it has been (and on occasion without happy results: I am thinking of the discussion summarized and brought to a negative conclusion by Hilding Celander, "Fröja och fruktträden," Arkiv för Nordisk Filologi *59 [1944]: 97–110) in the case of a goddess occupying the same theological level, Freyja: the use of folklore, the examination of the representations and still observable or recently described customs of the various Nordic countries with a view to discovering survivals, or analogies, capable of throwing light on the early pagan material. Perhaps it may seem to some rather late to take this path. The great vogue for such investigations has now passed. The memory of certain "post-Mannhardtian" abuses on the one hand, and the constitution of folklore as an autonomous subject for study with its own university chairs and specific tasks on the other, have loosened, indeed almost abolished the relationship between the two disciplines: the mythographers no longer dare to, the folklore specialists no longer wish to. In an article written in 1935 concerning those "spirits of the sea" familiar to all the Scandinavian peoples, and in particular the* havfrue, *under the title "Til de norske sjøvetters historie, vandring og stedegent,"* Maal og Minne, *pp. 1–25, Reidar Th. Cristiansen clearly indicated, accepted, and widened this divorce: he took no account at all of the problems of Njörðr and Nerthus. Yet useful observations may nevertheless be arrived at by a confrontation of the two bodies of material.*

Unlike Freyr, who was almost exclusively a landbound divinity, Njörðr, who was principally a sea god, does not seem to be an extension of a fragment of the third function in Indo-European theology. The sea and navigation were not, of course, foreign to the earliest Indo-Europeans, their vocabulary is

215

sufficient proof of that, but the great diversity of climatic, topographical, and economic conditions produced at the end of the migrations that scattered their descendants seem to have produced a fresh set of representations for each new set of imposed techniques: a matter of indifference to the earliest Romans, an antechamber to the life beyond for the Irish, an element in their cosmic structures for the Indians, the sea was something else again for the peoples whose frayed coastlines, all capricious promontories and deep gulfs, with friendly or hostile neighbors only too close on an opposite shore, demanded so much greater a degree of familiarity and daring from their seafarers: πόντος, *"road" from island to island, was how the Greeks saw the Aegean* θάλασσα. *And those who lived on the shores of the northern seas did not wait for Viking or varyag imperialism to learn the skillful exploitation of a mass of water that often seems to be but a series of communicating lakes. And the Scandinavians, like the Greeks, consequently peopled this shifting region of their demesne with strange figures, at once dangerous and helpful.[1] Poseidon and Njörðr, independently, were granted the government of it, and both, along the coasts of Attica or in the Norwegian fjords, in despite of Athene or of Skaði, participated in the delicate relationship of land and sea. Njörðr, and also Tacitus's Nerthus, must be envisaged in that setting, in that context. Just as it is most unlikely that Freyr, the Freyr* ingenti priapo, *should have been created, simply by promotion, from a minor vegetable spirit, so it is extremely probable, a priori, that the master of Nóatún, of the "Abode of Ships"—together with Hymir the owner of the great bowl, and Ægir too, with his sumptuous receptions—received both form and substance from the powerful dreams with which the sea inspires its familiars.*

I have retained the national and dialectal spellings of these spirits: Danish havfrue, Norwegian havfru(e) *(hence Lapp* avafruvva, afaruvva, aberuvva, *etc.),* Swedish havsfru *(Hýltén-Cavallius:* haf-fru) and sjöfru, sjöjungfru, sjörå . . .; *Danish and Norwegian* havmand, *Norwegian* havmann *(in Swedish* havsman *seems to be little used).*

Scandinavian sea folklore, the folklore of sea spirits and fishermen, naturally shares a great many common features with the homologous folklore of Germany, France, the British Isles, and so on: I cannot deal with such problems here, but other authors have done so, notably Fletscher S. Bassett, Legends and Superstitions of the Sea and Sailors in all Lands and all Times (1885); Paul Sébillot, Légendes, croyances et superstitions de la

1. Cf. Carla Costa, "La stirpe di Pontos," *Studi e Materiali di Storia delle Religioni* 39 (1968): 61–100.

mer (2 *vols.; 1887) and* Le folklore des pêcheurs (1901); *Walther Mitska,* Deutsche Fischervolkskunde (1940); *and Schifferund Fischerregeln,* Hessische Blätter für Volkskunde *39* (1941): *119–45.*

The material of this essay was first put forward in a lecture given at the University of Copenhagen, 30 November 1953, upon the kind suggestions of Kaj Barr and Louis L. Hammerich, then published in the Revue de l'Histoire des Religions *147* (1955): *210–26.*

Snorri defines the function of Njörðr briefly but clearly: he governs the blowing of the winds, and is thereby able to calm the sea and fire; he must be invoked before going on sea journeys or fishing; moreover, he is so rich and so well-endowed with possessions, *svá auðigr ok fésæll,* that he can give richness of soil and chattels to all those who invoke him to that end. The *Ynglingasaga,* which makes Njörðr into an extremely landbound king whose reign is agriculturally very prosperous, confirms that the Swedes attributed power over the harvest and man's wealth to him.[2]

Turning to folklore, we find that the folk traditions of all the modern Scandinavian peoples, including the Lapps,[3] feature characters, spirits, that possess either in totality or in large part the same complex domain and exercise the same functions: control of the winds, sailing, and fishing; wealth and power to bestow wealth, even on land.

In Helgeland there is a story[4] that a fisherman once drew up on the end of his line a curious being, about the size of a small child, fish below the waist and man above. Not only did he treat it well but also, the following night, when a voice from the sea called to it and the little wonder explained: "It's daddy calling me ...," he threw him back into the waves. In recompense, the father, the *havmann,* a masculine spirit of the sea, began by offering him a magic boat; but the man did not dare to accept it. At which the *havmann,* determined to make him a gift of some sort, told him about a spot to fish where he would always be certain of making a wonderful catch. And at the spot indicated the fisherman did indeed find so many fish that he was

2. *Gylfaginning* 11, p. 30; *Ynglingasaga,* 9. See above, pp. 24, 85.
3. Whose modern folklore, as with the mythology recorded in the seventeenth and eighteenth centuries, is dependent upon Norwegian and Swedish figures.
4. Knut Strompdal, *Gamalt fra Helgeland* 1 (= Norsk *Folkeminnelag,* cited henceforth as NF) 19 (1929): 130–31).

forced to break off his labors before having caught them all because his boat was so heavily laden it was threatening to sink.

A variant on this tradition, also from Helgeland,[5] makes the spirit a *havfru* rather than a *havmann*, but her generosity is the same and her gifts very similar. The *havfru* first presents the man with a boat, telling him that of all the boats in the world it is the soundest in a bad wind and the swiftest in a good one. When the young man does not dare to accept such a present, still wishing to reward him she makes him instead a gift that he cannot refuse, a gift of nature such as fairies give: he will be able to sail in any weather without fear of shipwreck. And even after that it was indeed true that he never returned from fishing until he had made his catch, heedless of storms, and lived to be very old.

There are numerous folk tales in which an angry sea spirit stirs up a storm or a kindly disposed one gives warning that a storm is on its way. No less numerous are those in which a sailor who has been taken for some variable reason to visit the underwater realm and dwelling of a sea spirit is dazzled by the wealth (gold, cattle, palace . . .) he beholds there. In other traditions, to which I shall return later, a sea spirit endows a man with wealth in general, or with the gift of always succeeding in business affairs.[6] Lastly, the spirits' domestic animals, and especially their sea-cattle, are famous everywhere; and when a shore farmer is fortunate enough to have a bull belonging to a sea spirit to serve his cows, then he will always have calves of exceptional value.

All this, as you see, falls clearly enough within the earlier functional domain of Snorri's Njörðr, and possesses the same variety and scope. But is it permissible to say that there is any continuity, any affiliation of the one to the other? That the pagan god was an earlier form of the modern spirits? Or are these figures and their stories in fact the relatively recent things for which Reidar Christiansen accepted them in 1935, figures and stories that have come from the Celtic countries or have been put together from folklore fragments borrowed from other kinds of spirits, from the *bergfolk*, for example?

Needless to say, even if such continuity does exist where the

---

5. Ibid., pp. 129–30.
6. See below, p. 223 and n. 27.

essentials are concerned, this does not mean that a great many changes have not taken place. As the Norwegian scholar pointed out, folklores are living, moving things, all constantly drawing on and influencing one another. These half-fish, half-man (and generally half-woman) sea spirits that Snorri had still not heard of, but that we find mentioned very soon after him, probably owe much of their outward aspect to the sirens of the Mediterranean sailors. And it may also be that the Celts have enriched the appearance, or the mode of action, or the adventures of such Scandinavian sea dwellers with this or that detail, even though Reidar Christiansen seems to me to have gone a little far and a little too precipitately in that direction. In any case, however, such influences cannot obscure two noteworthy facts:

1. Even since quite early pagan times the sea has always been a continuing element of prime importance in Norwegian and Danish life. It is therefore, *a priori*, improbable that there was at any particular moment a complete loss of the traditions relating to the spirits that preside over the sea in its relationship with mankind (sailing and fishing);

2. I stressed just now that the modern sea spirits, such as the Norwegian ones, for example, present almost in its entirety the complex of functions that once constituted the province of Njörðr: not only mastery over the wind, sailing, and fishing, but also wealth and the power to confer wealth and prosperity on mortals, even on land. It is again, *a priori*, improbable that this complex should have disappeared suddenly toward the end of the twelfth century, only to reform itself later with almost exactly the same structure.

But we have something stronger than probabilities, more conclusive than these commonsense deductions always open to dispute. We have a document that appears to have been left unemployed and accorded no importance in our studies, even though it is recorded in a very well-known collection of folklore material, the *Norsk Folkeminnelag*. In volume 51, published in Oslo in 1943 under the title *Makter og Menneske*,[7] Halldar O. Opedal recorded a quantity of very valuable data relating to the life of the inhabitants of Hardanger, and particularly with regard to fishing. On p. 49, doubtless on the authority of

7. = *Folkeminne fra Hardanger* 5.

the informant Anna L. Reinos,[8] of Odda, he presents the following material:[9]

> The old folk [folk in the olden days?] were always rather lucky[10] when they went fishing. One night old Gunnhild Reinsnos (born in 1746) and Johannes Reinsnos were fishing in the Sjosavatn. They had taken a torch and were fishing with live bait.[11] The fish bit well,[12] and it wasn't long before Gunnhild had a week's supply of fish for her pot. So she wound her line around her rod[13] with the words: "Thanks be to him, to Njor, for this time."[14]

It is certain that we have here a piece of folklore related by a sincere informant and enacted by an authentic performer. "Old Gunnhild," who was doubtless not so old at the time of her memorable fishing venture, had never read a mythology book. She simply thanked her invisible benefactor under the name that was customary in her world, customary with her, and that name was *Njor*. In consequence, we know that in the folklore of the Hardanger[15] fishermen, up until the second half of the eighteenth century, the sea spirit possessing one of the principal characteristics of such spirits today—that of bestowing a good catch—still bore the name of the ancient pagan god whom Snorri tells us had to be invoked "before sailing and fishing." It is of course regrettable that this document is an isolated one. But if we think how very little evidence exists at all of Norwegian folk beliefs two hundred years ago, then this single note, which leaves room for

8. This person's name occurs at all events in the list of informants prefacing the first volume of *Folkeminne fra Hardanger* (= NF 23 [1930]: 5). The material doubtless constitutes a Reinsnos family tradition.

9. *Dei gamle hadde jamleg hov med fisket. Gamle Gunnhild Reinsnos (f. 1746) og Johannes Reinsnos sat ei natt med Finntoppudri og fiska i Sjosavatn. Dei hadde loge med seg og fiska med makk. Fisken beit hivande, og det var kje lenge bia før Gunnhild hadde kokefisk for heila vekn. Då vatt ho snøret på troda og sa: "No ska han Njor ha takk fij denn' vændo."* I asked Kristian Hald and Kaj Barr to help me with this dialect text, and I have given their translation, as well as their explanation of the meaning of several individual words in the following five notes.

10. *Hov* must be the same word as *hov,* "moderation," in the *Norsk Ordbog* of Ivar Aasen (1873).

11. Old Scandinavian, *logi.*

12. *Hivande,* "with rapidity"; cf. *hiva i veg,* "to set off at a gallop."

13. Old Scandinavian, *troda.*

14. *Venda,* "once, on one occasion," a familiar meaning in Hardanger according to Aasen.

15. It will be noted that it is only a short distance from the entrance to Hardanger fjord to the island of Tysnes, once Njarðarlaug, which Magnus Olsen in the first and still excellent part of his 1905 memoir (paras. 1–3, pp. 3–21) has shown to have been probably an important center of Njörðr worship. See above, p. 25, n. 19.

no doubts as to its genuineness, is sufficient to establish a continuity between Njörðr and the *havmann*.

This being so, we are justified in turning to the folklore of such sea spirits for new means of solving some of those traditional problems that philologists and historians of religion are continually debating, with no decisive outcome in sight, relating to the god Njörðr.

And first and foremost, his relationship to Nerthus and the famous mystery of the sexes of these two divinities. Njörðr is a god. The Nerthus of Tacitus[16]—and we have no reason to doubt the reliability of his information—is a goddess, described as a *Terra Mater*, but whose aquatic, marine characteristics are also unmistakable (*est in insula Oceani castum nemus* . . .; and also the *secretus lacus* into which goddess, chariot, and slaves are all plunged), so that, like Njörðr, she is active in two domains.

None of the explanations put forward for this divergence is satisfactory. Axel Kock saw it as the result of a grammatical change: the regular passing into the masculine, in Old Scandinavian, of all stems with -*u*- endings;[17] but that is to grant language an excessive power over mythology. Jöran Sahlgren, in the process of criticizing Kock, reconstructed an evolution from the "onomastic taboos" with which he was concerned at that time;[18] but apart from the extreme complication of the process presupposed, the inhabitants of this theological zone are not generally exposed to such taboos. Making generous use of a fairly monstrous-looking cave drawing from Bohuslän—even though we have no evidence to indicate that it represents a divinity, or even a single character—Edv. Lehmann put forward the notion that the Germanic tribes began by honoring an hermaphrodite deity, *tvekonned*, with a penis and breasts, that later evolved in different directions on the Continent and in Norway;[19] but neither Nerthus nor Njörðr displays the slightest vestige of hermaphroditism.

Since we have established our justification for the notion that modern sea-spirit folklore is to some extent continuous with the

---

16. *Germania* 40, pp. 2–5.

17. "Die Göttin Nerthus und der Gott Njörðr," *Zeitschrift für deutsche Philologie* 28 (1896): 289–94.

18. "Förbjudne namm," *Namn och Bygd* 7 (1918): 1–40; 4; Nerthus, *Freyr och Freyja*, pp. 22–27.

19. "Tvekonnede frugtbarhesguder i Norden," *Maal og Minne* (1919), pp. 1–4.

mythology of Njörðr, a simpler solution now appears: even today, in the north, the sea spirit is sometimes of one sex and sometimes of the other, and the same incidents, the same interventions, the same forms of generosity are attributed to both the male and female forms.[20] In their very valuable book, *Nordens Gudeverden*,[21] Axel Olrik and Hans Ellekilde have noted that it is on the coasts of Jutland and the western coasts of Norway that the *havmand* is of greatest importance. And that is true, but he does appear everywhere.

With regard to this point, in Sweden I have been unable to make a thorough examination of more than the manuscript fiches in the Folklore Archives at Uppsala, which do contain, however, evidence collected from all the country's various provinces;[22] but here again I found the usual stories with male and female spirits alternating in the main rôle. As an example, in one story of which the archives contain many variants, a spirit halts, immobilizes a ship, and makes it impossible for it to sail at all until the captain has promised to buy and bring back a quantity of salt (or grain . . .); when the ship returns to the appointed meeting-place, having been freed and having accomplished the requested task, the spirit takes delivery of its order and then, as payment, takes a member of the crew down to its home under the sea; this human emissary marvels at the wealth of the undersea realm and is sometimes given the gift of personal wealth or of good luck in business.[23] And though the spirit in this story is more generally female, there are also versions in which it is a man, a "gentleman," *en fin herre*.[24] The same ambiguity was recorded, a century ago, in Gunnar Olof Hyltén-Cavallius's *Wärend och Wirdarne* with regard to the spirits of the great inland lakes, the folklore of which to a great extent overlaps with that of the sea spirits: after having given an account of the female *sjörå* of Tjurken lake (who does her own washing and spreads it out on the reefs or islands before a

20. This essential fact is ignored in the article by Reidar Th. Christiansen cited above, p. 215.

21. *Vætter og Helligdomme* I (1926–51): 432.

22. Landsmåls- och Folkminnesarkivet (= ULMA). I express my gratitude to Dag Strömbäck and Mrs. Åsa Nyman for the work facilities accorded me in these archives.

23. ULMA, 21.237, pp. 1–5 (from Vilhelmina, Lappland, 1951): it is the cabin boy who is brave enough to go down to the bottom of the sea; as a reward he receives the gift of succeeding in all he undertakes; he sets up a business on land, becomes very rich, but eventually violates a taboo and ends up blind.

24. As in the text cited in preceding note; ibid., 1368, 4, p. 8 (from Möja, Värmdö, Uppland, 1927).

storm . . .), he says:[25] "On other lakes, when the weather is about to change, a figure will appear, sometimes a man and sometimes a woman, wearing immaculately white clothing and with long, loose hair; he [*han*] is either seated or standing on the water, at intervals bending down to sprinkle his body."[26]

In Denmark and Norway—I have already cited the twin versions of the supernatural catch story from Helgeland[27]—the *havmand* and the *havfru(e)* are no less interchangeable. In the type of story that Olrik and Ellekilder refer to as *Vantrevensagnen*,[28] the sea spirit appears beside a ship moaning and shivering, saying that it is cold; sometimes it has only one trouser leg, which it changes with extraordinary speed from one leg to the other. A sailor, seized with pity, cuts off one of his own trouser legs and throws it down to the unfortunate spirit (sometimes he throws an old pair of trousers that happen to be on board; sometimes a glove, when it is a glove the spirit is asking for; sometimes a skin . . .). The grateful spirit immediately informs its benefactor, either in verse or prose, of the imminence of a storm from the north. The ship just has time to regain the shore and take shelter when a terrible wind does in fact spring up and cause innumerable shipwrecks. In Norway, as far as I can make out, this story generally involves a *havmand*, though occasionally a *havfru(e)*,[29] and in Denmark, in Evald Tang Kristensen's *Danske Sagn*,[30] we find two almost identical variants, one immediately after the other, in one of which the spirit is female and in the other male.

This situation may suggest a way of resolving the Nerthus-Njörðr problem rather more simply, suggesting as it does that an evolutionary explanation of it is unnecessary, since the unimportance of their sex, or rather the possibility they have of embodying themselves in either male or female form, seems to be a constituent characteristic of these beings. Which would quite simply mean that whereas Tacitus's informants happened to tell him about a female form of *Nerþuᴢ* inhabiting an island off the mainland, the Eddic mythology

---

25. *Wärend och Wirdarne* 1 (1864): 248 (para. 62); on the *Haf-fru*, pp. 245–48 (para. 61).
26. Cf. *ULMA*, 6337 (from Fläckebo, Västmanland, 1933): "According to opinion here the *sjörå* is a female being, but the *sjötroll* can equally well be male or female."
27. See above, pp. 217–18.
28. *Op. cit.*, p. 432.
29. K. Weel Engebretsen and Erling Johansen, *Sagn fra Ostfold* (= NF, 59, 1947), p. 45.
30. 2 (1893); 143–44.

spread the knowledge of a male form beside which, in folk tradition, there also subsisted a female form that has continued to flourish until our day.

There is another customary characteristic of the sea spirit that confirms the authenticity, and throws light on the meaning, of one of the rare mythical stories concerning Njörðr that has come down in written form: that of the unfortunate marriage by which this divinity, essentially a man of the sea, is allied with the only-too-landbound Skaði (whose name seems certainly to have contributed, in one way or another, to that of Scandinavia).[31]

With rare exceptions,[32] the sea spirit, male or female, is not explicitly presented as being married to another being of its own kind. Whenever a sailor is taken down to visit the splendors of the undersea world, he sees only the spirit who has issued the invitation—"he" or "she" according to the variant—but never a wife or husband, and the spirit behaves as though it lived a solitary and celibate existence.

When he (or she) does have sexual or emotional liaisons, it is with a human, land-inhabiting being, a man or a woman, and these ill-matched unions are generally not lasting and come to an unhappy end. In one story, from Evald Tang Kristensen's *Danske Sagn*, the *havfrue* falls in love with a fisherman, appears to him on several occasions, and finally succeeds in taking him down to her magnificent undersea palace, where he remains for some while. One day he asks leave to go up and revisit his home on land. She agrees, on condition that he does not go into the church and does not sing any psalms. He breaks his promise, then rushes down to the shore; but the sea is boiling with fury and he is drowned.[33] Moreover, Kristensen has added a note to the effect that this *havfrue* version is merely a distortion of the much more widespread *havmand* version that is the

---

31. See above, p. 35, n. 38.

32. P. ex. Kristensen, *Danske Sagn*, N.R., 2 (1928–29): 103–4. Sometimes the male sea spirit is accompanied by his sons, the wife not appearing, as in the fine Lapp tale from Jens Andreas Friis, "Lappiske Eventyr og Folkesagn" (1871), pp. 19–23 (no. 6: *Čacče-haldek eller Havfolk*, from Naesseby), translated by Josef Calasanz Poestion in *Lappländische Märchen, Volksagen, Räthsel und Sprichwörter* (1886), pp. 46–49 (8: "Meerleute").

33. 2 (1893): 147. This type, with embargoes on the Melusine model, is rare in Scandinavian legends of marriage between humans and spirits (sea spirits or otherwise), whereas it is predominant in the parallel Celtic legends.

basis of one of the old Danish *Folkeviser, Agnete og Havmanden*.[34] And it is naturally this *havmand* version that is the more interesting for the purposes of comparison with the Njörðr-Skaði myth.

Married in most unusual circumstances, these two divinities have a total incompatibility of character that is expressed in a famous poetic duet. Skaði, the land-dweller, the mountain-maiden, cannot bear life in Nóatún, "the Place of Ships," the city where Njörðr lives, somewhere on some fabled shore, and where the cries of the gulls torment her ears. Njörðr, on the other hand, being a sea-dweller, cannot live far from the sea, cannot bear the land full of howling wolves. They agree to alternate between their two homes, to live for nine years (or nine nights) on the coast, then nine inland. But even in this attenuated form Skaði is unable to bear the ordeal: she leaves her husband in order to return for good to the mountains where she grew up.[35]

In the Danish ballad, the story has been Christianized and the church plays a large rôle. But despite Svend Grundtvig's introduction, which is in any case concerned solely with poetic *form*, the material is neither Slavic nor German in origin; on the contrary, it is from Scandinavia that it originally spread, and very thinly too, toward the south and southeast.[36] In Denmark itself the ballad is linked with a number of prose tales that have been labeled rather too precipitately as secondary formations, but that in fact are probably parallel to it; and in particular with tales of the same type that have been found along the Norwegian coasts and in southwest Sweden.

As far as Denmark is concerned, I am thinking of the story collected by Just Mathias Thiele entitled "Havmandens Klage,"[37] in which we find the "diptych of laments," a feature so characteristic of the Njörðr-Skaði myth: (1) Grethe has followed the *havmand* to the bottom of the sea; a few years later, while she is minding her children, she hears the sound of the bells from the land and her father weeping; she laments, and her husband asks her why; (2) When the *havmand* has given her leave to visit her home, and she does not answer the three summonses that he comes onto the land to address to her, he

---

34. *Danmarks gamle Folkeviser* 2 (1856): no. 38, pp. 48–57.
35. See above, pp. 21–22, 34–35.
36. Three German ballads, one from Silesia; two Slavic, one again in Silesia, the other in Slovenia. More recently, tales using the same theme have been found in Russia.
37. *Danmarks Folkesagn* (2d. ed.; 1843), pp. 259–60.

in his turn voices his lament: he goes back down to the bottom of the sea weeping warm tears, and the sailors often hear *hans Graad og Væklage*.

In Norway, in a story from Helgeland,[38] the *havmann* has taken a girl named Åshild to the bottom of the sea with him and her parents do not know what has become of her. One night the *havmann* comes to the mother's house and asks her to come with him at once: his wife is about to give birth, and there are no Christians at the bottom of the sea.... The old woman goes with him and helps with the delivery. Her daughter goes with her when she leaves, and later fails to return to her husband again. One Sunday, in a terrible storm, Åshild and her mother are in church. The *havmann* appears with a whole band of *havfolk* to take Åshild back into the other world. Fortunately, however, there are some holy men in the church who make the sign of the cross and drive the *havfolk* away. Nevertheless, a little while afterward, Åshild does return to her husband and is never seen in her village again.

In Sweden, in Tjörn, on the coast north of Göteborg,[39] the story line is similar, but it is the sea spirit who comes to live with the woman on land, and his homesickness for his native element only manifests itself when the time comes for him to die. Some fishermen catch on their hook and bring home with them a *hafman* who had been busy guarding his father's underwater herds. They keep him on land, baptize him, and marry him to one of their own women. He himself provides the name he is given: "Håfvålen." Being a *hafman*, he does as Njörðr would have done in earlier times and always tells the fishermen the best places to fish, as well as displaying great skill in forecasting the weather. But when he is on the point of death he asks them to take him back out to sea, to the spot where he was fished up, a point in the Skagerak today named "Håfvålen" after him. The fishermen do as he asks, but scarcely have they replaced him in the water when a terrible storm blows up in which they expect to perish. The descendants of the *hafmann* and his wife are still alive and are recognizable by their mongoloid features.

Is it not as one of this series that we should begin to see the union

38. Jogan Hveding, *Folketru og Folkeliv på Hålogaland* 2 (= NF, 53, 1944): 38.
39. *Bidrag till kännedom om Göteborgs och Bohusläns fornminnen och historia* 4 (1890): C. Ljungman, *Folksägner från Tjörn*, p. 440 ("om hafsfolket").

and separation of Njörðr and Skaði, of the *marinus* and the *terrena* who can never agree, each the prey of an irresistible homesickness for his or her element, and the woman, at some unbearable moment, breaking the conjugal tie? I do not claim, of course, that the folktales derive from the myth, from the Njörðr-Skaði duet as preserved in Snorri's *Edda*, and reflected in the duet of Hadingus and Ragnilda in Saxo. But it is probable that from time immemorial the typical sea-god or sea-spirit myth has involved an ill-matched marriage of this kind, doomed to an unresolvable tug-of-war between sea and land, to disunion, and to separation.[40] This coincidence provides a fresh reason for regarding Snorri's lyrical account of the disagreement between the god of Nóatún and the giantess from the Norwegian mountains as authentic, as genuinely mythic and no mere literary invention.

The information Tacitus possessed concerning Nerthus was principally concerned with her visits among mankind: at regular intervals, no doubt,[41] escorted by her priest, she leaves the mysterious grove on her island and goes on a journey through the amphictyony in a chariot drawn by cows. During this time a great peace reigns: the tribes give themselves up to the joys of the hospitality they lavish upon her. Then she returns to her sanctuary, to the *secretus lacus* into which she is plunged, together with her chariot and also, *statim*, never to be seen again, the slaves who have helped in the sacred ceremony: *arcanus hinc terror sanctaque ignorantia, quid sit illud, quod tantum perituri vident*. Tacitus is obviously thinking of the objects revealed during Mediterranean mysteries. But perhaps the *servi* are no more in the Germanic rites than the figures we can glimpse in the Scandinavian rite filtered through folklore: the mortals that the *havfrue* summons and draws down with her to the bottom of the sea so that they may marvel at all the splendors of her palace, and sometimes to enjoy her love, similarly "unknown" to the rest of mankind: not victims in a sacrifice but volunteers leaving for the magical adventure that awaits them beneath the water as joyously as Christian martyrs on their way to heaven.

40. There is room for a fascinating structural study of the marriages of this type in the various mythologies, beginning with that of Pluto and Persephone.
41. Tacitus does not say when or how often, but such customs are usually of regular occurrence.

Then we also find in Scandinavian folklore the regular visit made by the *havfrue* to dry land, to the mortals on the shore. Except that in these Christian times her visit is not only not desired but feared; it is no longer a friend coming to enjoy *conversationem mortalium*; it is an evil spirit who comes to do them harm, and whom, far from welcoming, they attempt to keep away. The *havfrue's* visit in Norway and Sweden[42] takes place on Michaelmas night, *Mikkjelsmessnatta*, "when the wind blows from the south": then she comes, drawn with a team of her own cows, the famous "cows of the sea," which eat all the food that has been left by men in the byres for their own cattle. Ought we not to see this as a counterpart, deritualized and reattributed to the forces of evil, of that ancient hospitality the goddess came to demand in her chariot also drawn by cows, *bubus feminis*?

The method used by the peasants to ward off these disastrous visits is no less noteworthy. At Nesna, in Helgeland, the practice is described by Knut Strompdal as follows:[43]

> There was one day in the year when the *havfrue* always came up onto dry land so that her cattle could eat their fill. So the evening before, the folk always put steel in the hay they had stored, so that the *havfrue* could not go near it and take it, because if there was steel in the heap, then she kept her distance.

From Möja, among the islands scattered offshore from Stockholm, we have an account dating back a hundred years or so[44] describing how the *havsfrue* brought her cattle up to graze on the island. One day a man hurled his metal cleaver at the biggest beast. Immediately all the others disappeared, while the one he had hit remained and became his property.

There is also a fine story in the Folklore Archives of Uppsala from the same *skeppslag*, from the same source, that goes, in summary, as follows:[45] at the end of the fishing season a young man has been spitefully marooned by his companions on one of the islands that is uninhabited for the rest of the year. He has no boat and keeps alive as best he can by bringing down birds with a bow and arrow. One day

42. Johan Theodor Storaker, *Tiden i den norske folketro* (= NF 2 [1921]), p. 112; Anton Rǿstad, *Frå gamal tid, folkeminne frå Verdal* (= NF 23 [1931]), p. 85; Gunnar Olof Hytén-Cavallius, *Wärend och Wirdarne* (above, p. 223, n. 25) 1: 245.
43. *Gamalt frå Helgeland* 2 (= NF 40 [1938]): 98–99 (no. 497).
44. ULMA, 1368: 4, pp. 1–4 (1927, from an informant born in 1841).
45. Ibid.

when he is in his hut the door opens and a procession appears, led by the *havsfrue* wearing a golden crown: she has come to celebrate her wedding (to whom? the young man?), and the procession drags in a bullock in order to butcher it and feast on it. The young man snatches up his bow; happily he has some steel about him—a big needle; he uses it as an arrow and hits the crown. Immediately the ἱερὸς γάμος disperses, everything vanishes except the crown and the already slaughtered bullock. The young man is saved: he now has enough food to last until the next fishing season, when the fleet will pick him up.

Thus that which protects one from the feared visit of the Lady from the Sea, what puts her to flight, her and her cows, is steel.[46] Now let us return to Tacitus and look again at the passage in which he describes the peace of Nerthus—with a precision that has perhaps not been sufficiently heeded: *non bella ineunt, non arma sumunt; clausum omne ferrum; pax et quies tunc tantum nota, tantum amata.* It is clear that Tacitus is thinking solely of peace and war, but he says, perhaps repeating the words supplied by his informant verbatim, *clausum omne ferrum*; not only weapons but all iron, as though the visit of Nerthus were incompatible with the mere presence of that metal. Was the reason not perhaps because, even as early as pagan times, iron, whether used for military purposes or not, would have prevented the approach of the desired divinity, as today steel is the best means of preventing the feared approach of the *havfrue*? It is possible that *ferrum* here is not just a rhetorical, redundant repetition of *arma* but exact reporting of a ritual fact, exceeding in significance the *pax et quies* of men.

46. The belief in the protective virtue of iron or steel, of their power to repel spirits, is very widespread.

SAXONIS, GESTA DANORUM

I, v-viii

V: 1. Filii Gram, Guthormus et Hadingus, quorum alterum Gro, alterum Signe enixa est, Suibdagero Daniam obtinente, per educatorem suum Brache nave Suetiam deportati Wagnophtho et Haphlio gigantibus non solum alendi, verum etiam defensandi traduntur.

2. Quorum summatim opera perstricturus ne publicae existimationi contraria aut veri fidem excedentia fidenter astruere videar, nosse operae pretium est, triplex quondam mathematicorum genus inauditi generis miracula discretis exercuisse praestigiis.

3. Horum primi fuere monstruosi generis viri, quos gigantes antiquitas nominavit, humanae magnitudinis habitum eximia corporum granditate vincentes.

4. Secundi post hos primam physiculandi sollertiam obtinentes artem possedere Pythonicam. Qui quantum superioribus habitu cessere corporeo, tantum vivaci mentis ingenio praestiterunt. Hos inter gigantesque de rerum summa bellis certabatur assiduis, quoad magi victores giganteum armis genus subigerent sibique non solum regnandi ius, verum etiam divinitatis opinionem conscicerent. Horum utrique per summan ludificandorum oculorum peritiam proprios alienosque vultus variis rerum imaginibus adumbrare callebant illicibusque formis veros obscurare conspectus.

5. Tertii vero generis homines ex alterna superiorum copula pullulantes auctorum suorum naturae nec corporum magnitudine nec artium exercitio respondebant. His tamen apud delusas praestigiis mentes divinitatis accessit opinio.

6. Nec mirandum, si prodigialibus eorum portentis adducta barbaries in adulterinae religionis cultum concesserit, cum Latinorum

Edition Jøgen Olrik et Hans Ræder, 1931, p. 20–35.

quoque prodentiam pellexerit talium quorundam divinis honoribus celebrata mortalitas. Haec idcirco tetigerim, ne, cum praestigia portentave perscripsero, lectoris incredula refragetur opinio. His praetermissis propositum repetam.

7. Occiso Gram Suibdagerus Daniae Suetiaeque imperiis auctus fratrem coniugis Guthormum, eadem saepius flagitante, exsilio abductum tributaque pollicitum Danis praefecit, Hadingo patris ultionem hostis beneficio praeferente.

VI: 1. Hic primis adolescentiae temporibus felicissimis naturae incrementis summam virilis aetatis perfectionem sortitus, omisso voluptatis studio, continua armorum meditatione flagrabat, memor se bellicoso patre natum omne vitae tempus spectatis militiae operibus exigere debere.

2. Cuius fortem animum Harthgrepa Wagnhofthi filia amoris sui illecebris emollire conata sedula affirmatione certabat oportere eum primum genialis tori munus suis erogare connubiis, quae infantiae eius exactioris curae fomenta porrexerit primaque subministrarit crepundia. Nec simplici verborum exhortatione contenta carminis quoque modo sic orsa:

Quid tibi sic vaga vita fluit?
Quid caelebs tua lustra teris,
arma sequens, iugulum sitiens?
Nec species tua vota trahit;
eximia raperis rabie,
labilis in Venerem minime.
Caedibus atque cruore madens
bella toris potiora probas
nec stimulis animum recreas.
Otia nulla fero subeunt,
lusus abest, feritas colitur;
nec manus impietate vacat,
dum Venerem coluisse piget.
Cedat odibilis iste rigor,
adveniat pius ille calor
et Veneris mihi necte fidem,
quae puero tibi prima dedi
ubera lactis opemque tuli,
officium genetricis agens,
usibus officiosa tuis.

3. Quo corporis eius magnitudinem humanis inhabilem amplexibus referente, cuius naturae contextum dubium non esset giganteo germini respondere: «Non te moveat», inquit, «insolitus meae granditatis aspectus. Nunc enim contractioris, nunc capacioris, nunc exilis, nunc affluentis substantiae, modo corrugati, modo explicati corporis situm arbitraria mutatione transformo; nunc proceritate caelis invehor, nunc in hominem angustioris habitus condicione componor». Adhuc haesitante eo fidemque dictis habere cunctante, tale carmen adiecit:

> Ne paveas nostri iuvenis commercia lecti.
> Corpoream gemina vario ratione figuram
> et duplicem nervis legem praescribere suevi.
> Nam sequor alternas diverso schemate formas
> arbitrio variata meo; nunc sidera cervix
> aequat et excelso rapitur vicina Tonanti,
> rursus in humanum ruit inclinata vigorem
> contiguumque polo caput in tellure refigit.
> Sic levis in varios transmuto corpora flexus
> ambiguis conspecta modis: nunc colligit angens
> stricti membra rigor, nunc gratia corporis alti
> explicat et summas tribuit contingere nubes;
> nunc brevitate premor, nunc laxo poplite tendor
> versilis inque novos converti cerea vultus.
> Nec me mirari debet, qui Protea novit.
> Nunc premit effusos, modo clausos exserit artus
> forma situs incerta sui speciesque biformis,
> quae nunc extricat, nunc membra revolvit in orbem.
> Exsero contractos artus tensosque subinde
> corrugo, vultum formis partita gemellis
> et sortes complexa duas: maiore feroces
> territo, concubitus hominum breviore capesso.

4. His assertis Hadingi concubitu potita tanto iuvenis amore flagravit, ut, cum eum revisendae patriae cupidum comperisset, virili more culta prosequi non dubitaret laboribusque eius ac periculis interesse voluptatis loco duceret. Quo comite susceptum iter ingressa penatibus forte pernoctatura succedit, quorum defuncti hospitis funus maestis ducebatur exsequiis. Ubi magicae speculationis officio superum mentem rimari cupiens, diris admodum carminibus ligno insculptis iisdemque linguae defuncti per Hadingum suppositis, hac voce eum horrendum auribus carmen edere coegit:

5.   *Inferis me qui retraxit, exsecrandus oppetat*
            Tartaroque devocati spiritus poenas luat.
              Quisquis ab inferna sede vocavit
              me functum fatis exanimemque
              ac rursum superas egit in auras,
              sub Styge liventi tristibus umbris
              persolvat proprio funere poenas.
              En praeter placitum propositumque
              quaedam grata parum promere cogor.
              Ex hac namque pedem sede ferentes
              angustum nemoris advenietis,
              passim daemonibus praeda futuri.
              Tunc quae nostra chao fata reduxit
              et dedit hoc rursum visere lumen
              mire corporeis nexibus indens
              Manes elicitos sollicitando,
              quod nisa est temere, flebit acerbe.
            Inferis me qui retraxit, exsecrandus oppetat
            Tartaroque devocati spiritus poenas luat.
              Nam cum monstrigeni turbinis atra lues
              intima conatu presserit exta gravi
            atque manus vi vos verrerit, ungue fero
            artubus avulsis corpora rapta secans,
              tunc, Hadinge, tibi vita superstes erit,
              nec rapient Manes infera regna tuos,
              nec gravis in Stygias spiritus ibit aquas.
              Femina sed nostros crimine pressa suo
              placabit cineres, ipsa futura cinis,
              quae miseris umbris huc remeare dedit.
            Inferis me qui retraxit, exsecrandus oppetat
            Tartaroque devocati spiritus poenas luat.

6. Igitur cum apud praedictum nemus compacto ramalibus tecto noctem agerent, inusitatae granditatis manus domicilium penitus pererrare conspecta. Quo monstro territus Hadingus nutricis opem implorat. Tunc Harthgrepa artus explicans ac magno se turgore distendens manum artius apprehensam alumno praebuit abscindendam. Ex cuius taeterrimis vulneribus plus tabi quam cruoris manavit. Cuius facti postmodum ab originis suae consortibus laniata poenas perpendit; neque illi aut naturae condicio aut corporis magnitudo, quo minus infestos hostium ungues experiretur, opitulata est.

7. Spoliatum nutrice Hadingum grandaevus forte quidam, altero orbus oculo, solitarium miseratus Lisero cuidam piratae solemni pactionis iure conciliat. Siquidem icturi foedus veteres vestigia sua mutui sanguinis aspersione perfundere consueverant, amicitiarum pignus alterni cruoris commercio firmaturi. Quo pacto Liserus et Hadingus artissimis societatis vinculis colligati Lokero, Curetum tyranno, bellum denuntiant. Quibus superatis, fugientem Hadingum praedictus senex ad penates suos equo devehendum curavit ibique suavissimae cuiusdam potionis beneficio recreatum vegetiori corporis firmitate constaturum praedixit. Cuius argurii monitum huiusmodi carmine probavit:

8.
> *Hinc te tendentem gressus profugum ratus hostis*
> *impetet, ut teneat vinclis faucisque ferinae*
> *obiectet depascendum laniatibus: at tu*
> *custodes variis rerum narratibus imple,*
> *cumque sopor dapibus functos exceperit altus,*
> *iniectos nexus et vincula dira relide.*
> *Inde pedem referens, ubi se mora parvula fundet,*
> *viribus in rabidum totis assurge leonem,*
> *qui captivorum iactare cadavera suevit,*
> *inque truces armos validis conare lacertis*
> *et cordis fibras ferro rimare patenti.*
> *Protinus admissa vapidum cape fauce cruorem*
> *corporeamque dapem mordacibus attere malis.*
> *Tunc nova vis membris aderit, tunc robora nervis*
> *succedent inopina tuis solidique vigoris*
> *congeries penitus nervosos illinet artus.*
> *Ipse struam votis aditum famulosque sopore*
> *conficiam et lenta stertentes nocte tenebo.*

9. Et cum dicto relatum equo iuvenem pristino loco restituit. Tunc Hadingus amiculi eius rimas, sub quo trepidus delitebat, per summam rerum admirationem visus perspicuitate traiciens animadvertit equinis freta patere vestigiis, prohibitusque rei inconcessae captare conspectum plenos stuporis oculos a terribili itinerum suorum contemplatione deflexit.

10. Qui cum a Lokero captus omnem praedictionis eventum certissimis rerum experimentis circa se peractum senisset, Handwanum, Hellesponti regem, apud Dunam urbem invictis murorum praesidiis

vallatum moenibusque, non acie resistentem bello pertentat. Quorum
fastigio oppognationis aditum prohibente, diversi generis aves loci
illius domiciliis assuetas per aucupii peritos prendi iussit earumque
pennis accensos igne fungos suffigi curavit; quae propria nidorum
hospitia repetentes urbem incendio complevere. Cuius exstinguendi
gratia concurrentibus oppidanis, vacuas defensoribus portas reli-
querunt. Adortus Handwanum cepit eique redemptionis nomine
corpus suum auro rependendi potestatem fecit, cumque hostem tollere
liceret, spiritu donare maluit: adeo saevitiam clementia temperabat.

11. Post haec, multo Orientalium robore debellato, Suetiam reversus Suibdagerum apud Gutlandiam ingenti classe obvium pugna
adortus oppressit sicque non solum exterorum manubiis, verum
etiam paternae fraternaeque vindictae trophaeis ad eminentem
claritatis gradum provectus exsilio regnum mutavit, cui patriam non
ante repetere quam regere contigit.

VII: 1. Ea tempestate cum Othinus quidam Europa tota falso divinitatis titulo censeretur, apud Upsalam tamen crebriorem deversandi
usum habebat eamque sive ob incolarum inertiam sive locorum
amoenitatem singulari quadam habitationis consuetudine dignabatur.
Cuius numen Septentrionis reges propensiore cultu prosequi cupientes
effigiem ipsius aureo complexi simulacro statuam suae dignationis
indicem maxima cum religionis simulatione Byzantium transmise-
runt, cuius etiam brachiorum lineamenta consertissimo armillarum
pondere perstringebant. Ille tanta sui celebritate gavisus mittentium
caritatem cupide exosculatus est. Cuius coniunx Frigga, quo cultior
progredi posset, accitis fabris aurum statuae detrahendum curavit.
Quibus Othinus suspendio consumptis statuam in crepidine colloca-
vit, quam etiam mira artis industria ad humanos tactus vocalem
reddidit. At nihilominus Frigga, cultus sui nitorem divinis mariti
honoribus anteponens, uni familiarium se stupro subiecit; cuius
ingenio simulacrum demolita aurum publicae superstitioni conse-
cratum ad privati luxus instrumentum convertit. Nec pensi duxit
impudicitiam sectari, quo promptius avaritia frueretur, indigna
femina, quae numinis coniugio potiretur. Hoc loci quid aluid adie-
cerim quam tale numen hac coniuge dignum exstitisse? Tanto quondam errore mortalium ludificabantur ingenia. Igitur Othinus, gemina
uxoris iniuria lacessitus, haud levius imaginis suae quam tori laesione

dolebat. Duplici itaque ruboris irritamento perstrictus plenum ingenui pudoris exsilium carpsit eoque se contracti dedecoris sordes aboliturum putavit.

2. Cuius secessu Mithothyn quidam praestigiis celeber, perinde ac caelesti beneficio vegetatus, occasionem et ipse fingendae divinitatis arripuit barbarasque mentes novis erroris tenebris circumfusas praestigiarum fama ad caerimonias suo nomini persolvendas adduxit. Hic deorum iram aut numinum violationem confusis permixtisque sacrificiis expiari negabat ideoque iis vota communiter nuncupari prohibebat, discreta superum cuique libamenta constituens. Qui cum Othino redeunte, relicta praestigiarum ope, latendi gratia Pheoniam accessisset, concursu incolarum occiditur. Cuius exstincti quoque flagitia patuere, siquidem busto suo propinquantes repentino mortis genere consumebat tantasque post fata pestes edidit, ut paene taetriora mortis quam vitae monumenta dedisse videretur, perinde ac necis suae poenas a noxiis exacturus. Quo malo offusi incolae eguestum tumulo corpus capite spoliant, acuto pectus stipite transfigentes; id genti remedio fuit.

3. Post haec Othinus, coniugis fato pristinae claritatis opinione recuperata ac veluti expiata divinitatis infamia, ab exsilio regressus cunctos, qui per absentiam suam caelestium honorum titulos gesserant, tamquam alienos deponere coegit subortosque magorum coetus veluti tenebras quasdam superveniente numinis sui fulgore discussit. Nec solum eos deponendae divinitatis, verum etiam deserendae patriae imperio constrinxit, merito terris extrudendos ratus, qui se caelis tam nequiter ingerebant.

VIII: 1. Interea Asmundus, Suibdageri filius, in ultionem patris pugna cum Hadingo congressus, ut filium Henricum, cuius caritatem etiam proprio spiritui praeferebat, fortissime dimicantem occidisse cognovit, avido fati animo lucem perosus tali carmen voce compegit:

> Quis nostra fortis ausit arma sumere?
> Nil proficit cassis vacillanti nitens,
> lorica iam nec commode fusum tegit;
> armis ovemus interempto filio?
> Cuius mori me cogit eminens amor,
> caro superstes ne relinquar pignori.
> Utraque ferrum comprimi iuvat manu;

nunc bella praeter scuta nudo pectore
exerceamus fulgidis mucronibus.
Ferocitatis fama nostrae luceat;
audacter agmen obteramus hostium,
nec longa nos exasperent certamina
fugaque fractus conquiescat impetus.

2. Quo dicto geminam capulo manum iniciens, absque periculi respectu reflexo in tergum clipeo, complures in necem egit. Igitur Hadingo familiarium sibi numinum praesidia postulante, subito Wagnofthus partibus eius propugnaturus advehitur. Cuius aduncum Asmundus gladium contemplatus hanc in vocem carmine clamabundus erupit:

3.   *Quid gladio pugnas incurvo?*
                     Ensiculus fato tivi fiet,
                     framea torta necem generabit.
                     Hostem namque manu superandum
                     carminibus lacerari fidis,
                     plus verbis quam vi connisus,
                     in magica vires ope ponens.
                     Quid me sic umbone retundis
                     audaci iaculo minitando,
                     cum sis criminibus miserandis
                     obsitus et maculis refertus?
                     Infamis sic et nota sparsit
                     putentem vitiis labeonem.

4. Haec vociferantem Hadingus hasta traicit amentata. Sed nec mortis Asmundo solatia defuere. Siquidem inter exiguas vitae reliquias vulneratum interfectoris pedem perpetua claudicatione mutilavit clademque suam parvulo ultionis momento memorabilem reddidit. Ita alterum membri debilitas, alterum vitae finis excepit. Corpus eius sollemni funere elatum apud Upsalam regiis procuratur exsequiis. Cuius coniunx Gunnilda, ne ei superesset, spiritum sibi ferro surripuit virumque fato insequi quam vita deserere praeoptavit. Huius corpus amici sepulturae mandantes mariti cineribus adiunxerunt, dignam eius tumulo rati, cuius caritatem vitae praetulerat. Iacet itaque Gunnilda aliquanto speciosius virum busti quam tori societate complexa.

5. Post haec, Hadingo victore Suetiam populante, Asmundi filius,

Uffo nomine, conserendae manus diffidentia adductus in Daniam exercitum traicit hostilesque lares incessere quam proprios tueri satius duxit, opportunum propulsandarum iniuriarum genus existimans, quod ab hoste pateretur, hosti inferre. Ita Danis ad propria defensanda redire compulsis salutemque patriae exterarum rerum dominio praeferentibus, domesticum solum hostilibus armis vacuefactum repetiit.

6. Igitur cum Hadingus e bello Suetico regressus aerarium suum, quo bellis ac spoliis quaesitas opes excipere consuevit, furto violatum animadverteret, continuo custodem eius Glumerum suspendio consumpsit callidoque commenti genere edixit, ut, si quis e noxiis ablata referre curasset, honoris locum, quem Glumerus possederat, obtineret. Quo promisso sontium quidam beneficii percipiendi quam criminis tegendi studiosior redditus pecuniam regi reportandam curavit. Quem conscii in summam principis amicitiam receptum putantes nec uberius quam fidelius honoratum credentes et ipsi pari praemii spe relatis pecuniis reatum detegunt. Quorum confessio primum honoribus ac beneficiis excepta, mox suppliciis punita haud parvum vitandae credulitatis documentum reliquit. Dignos dixerim, qui solutae taciturnitatis poenas patibulis luerent, quos cum silentii salubritas tutos praestare posset, vocis stoliditas in exitium pertraxit.

7. His gestis Hadingus per summum integrandi belli apparatum hiberna permensus, verno sole frigoribus liquatis, Suetiam repetit ibique lustrum militando confecit. Cuius milites, diuturnae expeditionis negotio consumptis alimentis, ad ultimam paene tabem redacti silvestribus fungis famem linire coeperunt. Tandem per summam necessitatis indigentiam commanducatis equis, ad postremum canina cadavera corporibus indulserunt. Sed neque humanis artubus vesci nefas habitum. Itaque Danis in extremas desperationis angustias compulsis, nocte concubia sine auctore tale castris carmen insonuit:

> Taetro penates omine patrios
> liquistis, hoc rus Marte sequi rati.
> Quae vana mentes ludit opinio?
> Quae caeca sensus corripuit fides,
> hoc arbitrantes posse solum capi?
> Non amplitudo Suetica cedere,
> non exterorum Marte valet quati.
> At summa vestri defluet agminis,

cum Marte nostros coeperit aggredi.
Nam cum ferocem vim fuga solverit
et proeliorum pars vaga labitur,
in terga dantes Marte prioribus
caedis potestas liberior datur;
maiorque ferri parta licentia,
cum sors rebellem praecipitem fugat,
nec tela tentat, quem metus abstrahit.

9. Quod praesagium crebra Danorum caede sequens lucis eventus implevit. Nocte postera vocem huiusmodi incerto auctore editam Suetica auribus iuventus excepit:

Quid me sic Uffo provocat
seditione gravi,
poenas daturus ultimas?
Confodietur enim
multa premendus cuspide
exanimisque ruet
audaciam coepti luens.
Nec petulantis erit
livoris intactum scelus,
augurioque meo,
cum bella primum gesserit
contuleritque manum,
excepta membris spicula
corpus ubique petent,
crudosque hiatus vulnerum
fascia nulla premet,
nec ampla plagarum loca
contrahet ulla salus.

10. Eadem nocte congressis exercitibus, duo senes humano habitu taetriores capitibus coma vacuis inter siderum micatus triste visu calvitium praeferentes contrariis votorum studiis monstriferos divisere conatus. Siquidem alter Danorum partibus intendebat, alter Sueonum studiosus exstabat.

11. Victus Hadingus, cum in Helsingiam confugisset ibique solis fervore percalefactum corpus frigida maris aqua sublueret, inauditi generis beluam crebris ictibus attentatam oppressit necatamque in castra perferendam curavit. Quem facto ovantem obvia femina hac voce compellat:

Seu pede rura teras, seu ponto carbasa tendas,
infestos patiere deos totumque per orbem
propositis inimica tuis elementa videbis.
Rure rues, quatiere mari, dabiturque vaganti
perpetuus tibi turbo comes, nec deseret umquam
vela rigor nec tecta tegent, quae si petis, icta
tempestate ruent, diro pecus occidet algu.
Omnia praesentis sortem vitiata dolebunt.
Ut scabies fugiere nocens, nec taetrior ulla
pestis erit. Tantum poenae vis caelica pensat.
Quippe unum e superis alieno corpore tectum
sacrilegae necuere manus: sic numinis almi
interfector ades! Sed cum te exceperit aequor,
carceris Aeolici laxos patiere furores.
Te Zephyrus Boreasque ruens, te proteret Auster,
et coniuratos certabunt edere flatus,
donec divinum voto meliore rigorem
solveris et meritam tuleris placamine poenam.

12. Regressus igitur Hadingus eodemque cuncta tenore perpessus tranquilla quaeque proprio turbidabat adventu. Siquidem navigante eo oborta nimbi vis ingenti classem tempestate consumpsit. Naufragum hospitia petentem subita penatium strages excepit. Nec ante malo remedium fuit, quam scelere sacrificiis expiato cum superis in gratiam redire potuisset. Siquidem propitiandorum numinum gratia Frø deo rem divinam furvis hostiis fecit. Quem litationis morem annuo feriarum circuitu repetitum posteris imitandum reliquit. Frøblot Sueones vocant.

13. Cumque forte gigantum quendam Nitherorum regis Haquini filiam Regnildam pactum animadverteret, indignam rei condicionem perosus per summam futurae copulae, detestationem ingenuo ausu nuptias praecucurrit Norvagiamque profectus tam foedum regiae virginis amatorem armis oppressit. Adeo namque virtutem otio praetulit, ut, cum regiis deliciis frui liceret, non solum suas, verum etiam alienas iniurias propulsare omni voluptate iucundius duceret. Auctorem beneficii puella crebris offusum vulneribus ignara medendi cura prosequitur. Cuius ne notitiam sibi temporis interiectus eriperet, crus eius annulo vulneri incluso obsignatum reliquit. Eadem postmodum, a patre eligendi mariti libertate donata, contractam convivio iuventutem curiosiore corporum attrectatione lustrabat, deposita

quondam insignia perquirens. Spretis omnibus Hadingum latentis annuli indicio deprehensum amplectitur e que se coniugem donat, qui coniugio suo gigantem potiri passus non fuerat.

14. Apud quam deversante Hadingo, mirum dictu prodigium incidit. Siquidem cenante eo femina cicutarum gerula propter foculum humo caput extulisse conspecta porrectoque sinu percontari visa, qua mundi parte tam recentia gramina brumali tempore fuissent exorta. Cuius cognoscendi cupidum regem proprio obvolutum amiculo refuga secum sub terras abduxit, credo diis infernalibus ita destinantibus, ut in ea loca vivus adduceretur, quae morienti petenda fuerant. Primum igitur vapidae cuiusdam caliginis nubilum penetrantes perque callem diuturnis adesum meatibus incedentes quosdam praetextatos amictosque ostro proceres conspicantur; quibus praeteritis loca demum aprica subeunt, quae delata a femina gramina protulerunt. Progressique praecipitis lapsus ac liventis aquae fluvium diversi generis tela rapido volumine detorquentem eundemque ponte meabilem factum offendunt. Quo pertransito binas acies mutuis viribus concurrere contemplantur, quarum condicionem a femina percontante Hadingo: «Ii sunt», inquit, «qui ferro in necem acti cladis suae speciem continuo protestantur exemplo praesentique spectuculo praeteritae vitae facinus aemulantur». Procedentibus murus aditu transscensuque difficilis obsistebat, quem femina nequicquam transsilire conata, cum ne corrugati quidem corporis exilitate proficeret, galli caput, quem secum forte deferebat, abruptum ultra moenium saepta iactavit, statimque redivivus ales resumpti fidem spiraculi claro testabatur occentu.

15. Regressus igitur Hadingus patriamque cum coniuge repetere orsus imminentium sibi piratarum insidias celeri navigatione cassavit. Qui licet iisdem paene flatibus iuvarentur, ipsum tamen aequora praesulcantem paribus velis occupare non poterant.

16. Inter haec Uffo, cum mirae pulchritudinis filiam haberet, potiturum ea, qui vita Hadingum spoliaret, edixit. Quo pacto Thuningus quidam admodum sollicitatus accita Byarmensium manu votivum studuit impetrare progressum. Quem excepturus Hadingus dum classe Norvagiam praeteriret, animadvertit in litore senem crebro amiculi motu appellandi navigii monitus afferentem. Quem, repugnantibus sociis damnosumque profectionis deverticulum affirmantibus, nave susceptum centuriandi exercitus auctorem habuit,

in ordinanda agminum ratione curiosius attendere solitum, ut prima per dyadem phalanx ac per tetradem secunda constaret, tertia vero octoadis adiectione succresceret, semperque priorem insequens duplicitatis augmento transscenderet. Idem quoque funditorum alas in extremam aciem concedere iussit iisque satittariorum ordines sociavit. Ita digestis in cuneum catervis, ipse post bellatorum terga consistens ac folliculo, quem cervici impensum habebat, ballistam extrahens, quae primum exilis visa, mox cornu tensiore prominuit, denos nervo calamos adaptavit, qui vegetiore iactu pariter in hostem detorti totidem numero vulnera confixerunt. Tunc Byarmenses arma artibus permutantes carminibus in nimbos solvere caelum laetamque aeris faciem trist iimbrium aspergine confuderunt. E contrario senex obortam nubium molem obvia nube pellebat madoremque pluviae nubili castigabat obiectu. Victorem Hadingum dimissus senex non vi hostili, sed voluntario mortis genere consumendum praedixit clarisque bellis obscura ac lonqinquis finitima praeponere vetuit.

17. Quo relicto Hadingus ab Uffone per colloquii simulationem in Upsalam accersitus, amissis per insidias sociis, noctis habitu protectus aufugit. Nam Danis aedis, in quam convivii nomine contracti fuerant, excessum petentibus, praesto erat, qui cuiusque exsertum foribus caput ferro demeteret. Cuius facti iniuriam proelio insecutus Uffonem oppressit eiusque corpus deposito odio conspicui operis mausoleo mandavit, amplitudinem hostis elaborato busti splendore confessus. Ita quem vivum hostili studio insectari solebat, exstinctum honoris impendio decorabat. Et ut sibi devictae gentis animos conciliaret, fratrem Uffonis Hundingum regno praefecit, ne imperium potius in exteros transfusum quam in Asmundi familia continuatum videretur.

18. Cumque sublato iam aemulo complures annos per summam armorum desuetudinem rerum agitatione vacuus exegisset, tandem diutinum ruris cultum nimiamque maritimarum rerum abstinentiam causatus et quasi bellum pace iucundius ratus talibus se ipsum culpare disidiae modis aggreditur:

> Quid moror in latebris opacis,
> collibus implicitus scruposis,
> nec mare more sequor priori?
> Eripit ex oculis quietem

agminis increpitans lupini
stridor et usque polum levatus
questus inutilium ferarum
impatiensque rigor leonum.
Tristia sunt iuga vastitasque
pectoribus truciora fisis.
Officiunt scopuli rigentes
difficilisque situs locorum
mentibus aequor amare suetis.
Nam freta remigiis probare,
mercibus ac spoliis ovare,
aera aliena sequi locello,
aequoreis inhiare lucris
officii potioris esset
quam salebras nemorumque flexus
et steriles habitare saltus.

19. Cuius uxor ruralis vitae studio maritimarum avium matutinos pertaesa concentus, quantum in silvestrium locorum usu voluptatis reponeret, hac voce detexit:

Me canorus angit ales immorantem litori
et soporis indigentem garriendo concitat.
Hinc sonorus aestuosae motionis impetus
ex ocello dormientis mite demit otium,
nec sinit pausare noctu mergus alte garrulus,
auribus fastidiosa delicatis inserens,
nec volentem decubare recreari sustinet,
tristiore flexione dirae vocis obstrepens.
Tutius silvis fruendum dulciusque censeo.
Quis minor quietis usus luce, nocte carpitur
quam marinis immorari fluctuando motibus?

20. Eodem tempore Tosto quidam, obscuro Iutiae loco ortus, ferocitate clarus emersit. Plebe namque vario petulantiae genere lacessita, late crudelitatis famam extulit tantaque malignitatis opinione percrebuit, ut Facinorosi cognomine notaretur. Sed nec exterorum iniuriis abstinens post foedam patriae vexationem etiam Saxoniam tentat. Cuius duce Syfrido laborantibus proelio sociis pacem petente, fore, quod ab ipso poscebatur, asseruit, dummodo sibi gerendi cum Hadingo belli societatem polliceri voluisset. Refragantem illum condicionique parere metuentem acri minarum gerere ad eam,

quam optabat, promissionem perduxit. Fit enim, ut, quod blande non struitur, minaciter impetretur.

21. A quo terrestri negotio superatus Hadingus, cum victoris classem inter fugiendum repertam perfossis lateribus navigationi inutilem reddidisset, conscensam scapham in altum direxit. Quem Tosto occidisse ratus, cum diu inter promiscua necatorum cadavera quaesitum reperire non posset, ad classem regressus animadvertit eminus myoparonem mediis maris aestibus fluctuantem. Quem cum deductis in altum navigiis persequi statuisset, fractionis periculo revocatus aegre litus repetiit. Tunc correptis integris coeptum viae genus exsequitur. Hadingus occupari se videns percontari comitem coepit, an nandi usu calleret, neganteque eo fugae diffidentia sponte eversi navigii concavas partes amplexus mortis fidem insequentibus fecit. Securum deinde Tostonem inopinatumque et spoliorum reliquiis avidius incubantem adortus, prostrato exercitu, praedam deserere coegit suamque eius fuga ulciscitur.

22. Nec Tostoni in vindictam sui animus defuit. Nam cum ob accepti vulneris magnitudinem reparandarum intra patriam virium copiam non haberet, legati titulo Britanniam petiit. In qua profectione navigationis socios in aleae lusum per lasciviam contraxit rixamque a tesserarum iactibus ortam funesta caede finire docuit. Ita placido exercitii genere discordiam per totum navigium diffudit, cruentamque pugnam mutatus lite iocus progenuit. Et ut aliquod ex alieno malo commodum caperet, correptis interfectorum pecuniis Collonem quendam piratica tunc temporis insignem ascivit. Quo comite parvo post in patriam reversus, cum Hadingo suam quam militum fortunam expendere praeoptante ex provocatione congressus occiditur. Nolebant enim priscae fortitudinis duces universorum discrimine exsequi, quod paucorum sorte peragi potuisset.

> Belua nata tibi rabiem domitura ferarum,
> quaeque truci rabidos atteret ore lupos.

At post pauca subiunxit:

> Fac caveas: ex te nocuus tibi prodiit ales,
> felle ferox bubo, voce canorus olor.

Rex mane sopore discusso cuidam coniectuararum sagaci visum exponit. Qui lupi nomine futurae ferocitatis filium interpretatus oloris vocabulo filiam denotavit, illum hostibus perniciosum, hanc patri insidiosam fore praesagiens.

24. Eventus augurio respondit: sequidem Hadingi filia Ulvilda privato cuidam Guthormo denupta, sive copulae indignitate, sive claritatis affectatione permota, maritum in parentis caedem absque pietatis respectu sollicitat, reginam se quam regis filiam censeri malle praefata. Cuius exhortationis modum iisdem paene verbis, quibus ab ipsa editus fuerat, explicare constitui; qui fere huiusmodi erat:

25. «O miseram me, cuius nobilitatem dispar copulae nexus obtenebrat! O infelicem, cuius stemmati rustica iugatur humilitas! O infortunatam principis prolem, quam tori lege plebeius aequiparat! Miserandam regis filiam, cuius decorem ignavus pater in obsoletos ac despicabiles transmisit amplexus! Infaustam matris subolem, cuius felicitati tori commercium derogat, cuius munditiam immunditia ruralis attrectat, dignitatem indignitas vulgaris inclinat, ingenuitatem condicio maritalis extenuat! At si quis tibi vigor inest, si qua mentem virtus possidet, si dignum te regis generum probas, socero fasces eripe, genus probitate redime, prosapiae defectum virtute aestima, sanguinis damnum animo pensa! Felicior est honos audacia quam hereditate quaesitus. Melius virtute culmen quam successione conscenditur. Aptius honores meritum quam natura conciliat. Adde quod senectutem subruere nefas non est, quae proprio in ruinam pondere suppressa devergit. Sufficiant socero tot temporum fasces; senilis tibi potestas obveniat, quae si te frustrata fuerit, alteri cedet. Lapsui vicinum est quicquid senio constat. Sat illi regnasse sit; tibi quandoque praeesse conveniat. Malo praeterea virum regnare quam patrem. Malo regis coniunx quam nata censeri. Melius est principem interius amplecti quam exterius venerari, gloriosius nubere regi quam obsequi. Ipse quoque tibi sceptrum quam socero malle debeas. Proximum sibi quemque natura constituit. Aderit coepto facultas, si facto voluntas accesserit. Nihil est quod non ingenio cedat. Instaurandum epulum est, exornandum convivium, providendi paratus, invitandus socer. Fraudi viam familiaritas simulata praestabit. Nullo melius quam affinitatis nomine insidiae teguntur. Adde quod temulentia promptum caedi iter aperiet. Cumque rex capitis cultui intentus fabulis mentem, barbae manum intulerit pilorumque perplexionem crinali spico seu pectinis enodatione discreverit, applicari ferrum visceribus

sentiat. Minor occupatis solet cautela perquiri. Dextera tua tot scelerum vindex accedat. Pium est ultricem miserorum manum extendere.»

26. Talibus insistente Ulvilda, vir suggestione victus insidiis operam pollicetur. Interea Hadingus generi dolum cavere somnio monitus, petito convivio, quod ei filia caritatis simulatione paraverat, armatorum non longe praesidia statuit, quibus adversum insidias, cum res exigeret, uteretur. Quo cibum capiente, satelles in fraudis ministerium accitus, occultato sub veste ferro, opportunum sceleri tempus tacitus exspectabat. Quo rex animadverso collocatis in vicino militibus signum lituo dedit. Quibus continuo opem ferentibus, dolum in auctorem retorsit.

27. Interea rex Sueonum Hundingus occasum Hadingi falso acceptum nuntio inferiis excepturus, optimatibus contractis, eximiae capacitatis dolium cereali liquore completum deliciarum loco medium convivis apponi praecepit, et ne quid celebritatis deesset, ipse ministri partibus assumptis pincernam agere cunctatus non est. Cumque exsequendi officii gratia regiam perlustraret, offenso gradu in dolium collapsus interclusum humore spiritum reddidit, deditque poenas sive Orco, quem falsa exsequiarum actione placabat, sive Hadingo, cuius interitum mentitus fuerat. Quo cognito Hadingus parem veneratori gratiam relaturus exstinctoque superesse non passus suspendio se vulgo inspectante consumpsit.

INDEX